SAINT JEROME IN HIS STUDY

LATIN WRITERS OF THE FIFTH CENTURY

BY

ELEANOR SHIPLEY DUCKETT,

M.A., PH.D., D.LIT.

SOMETIME SCHOLAR AND FELLOW OF GIRTON COLLEGE,
CAMBRIDGE, AND OF BRYN MAWR COLLEGE
PROFESSOR OF LATIN LANGUAGE AND LITERATURE IN SMITH COLLEGE

WITH AN INTRODUCTION BY

ERIC MILNER-WHITE, M.A., D.S.O.

ARCHON BOOKS
1969

SBN: 208 00845 4
LIBRARY OF CONGRESS CATALOG CARD NUMBER: 71-93462
[REPRODUCED FROM A COPY IN THE YALE UNIVERSITY LIBRARY]
PRINTED IN THE UNITED STATES OF AMERICA

To

FLORENCE ALDEN GRAGG

INTRODUCTION

Only in two ways can we read the mind of an age and of the people who toiled and suffered through it: by the nature of its events and by the contents of its literature. The events of the fifth century report little more than a record of wars and rumours of wars, of chaos and despair, of things that were barbarous and things that were shadows, of the blind movements of peoples, of all the sorrows that strike men dumb, and, not least, of the weakening of Christian confidence and saving faith. These things influenced the thought of the age chiefly by retarding and stifling it; only one great work issues from the century; and that, the *City of God*, is a vindication of the ways of God through the catastrophes and tears of earth.

Yet Miss Duckett, in her survey of its writings, has shewn the heart of the century to be neither uninteresting nor unimportant. As literature, these ˙may hold no high place; as interpretation of an age, they bear sure witness; as influence, they open the door to the Middle Ages and actually stretch forward to the figure of our English Milton. A general sketch of the mind of an age in right proportion, true emphasis, and clear line is no easy thing to do. But as the author has done it, it provides not only its own interest, but valuable material for such great subjects as "The Development of the Christian Mind" and "The History of Christian Prayer," unwritten as yet for want of any competent to write them, essential to the understanding of the building up of modern man, and left unconsidered hitherto by the modern historian.

Inevitably the literature of the fifth century reflects the bewilderment and pessimism of the age. The complete paralysis of the pagan outlook in the West is illustrated by the barrenness of both its poetry and its prose. The more powerful Christian pens betray pessimism even in the struggle against it. Chapter three, a brilliant study of the Poets of Biblical History, indicates the eagerness with which they fell back, for sure foundation and explanation of present evil alike, upon the stories of Creation and of the Fall. The ideal of "holy escape" is put into practice by Jerome, and urged with the combined force of example, learning and style. His story shews, no less, a world of strife infecting even the saints with its spirit. And when mankind was so clearly proving itself to be "one mass of perdition," the greatest mind of the age, and of most ages, fell back upon the starkest conceptions of human depravity and of divine predestination, of God's irresistible mercy to the elect and the unescapable condemnation of the remainder. The *City of God* is the apologia of a pessimist, of one who, as Troeltsch observes, has little thought of building a civilisation to replace that which was perishing, but points to a future life for happiness and rest out of an ancient civilisation plainly doomed to death. Orosius, his disciple, could scarcely have raised contemporary courage by a history of the world intended to prove that bad as were the calamities of to-day, those of past days were worse. Salvian's description of his times reads like a horror of great darkness.

No wonder that even the best minds looked only to retreat for remedy; and not wrongly, for the desert had become the hope of the world. Times so desperate called for protest and repentance by way of extreme ascetic rigour. A strange field for heroism it was that the Gospel found; a hard garden, the desert, for Christian hope to cultivate. The solitary and the cœnobite represented a despair that at least was full of faith, and so became the new sowing which bore fruit an hundredfold. These were the undaunted spirits who fashioned a new unnatural life of goodness to meet the unnatural evil. The doctrine of St. Vincent and the ascetic theology of Cassian rank as no less seminal to the devotion of the Middle Ages than St. Augustine's philosophy to their church polity. European development thus owes much to the age with which this scholarly review deals.

Let me add that it represents the author's work at Girton College, Cambridge, when for two years she held the Ottilie Hancock Fellowship for literary research. Her life as researcher in this period belongs to England, as teacher to America. Two countries, therefore, greet her first work of this kind, and look for a second.

E. MILNER-WHITE.

King's College,
Cambridge, England.
November 1, 1930.

AUTHOR'S FOREWORD

Two reasons may explain the writing of this book. First, in Professor Bury's words: "The fifth century was one of the most critical periods in the history of Europe. It was crammed with events of great moment, and the changes which it witnessed transformed Europe more radically than any set of political events that have happened since. At that time hundreds of people were writing abundantly on all kinds of subjects, and many of their writings have survived. . . ." The special interest, then, of the century that saw the Fall of the Western Empire, the hard dying of pagan worship and the growing pains of the Church Catholic in the world as in the cloister, in the West as in the East, gives foremost cause for study of these contemporary writings which illuminate its darkness, irrespective of their own individual worth to literature.

Secondly, the legacy of this century is in itself of interest and importance. It gave to us divers treatises of greater and of lesser Fathers of the Church. It gave, moreover, among its host of writings, a number that are well worthy of study by others than experts in Christian poetry and prose. Some of these works have been fully discussed by our authorities, some have of necessity received scant treatment in the broad and comprehensive descriptions of age succeeding age. From all of them a representative company, great and small, have been gathered in the picture offered here, set in the framework of the time. It is drawn for lay students, for those readers of pagan classics and ecclesiastic records who do not sit in theological halls and colleges, and are not given to deep consideration of technical works on Church history, who nevertheless may welcome a brief account of the course and content of Latin writings between pagan and mediæval days. We know, in some degree, the chief men of literature to the end of the fourth century of Imperial Rome; book after book is revealing more clearly the Latin writers of humanistic fame. There is good cause, I think, for the building of a bridge for passengers from one to the other across the fifth and following centuries that intervene.

Such a bridge has indeed already been constructed in great part by Professor Edward Kennard Rand's *Founders of the Middle Ages.* To him, as our special authority for these writers, I am most grateful for his kindly interest in my work. Its aim will be realized if it may fill in some details in the story which there and elsewhere he so skilfully describes. Our knowledge of the pro-mediæval literature has further been enlarged of late by the publications of F. J. E. Raby and of Fr. Kuhnmuench on early Christian Latin poetry. These and other books have been included in lists given at the end of my pages, not, of course, as full bibliographies, but as indication of the sources from which I have drawn my material and from which deeper knowledge may be gained. The translations are my own. The necessity of curtailing the *Notes* has caused me most regretfully to omit quotation of the Latin.

It remains to make glad acknowledgment of help received from either side of the ocean: To my college in America, and especially to its President, William Allan Neilson, for the granting of leave of absence from 1926 till 1928; to my college in England for the Ottilie Hancock Fellowship held by me during the same two years; to the Cambridge University Library and to the Smith College Library in Northampton for constant courtesy and aid.

To individual scholars I give warm thanks for various acts of charity rendered to my book, though on none but my own head rests the responsibility for the errors and omissions which await remark. Among authorities ecclesiastical, to the Reverend Eric Milner-White, Dean of King's College, Cambridge, I owe not only the generous gift of the Preface which introduces this study, but also the preliminary reading and criticism of my manuscript; to the Reverend Frank Gavin, Professor of Ecclesiastical History in the General Theological Seminary, New York, I give my thanks for willing encouragement of an amateur in his fields; from the Reverend Charles Carroll Edmunds, Editor of *The American Church Monthly*, I have received permission to reprint here part of Chapter VII, dealing with Cassian. Among authorities in matters literary, both sacred and secular, in addition to Dr. Rand, I am especially grateful to Professor Chauncey Brewster Tinker, of Yale University, for the aid given to my study of early Church history; to Miss Marjorie Hope Nicolson, Dean of Smith College, for the joy of her expert knowledge of Milton and of her counsel in many problems and perplexities; to Miss Mary Ellen Chase, Professor of English Language and Literature in Smith College, for the eager sense of form which has left its mark unacknowledged on every page from end to end; to Miss Georgia Dunham Kelchner and Miss Olava Ørbeck, of Cambridge, England, for the gracious hospitality to scholarship which made possible the completion of my work. To Florence Alden Gragg, my colleague, critic, and Chairman in travail of lecture-rooms and libraries, I have dedicated my book as an offering of gratitude for the fellowship in humanities which has made glad my sojourn in New England for now these many years.

E. S. D.

Northampton, Massachusetts
November 1, 1930.

CONTENTS

CHAPTER   PAGE

I. THE BACKGROUND OF THE FIFTH CENTURY WRIT-
   INGS   3

II. SECULAR POETRY   17
   The later works of Claudian; Claudian as poet of his-
   tory; his standpoint in religion. The *De Suo Reditu*
   of Rutilius Namatianus; the *Carmina* of Merobaudes;
   Apollinaris Sidonius.

III. THE POETS OF BIBLICAL HISTORY   51
   The *Chronica* of Sulpicius Severus; the *Alethia* of
   Claudius Marius Victor; Hilary and Cyprian of Gaul;
   the *Carmina* of Avitus; the *Paschal Song* and *Hymns*
   of Sedulius; the *Apology* and the *Praises of God* of
   Dracontius; the relation of these poets to Milton.

IV. HISTORICAL EVENTS IN CHRISTIAN POETRY . .   93
   Endelechius, *On the Death of the Oxen;* the *Epigram of
   St. Paulinus;* the poems *On the Divine Providence* and
   To My Wife; the *Commonitorium* of Orientius; the
   Thanksgiving to God of Paulinus of Pella.

V. CHRISTIAN PROSE: JEROME AND AUGUSTINE . .   108
   Jerome in Bethlehem; his *Letters* and works *Against
   Vigilantius, Against Rufinus, Against the Pelagians;*
   his relations with Augustine. Augustine in Hippo; his
   Letters and writings against the Donatists and the Pela-
   gians; the *City of God*.

VI. CHRISTIAN PROSE: OROSIUS AND SALVIAN . .   158
   The patristic philosophy of History; the *Histories* of
   Orosius; Salvian: *On the Government of God*.

VII. MONASTIC WRITINGS OF THE WEST IN THE FIFTH
   CENTURY   182
   Sulpicius Severus: *Life of St. Martin* and *Dialogues;*
   the School of Lerins—Eucherius, Faustus, Vincent; the
   Institutes and the *Conferences* of Cassian.

xiii

CHAPTER   PAGE

VIII. SECULAR PROSE: MARTIANUS CAPELLA . . . 224

The *Nuptials of Mercury and Philology;* its influence
in the Middle Ages.

NOTES 237

SELECT BIBLIOGRAPHY 255

GENERAL BIBLIOGRAPHY 264

INDEX 267

CHIEF HISTORICAL EVENTS

A.D.

395. Honorius Emperor in the West; Arcadius Emperor in the East.
400. First Consulship of Stilicho.
401. Invasion of Noricum and Rætia by Radagaisus.
Alaric invades Italy for the first time.
402. Battle of Pollentia between Alaric and Stilicho.
403. Alaric invades Italy for the second time.
404. Sixth Consulship of Honorius.
Banishment of John Chrysostom, Bishop of Constantinople.
405. Second Consulship of Stilicho.
Invasion of Italy by Radagaisus and the Ostrogoths.
406. Capture and execution of Radagaisus by means of Stilicho.
The Vandals, Suevians, and Alans in great numbers cross the Rhine to ravage Gaul.
407. Constantine usurper of imperial power in Gaul.
Death of Chrysostom in exile.
408. Stilicho put to death at Ravenna.
Alaric enters Italy for the third time; his first siege of Rome.
Athaulf, his brother-in-law, marches into Italy.
Death of Arcadius; Anthemius Regent for Theodosius II in the East.
409. Second siege of Rome by Alaric.
The barbarians cross the Pyrenees from Gaul to ravage Spain.
Pelagius crosses to Africa.
410. Third siege and sack of Rome by Alaric.
Death of Alaric at Cosenza.
411. Constantine conquered by the Roman general Constantius, captured, and put to death.
412. Athaulf and the Visigoths cross the Alps into Gaul, taking Galla Placidia as captive.
The usurper Jovinus declared Emperor in Gaul.
Cyril elected Patriarch of Alexandria.

xv

A.D.

413. Execution of Jovinus.
Revolt of Count Heraclian in Africa; defeated and put to death.
414. Marriage of Athaulf and Galla Placidia.
414-416. Pulcheria Regent for her brother Theodosius II.
415. The Visigoths ravage Southern Aquitaine, burn Bordeaux, and march into Spain.
Assassination of Athaulf; succession of Wallia.
Murder of Hypatia at Alexandria.
Acquittal of Pelagius at the Council of Diospolis in Africa.
416-418. Wallia's conquest of the Vandals and the Alans in Spain.
417. Marriage of Placidia and Constantius.
418. Death of Wallia; succession of Theodoric I.
Condemnation of Pelagius by Synod at Carthage.
419. The Visigoths settle in Aquitaine.
421. Constantius and Galla Placidia crowned as Augustus and Augusta.
Death of Constantius.
Marriage of Theodosius and Eudocia.
423. Death of Honorius.
424. Usurpation of imperial power at Ravenna by John, supported by Aetius.
425. Capture and execution of John.
Valentinian III Emperor in the West; Regency of Galla Placidia.
427-430. Successful campaign of Aetius in Gaul against the Goths and the Franks.
427. Rebellion of Boniface, Count of Africa.
428. Nestorius consecrated Bishop of Constantinople.
Boniface calls Gaiseric and the Vandals to his aid.
429. The Vandals under Gaiseric invade and ravage Africa.
Compiling of Codex of Theodosius.
430. Defeat of Boniface and siege of Hippo by Gaiseric.
431. Capture of Hippo by the Vandals.
The Third Œcumenical Council at Ephesus condemns Nestorius.
432. Struggle for power between Aetius and Boniface in Italy.
434. Aetius supreme at the Western Court.
435. Treaty between Valentinian and Gaiseric.
Campaign of Theodoric I and the Visigoths in Gaul.
436. Siege of Narbonne by Theodoric; relieved by Litorius.

437. Marriage of Valentinian III and Eudoxia, daughter of Theodosius II.
End of Regency of Galla Placidia.
439. Battle of Toulouse between the Visigoths and Litorius; Litorius taken prisoner.
Capture of Carthage by Gaiseric and the Vandals.
442. The Vandals receive by settlement a large part of Northern Africa.
449. "Robber" Council of Ephesus.
450. Death of Galla Placidia.
Death of Theodosius; Marcian Emperor in the East.
Marriage of Marcian and Pulcheria.
Valentinian's sister, Honoria, seeks help from Attila, Emperor of the Huns.
451. Fourth Œcumenical Council at Chalcedon.
452. Invasion of Italy by Attila.
453. Death of Attila.
Death of Pulcheria.
Succession of Theodoric II as King of the Visigoths.
454. Assassination of Aetius by Valentinian III.
455. Assassination of Valentinian; Petronius Maximus Emperor in the West.
Assassination of Petronius Maximus.
Invasion and sack of Italy by Gaiseric and the Vandals.
Avitus proclaimed Emperor in the West.
456. Avitus deposed by Ricimer and Majorian.
457. Death of Marcian; Leo I Emperor in the East.
Majorian Emperor in the West.
461. Majorian put to death by Ricimer; Severus Emperor in the West.
465. Death of Severus.
466. Euric murders Theodoric II and becomes King of the Visigoths.
467. Anthemius declared Emperor in the West.
472. Assassination of Anthemius.
Death of Ricimer.
473. Glycerius declared Emperor in the West without support of Leo.
474. Julius Nepos declared Emperor in the West by Leo.
Death of Leo.
Zeno Emperor in the East.

475. Orestes forces Julius Nepos to leave Rome and sets up his own son Romulus Augustulus as Emperor in the West.
476. Orestes killed by soldiers of Odovacar, and Romulus deposed.
477. Odovacar ruler of Italy under Zeno.
Death of Gaiseric.
480. Murder of Julius Nepos.
489-493. Struggle between Odovacar and Theodoric the Ostrogoth for the rule of Italy.
Siege of Ravenna; massacre of Odovacar's soldiers by Theodoric.
493. Capture of Ravenna by Theodoric, and slaying of Odovacar.

LITERARY DATES OF THE FIFTH CENTURY

A.D.

395-404.   Works of Claudian.
c. 400.   Endelechius: *De mortibus boum.*
           Sulpicius Severus: *Life of St. Martin.*
c. 403.   Sulpicius Severus: *Chronica.*
c. 408.   St. Paulinus: *Epigramma.*
c. 415.   *De Providentia Divina.*
400-419.   Last works of St. Jerome.
416.   Journey of Rutilius.
418.   Orosius: *Historiæ adversus Paganos.*
413-426.   St. Augustine: *City of God.*
c. 420-428. Works of Cassian.
c. 430-440? Claudius Marius Victor: *Alethia.*
434.   St. Vincent of Lerins: *Commonitorium.*
410-439?   Martianus Capella: *Nuptials of Mercury and Philology.*
420-440?   Orientius: *Commonitorium.*
425-450.   Sedulius: *Paschale Carmen.*
c. 437-446. Poems of Merobaudes.
439-451.   Salvian: *De Gubernatione Dei.*
460?   Paulinus of Pella: *Eucharisticos Deo.*
456-468.   Panegyrics of Apollinaris Sidonius.
c. 470.   *flor.* Paulinus of Périgueux.
c. 480-490. *flor.* Dracontius.
c. 500.   *flor.* Avitus.

LATIN WRITERS OF THE FIFTH CENTURY

CHAPTER I

THE BACKGROUND OF THE FIFTH CENTURY WRITINGS

The fateful record of these last days is a familiar tale. And indeed seldom has the course of any hundred years of history been marked by calamities of strife and destruction such as those which fell in quick sequence upon the Roman Empire after the death of Theodosius the Great had left its divided government in the incapable hands of the two boys his sons, Honorius, Emperor of Rome and the West, and Arcadius, ruler of Constantinople and the East. While in the East persecution and theological strife brought Alexandria face to face with Constantinople in fierce threefold campaign, and Chrysostom was banished and Nestorius condemned and Flavian deposed, while Ephesus and Chalcedon, mighty for ages unborn, made their present world ring with ghostly tales of "robbers" and rivals in Council, of faint-hearted Bishops and ruffian monks, while the further East rose in rebellion against Chalcedon's Declaration of Faith and New Rome vied for spiritual eminence with Rome, the West, forced to deal directly with matters physical, was slowly disintegrating through its weakness and lassitude in the face of barbarian arms. Of Rome's inner peril in this time long account has been given: of grinding economic burdens on the poor, of corruption of magistrates, of chaos in finance, of callous absorption in cultured ease among wealthy and highborn citizens, of shrinking of men of Roman blood from warfare, from worldly and civic

3

office, from wedlock and its service to the State. The Empire in truth scarce needed for its Fall the shocks that smote it from without.

Yet before the first two years of the opening decade had passed, the country around the Danube was overrun by the German Radagaisus and his following of Vandals, while in this same moment of stress the great barbarian hero of these ten years, Alaric the Visigoth, preferring his own fortunes to the Empire of his former allegiance, for the first time marched as an enemy across the border of Italian soil. Three times before his death Alaric invaded this land, terrifying its people and driving Honorius to seek amid the marshes of Ravenna refuge for the Imperial Court; three times he dared besiege the City herself; the third time he brought slaughter and ravagings unspeakable upon her panic-stricken habitants. In 405 Radagaisus led his Ostrogoths to devastate the north of Italy; in the following year broke forth the famous irruption of barbarian tribes, Vandals, Suevians, Alans, in their hosts across the Rhine for the ruin of the fertile fields of Gaul. Nor did the death of Alaric bring peace to the distracted world. His power, already reinforced by aid of Athaulf, his brother-in-law, then fell in its entirety to this new ruler of the Visigothic men-of-arms. From Italy they departed in triumph across the Alps into Gaul, bent on career of pillage and carrying as captive in their company the future bride of Athaulf the barbarian, Galla Placidia, step-sister of the Emperor himself. There with lust of arms they ravaged Aquitania in its southern parts and kindled with fire the great city of Bordeaux before proceeding on their course of havoc into Spain. Twice before this climax of trouble had a usurper arisen in Gaul to claim imperial power; and Constantine in Arles and Jovinus in Valence had been thrown down from their pretensions to meet a tyrant's fate.

Small wonder is it then that the literature of this time reechoes the cry of mourning of Italy and Spain and Gaul, as they looked on their plundered homes and their fields laid waste and wondered what was yet to come. Man after man, though his shadows were deepened for the enhancing of his art, yet reflected in his picture of words the undoubted suffering and sorrow of the day. Saint Jerome writes with a breaking heart from Bethlehem his marvel that such visitation should have come upon the City of the world; Rutilius hastens homeward from that City that he may succour his native district in Gaul, whence arrived such grievous news; Orientius, more than twenty years later, remembers in his Bishop's seat in Aquitaine that all Gaul was at this period but one pyre of flame and smoke. Small wonder, too, that men, as ever, should see in their troubles the indifference or the wrath of God, should even repent them of this new-found Christian religion and look dubiously back upon the preachers of the old heathen creed, who thundered in their ears that the gods of ancient days were taking vengeance on the Roman world for desertion of their rites whence its glory once had sprung. For slowly the pagan faith yielded its sway. In the fifth century's dawn the country fields recked little of the Christ for healing of their ills, as we learn from Endelechius, poet of the plague; in Rome the old patrician class of Senators found still in Claudian the honoured champion of their creed; still heathen feasts and ceremonies found worshippers, though Theodosius, though Honorius and Arcadius in turn shut close the pagan shrines, forbidding sacrifice.

But to heathen blasphemies against truth answer must be made; and who more fittingly in this time could explain the ways of God to ignorant men than Augustine, the leading figure in the troubled world of Western Christendom? In his see of Royal Hippo, encompassed as he was by the daily cares of the Church within and by combats against heresy and schism without, he could yet study for thirteen years how best to prove triumphantly that God still ruled his City on earth and that, despite appearances, it was well with the world of those who faithfully believed. Lesser men, too, were called by him to supplement his work, and we find the Spanish priest Orosius, a fugitive from his native land, writing in Africa the story of the world in which good has always triumphed and evil has always met its due reward; if then in the past, so should it be even likewise in that present time of seeming ill.

To troubles past were added fresh tidings of gloom. The death of Honorius in the West was followed by usurping of imperial power at Ravenna on the part of the upstart John, whose capture and execution took toll of Roman energy before the boy Valentinian the third, son of Galla Placidia and her second husband Constantius, co-Emperor with Honorius for brief space, was seated under his mother's care upon the throne. Straightway Goths and Franks stirred up new conflict in Gaul; in Africa Count Boniface, the Roman viceroy, heeded in no respect the summons homeward from the Empress-Regent, and, when pressed by force, took the fatal step of allowing Gaiseric and his Vandals to cross from Europe to his aid. Promptly they came in their multitude, and to no purpose Boniface accepted terms of reconciliation with the Imperial Court at home; for in the following year the sounds of the Vandal siege of Hippo echoed about Augustine as he drew near to his death.

The African city was captured, and covenant between

Gaiseric and Valentinian soothed for a moment the eager
ambition of the Vandal chief; yet four years later we hear of
his victorious entry into Carthage herself, and a second
treaty gave mighty power and vast tracts of Northern Africa
into his hands. By this time Theodoric the first as leader
of the Visigothic hordes had led them in zealous imitation
of his forebears Alaric and Athaulf to besiege Narbonne, and
near Toulouse to capture the Roman general Litorius at the
time when Carthage met its fall. Surely such constant
disaster must point, not to wrath of heathen gods, powerless
to wreak vengeance for their eclipse, but to the very real
anger of One Almighty Father at the abandoned wickedness
of his sons on earth. Such was the rebuke of Salvian, priest
of Marseilles, flung forth about this time in burning words
which sought to cauterize the loathsome sore of Roman
morals in Gaul and Italy and Africa; against the background
of Roman vice and perversity barbarians appear in his pages
as shining lights of honour and purity and love. So also in
loyalty to truth rather than to false pride of patriotism a
writer from Gaul, the nameless author of the *Epigram*, had
told in verse of the woeful doings of men and women in the
district whence he came.

And yet there is, at least in the pages of literary records,
a more cheerful side to this picture of crime and distress.
If Christian thinkers dwelt on the troubles of Rome, as sent
for discipline or punishment, the thoughts of other patriots
chose rather to linger with the deeds of those who had
protected her in these dire attacks of barbarian force. If
Radagaisus and Alaric were mighty men, their might but
served to magnify the splendour of the strength that had
repeatedly stayed their advance; it inspired the poet
Claudian to tell in ringing words of the exploits of Rome's
defender Stilicho, to whom despite a Vandal ancestry Theo-

dosius had married his niece and entrusted the welfare of his sons and their imperial rule. To meet the onslaughts of Visigoths in Gaul and to contend against the dread coming of Attila and his Huns, there arose another hero, Aetius, once champion of the tyrant John, but afterwards for long course of time the great minister and general of the Empress Placidia during her Regent's power, till he fell, four years after her death, assassinated by Valentinian's hand. And again a great man found his singer, for the Spaniard Merobaudes told while Aetius yet lived of the triumphs of his arms. Still a third instance shows that an age of inferior literature finds joy in dwelling on details touching its heroes and their deeds; it turns to men and their tiny acts that it may praise them in loud-sounding lines, when the causes and thoughts that underlie men's doings are too great for their facile pen. In such baser use Apollinaris Sidonius employed his artificial skill in verse to tell of the lives and doings of three Emperors who followed now their short careers in Rome.

For in the year after his murder of Aetius, Valentinian himself met death at the hand of Petronius Maximus, Patrician and ex-Prefect of Rome. Two uneasy months Petronius held in name imperial rulership, till in the panic caused by the descent of Gaiseric and his Vandal hosts upon Italy he forsook all and fled, to fall in his turn by an unknown hand at the City gates. The onrush of Gaiseric was stayed by Leo the Great, Bishop of Rome, even as three years before he had held Attila from entering with his hordes. But the City found no secular head to render help in her distress; and it was the Goths under Theodoric the second, successor of his father of the same name, and friend of Aetius and Rome, who proclaimed in Gaul as Emperor of the West Avitus, fellow-soldier of Aetius in his campaign against the Huns, and father-in-law of this Sidonius who sang his glory in official state.

But however warmly Gaul might hail Avitus as its Chief, Rome would have none of him, and the next year saw him deposed, the captive of Majorian and of Ricimer, great soldier and greater politician of barbarian blood. Once Ricimer had held military command under Avitus, now his prisoner, and, though he might not because of his ancestors hold in his own person the imperial power, he was destined to make and unmake ruler after ruler in these days. So now he set up Majorian after brief delay upon the throne of the West; and again Sidonius thought fit to celebrate in laureate verse a monarch, the man who had undone his family pride. Majorian also failed to lead to triumph the soldiers of Rome against Gaiseric, that ever-present enemy who still ruled for their terror in Africa and menaced the Western world; through this failure he was condemned to die by Ricimer's command, and Severus by the same overruling agency was set to reign in his stead. No deed of fame could mark his years of dominion, as he had neither character nor force. Upon his death, amid the general strife of candidates, none was appointed to follow him, till two years later Leo, Emperor of the East, and in this interval sole sovereign of the Roman world, declared that Anthemius, son-in-law of his predecessor on the Eastern throne, should reign over the West, and won consent from Ricimer by promising him marriage with a daughter of the future royal house.

Now again we hear Sidonius as poet of imperial destinies, this time, moreover, as champion of his native Gaul. Here the second Theodoric had fallen before the violence of Euric, his brother; and Euric desired to see himself king of all the Gallic realm, a fate abhorred by all true Gallic sons of Rome. Therefore Sidonius, now Bishop of Clermont in Auvergne, a district especially dear to Euric's ambitious heart, journeyed to the Imperial City with other dignities of Gaul to plead his country's cause before this new occupant of the throne; his third pæan of praise was told in honour of the son of the East, Anthemius, for this end. It won for its writer the Prefecture of Rome, but it did not save Auvergne from Euric's hand; and the year 475 saw the passing of its rich territory from control of Julius Nepos, last Emperor of Rome, to the rule of the great Gothic Lord.

And not only were there in the fifth century those who turned to praise of men for this world's military deeds. Before it dawned, the evil and rampant luxury of the day had driven those of nobler ideals or impatient spirit to seek refuge in the simpler life. Already in many a desert place of Asia and Africa were found the huts of solitaries pledged to live in accordance with the strictest meaning of the threefold monastic vow; and in great cities, in Alexandria, in Constantinople, in Rome, were numbers who remained in, but not of, the world of strife and murder and profligate desire. It was needful that from the thousands who thus sought peace some should put into written words the ideals for which they laboured, if haply others might see and be saved by some like means. From the retreat of Bethlehem Jerome sent forth that famous stream of writings of exegesis, theology, devotion; not till his death in 420 did its abundance fail. From Africa, land of his birth, Augustine not only with the *City of God* encouraged those who scarcely believed, but by constant letters and more formal works on matters of Faith and Order toiled to defend the Church from her enemies for Christ; from Egypt Cassian returned to teach the future monks of Gaul what he had learned at the feet of abbots of the desert and the Nile.

At home heroes of holy life drew after them disciples whose praises excelled anything that poets of secular verse had told. Saint Martin found his Sulpicius and Paulinus of Périgueux, Honoratus his Hilary to tell the wonders of the life of monks in the West. Such counsels, given in theory and shown forth in practice, were accompanied also at home by writings that endeavoured to teach and help Christian men, struggling in combat against hydra-headed heresy. Thus Vincent in the tranquil haven of his island refuge thought it well to remind himself and all who were distressed of the essential truths of the Catholic Faith ever and everywhere held fast by the saints.

The calm of those dwelling in religious retreat was shared in spirit by a number who from various angles have left us a picture of peace among all the troubles that encircled their lives. Even in this distracted century no fewer than five writers were able to think in leisurely fashion on the Bible story and repeat it for the benefit of men. Of the work of these the epic of Avitus on the Creation and the Fall of Man is too little known in our time. He lived to see Anthemius fall by violence, and Ricimer meet a natural end, to dwell for a moment on the passing figures of two Emperors of a day, Olybrius and Glycerius, names hardly known to history in their brief holding of fame, to find the last lawful actor on the imperial stage, Julius Nepos, driven from his throne by the usurper Romulus "Augustulus," and finally with his death bringing to a close the long-drawn-out tragedy of the Roman Empire in the West. Four years before this end the usurper himself yielded to the Scirian champion Odovacar, suffered by Zeno, now Emperor of the East, to administer the West under his own supreme command as Overlord of Rome both Old and New.

Thenceforth Avitus and his friends in Gaul must scarcely

have dared to believe the tidings they heard of the rending asunder of Italy by the struggle for its rule between two barbarians, Odovacar and Theodoric the Ostrogoth, of the ghastly siege of Ravenna where for so many years had reigned the Imperial Court of Rome, of the massacre by Theodoric in their hundreds of Odovacar's men, of the final capture of the City in the Marshes and the slaying of the Scirian by Theodoric's own deed. And yet in his bishopric in Gaul he could tell in Latin hexameters of earliest Man and ancient Israel, could even pour forth a book of praise to comfort his sister in Religion for her unwedded life. In Marseilles in this same century Claudius Marius Victor laboured to repeat like truths for the instruction of his age; Sedulius told both of the Old Covenant and the New in his *Passover Song;* in Africa the tale of God's work of the Six Days was repeated by Dracontius for the glory of the Creator and for the softening of the wrath of one of those Vandal monarchs whose line followed in sequence upon Gaiseric's victorious descent.

Nevertheless, these writers could find reason for their labour if they might revive before their fellows the dealings of God with men of old; but there were others who seemed to dwell on words in prose and verse for their own pleasure's sake. Amid the threats of an ever-encroaching enemy that crept nearer and nearer to his home in Auvergne with conquest after conquest, Sidonius and his friends, as we learn from those most valuable *Letters* of his pen, lived on peacefully in scholarly pursuits, now exchanging epistles, now efforts at composition both serious and trifling and criticism on the same, with travelling and pastime of the hunt to vary the routine of their days. One can but agree with the argument that familiarity with barbarians must have added unconscious to conscious contempt for these invaders and their

uncultured ways in the minds of aristocrats of Gaul. Equally filled with thoughts of his own things was the meditation in metrical form by which Paulinus of Pella gave thanks to God for his conversion from a life of careless ease to the Christian acceptance of the toils and sufferings which beset his later years.

But even these works did tell at least of troubles of the world from which they came. Most out of keeping, however, with sorrow was that quaint medley of cheerful tale in which during the vital struggle of the time, it may be while Africa was falling into Vandal hands, Martianus Capella compiled for future generations of studious minds the principles of the Seven Liberal Arts. For true it is that even in the death agonies of mighty powers men still seek relief in pastimes and preoccupations that form a contrast also for us who read of them side by side with the records of the troubles then present and yet to come in the Empire's last end.

Here then we have some momentary glimpse of a few of the many writings of this strenuous time: words of complaint, warning, and consolation from those who gaze steadily upon its picture of gloom, words of praise and hope from those who look back upon its glories of old and trust still in the leaders of the age, books of instruction for the simple and for the scholar, for the pagan and for the people of God, didactic statements of history and pleasant dallyings with journeys from day to day—in truth, a varied tale.

Why therefore, if the content of these writings shows such diversity of thought, is the treatment so superficial in great part, the form so full of artifice and striving for effect, so lacking in depth and dignity? It is certain that the hand of rhetoric lay heavily upon writers of both verse and prose without number. Among such Sidonius and Avitus in their *Letters*, Merobaudes in his metrical periods, still show us their laboured work, valuable only for the aid it gives to historians' search; of such again in passing measure was Capella whom medieval students of erudition loved so long and faithfully. Compared with the romantic feeling of Ausonius, with the exuberant fervour of Prudentius' zeal for the Faith, which even in the declining days of the fourth century had given new life to literature, the lines of Claudian ring but coldly in their sonorous march, the elegiacs of Rutilius reecho in formal imitation of classic models of by-gone days.[1] For the freshness of life was wanting. To the glory of an Empire's hope, old yet new, centred in Augustus, had succeeded the lordship of little men, ruling an Empire by help of alien blood, by force of soldiers from afar. It is significant that this fifth century's literature comes in so tiny measure from Italy herself; the members of the Empire still lived, though uninspired by hope from the heart and centre of all. And so writers of imperial deeds played with courtly phrase and tricks of style to catch a big man's fancy since they lacked the union of one compelling loyalty. To the freshness of that zeal which drove on Lucretius to watch in nightlong search for truth, had succeeded surfeit of training in knowledge won by effort of ages past, in minds that no longer knew joy of creative thought on higher things and so tried to find content in rhetoric and precious effect of tongue and pen. To the hope of the countryside which in days of old had given to Rome so glorious a theme, had succeeded a great fear in the hearts of lowly men, as they looked on the threatened loss of home, of sustenance, of their land and City herself, from menace of government within, of enemies without; while men of loftier place foresaw the future and deemed it folly to resist the tide of fate. Upon the glory of the first enthusiasm for the Christian Faith, which had sent martyrs joyously to prove their steadfastness by death, had followed already the sense of familiarity which evoked compliance with external rite as matter of usage and tradition but scarcely stirred the inner workings of the heart. No longer was it cause of peril to safety or success that one should profess the newer creed. The pendulum had swung the other way.

Yet there are exceptions indeed for which we may be thankful. In poetry, the majesty of Rome raised Claudian in higher and Rutilius in lower degree to write lines in keeping with their cause; the glory of God's Creation made its poets at times worthy of their name. In prose, who can doubt the power with which Augustine vindicated the Christian Faith, or can fail to feel with the vigour of Jerome or the simple eagerness of Saint Martin's follower? It is true also that Salvian and Orosius thought but little of form in their ardent thought upon their task, that Cassian willed to write a plain tale for his teaching's sake, that Sedulius tried in the same way to reach all men alike.

For it cannot be denied that to the inspiration of Christian thought, replacing in bond of union the dying pagan faith, the people of Latin tongue owed the fact that in the days which followed Claudian they left not themselves altogether without witness of their power in written word, whether called forth for encouragement or rebuke or in pointing of milestones by those who led the way along the newer paths. To Claudian, to Rutilius Namatianus, it was the Imperial City, Rome, that had made one of all civilized lands; to Orosius it was the Christian Faith that gave him to "find in all the earth his Fatherland." From the last throes of the conflict between pagan and Christian, from the first combats of the Christian creed, steadily rising above the horizon of men's apprehension, with the teachings it rejected from its own domain, from the age-long struggle between the glamour of the world and the spirit of renunciation, from the joy in the personal sense of adventure in fields of religion waiting to be explored by those who dared to penetrate a little deeper than the disciples of convention, were born the utterances which these pages will describe. Often artificial, often crude in their form, they are yet fruitful of interest, not only in regard to their teaching of spiritual truth, but for the sake of those candle lights which in some measure relieve the darkness of history and literature in this disastrous time.

CHAPTER II

SECULAR POETRY

At the advent of the fifth century among perils of robbers and barbarians the Roman hero of the hour was Stilicho, and therefore no story of its literature may neglect mention of his poet, Claudius Claudianus. Now Claudian, of course, belongs in great part to the fourth century, and, moreover, has been fully discussed and criticized in many works,[1] so that we need recall here only those poems which belong to our period. They are few, but most important, and include some of his best work: the three books on the Consulship of Stilicho, the poem on the Gothic War, the panegyric on the Sixth Consulship of Honorius, the two poems relating to Serena, wife of Stilicho, and sundry of the *Carmina Minora*.[2]

No work of Claudian can be dated later than the fifth year of the century; as Glover states: "he suddenly appears a ripened poet in 395 and after nine years of great fertility as suddenly disappears in 404."[3] We are told that he was born in Egypt and was a citizen of Alexandria;[4] from his own words we learn that he began his literary life by writing Greek poetry, of which some fragments of more or less credited authorship yet remain, and that he turned to Latin when Probinus was consul in 395.[5] Thenceforth he gradually practised his hand in its twofold work—for the glory of his friends and the disrepute of foes. Friendship found expression in further praise of Probinus and of Olybrius in their consulship: a beginning of laud of noble senators which was steadily maintained throughout the poet's career by his

17

joy in Stilicho's regard for the Senate and by his own deference to that body, amply repaid by his popularity among the aristocrats of Rome.[6] On the other side we find the invective which pursued the murdered Rufinus, Prætorian Prefect of Constantinople, and the careful justification of this deed, incited by Stilicho himself.

So vigorous a start was followed by the glorifying of Honorius, Emperor of the Rome that ever did and ever shall lead the world despite the menaces of East and West, of Stilicho who shall carry out the triumph of Rome's victory over her present dangers, of Honorius as bridegroom and as consul in repeated years, of Stilicho as hero of the war against the rebel Gildo in Africa. Denunciation likewise did not cease in telling of the vile turpitude of the hated successor of Rufinus in Arcadius' good graces, Eutropius, the "bald old eunuch," under whom the East still planned and plotted against the career of the Vandal leader of the West.

In this way by the year 400 we find Claudian's power at its height. So far is he now from betraying weakness through his early training in a foreign tongue that his complete mastery of the Latin language and its art of poetry neither falters nor errs as he sweeps along in the splendid force of his finely wrought hexameter.[7] In the realm of State his position likewise was assured; he had won favour in the Imperial Court, then settled at Milan, and during the last years of his career was distinguished both as a *vir clarissimus*, or member of the third (and lowest) Senatorial order, and as a tribune and notary of the Imperial Council.[8] In 400, moreover, external affairs were at a point most advantageous for himself and his patron.[9] In the East Eutropius had fallen before the hatred of Gaïnas, Master of Soldiers, and the jealousy of the Empress Eudoxia; in the

West Alaric had not yet begun his descents upon Italy. It was doubtless in high hope that he returned from long absence to magnify the state of Stilicho, consul in this year. If Stilicho is "Scipio's heir," as we are told, then his poet must follow Ennius. The underlying thought is significant. Claudian can now boldly step forward as an official panegyrist of merited place and power.[10]

The praises of the First Consulship of Stilicho are divided into three books, comprising some twelve hundred lines in all. The first tells of the merits of the Consul with the poet's accustomed exaggeration:

> Each man his special gift
> Ennobles: comeliness, or strength in arms,
> Or sternness, loyalty, or skill in law,
> Or children, or pure wedlock, one to each,
> In their divided lot; thou holdest all.[11]

For this hero, Claudian declares, was the admiration of all who saw his tall erect figure passing along the streets of Rome, while he was yet but a simple soldier. His father might well count it sufficient glory that Stilicho was born his son; the Emperor chose him as bridegroom for his niece and adopted daughter from out all the world of youth; the people of his day were not conscious of the passing of Theodosius when Stilicho held the reins of power. Even his enemies flocked to submit when once they had looked upon his face and seen the wonder of his deeds. In solemn procession his triumphs pass in review before us: his mission to the East, his vengeance on the Bastarnæ for their murder of Theodosius' general Promotus, his campaigns in Thrace and on the lower Danube. In truth, had not the "secret traitor," Rufinus to wit, deceived imperial ears, we are assured that Alans, Goths, and all the horde of barbarians in

the country would have disappeared from the ken of mankind. So great the varied army he led forth that its like
had never been beheld from East to West! All the East was
gathered therein, Colchians, Spaniards, dwellers in Armenia
and in Araby, the painted Mede and Indian of swarthy
face. Yet so great peace and reverence were found under
his rule that no settler suffered loss, no rebellion stirred his
ordered ranks. Thus did he "deliver" Greece from Alaric's
menace, and pacify the district of the Rhine, and crush in
Africa the peril to the Imperial City of famine by the closing
of her store. The floodtide of Claudian's praise is reached
in the lines which show his hero unmoved by either the
Gildonic threatening in the West or by fear of treachery in
the unfriendly Empire of the East:

> What first, O Stilicho, shall I admire?
> That guarded wisdom ever conquered guile,
> That secret document and hand afire
> With gold could nowise lurk unseen? That naught
> Unworthy of this Latin land in time
> Of so great terror thou didst ever say,
> That proudly answer thou hast rendered high
> To men of Eastern race, nor straightway failed
> To prove thy words in deed, contemptuous still
> Though wealthy lands they held and dwellings famed:
> An easy loss to bear, while public weal
> Was never bent to thine own secret aim.[12]

It is a pity that lines so noble in their native dress should
be forced to meet the chilling criticism of scholarship regarding their foundation of truth. Yet it is of course known
to all students of the time that Stilicho did not go near
Africa to conquer Gildo in 397, but entrusted the campaign
to Mascezel, Gildo's brother and betrayer; it has even been
suggested that Stilicho from jealousy caused Mascezel to be

put to death.[13] It is also known that Stilicho during his first
expedition into Northern Greece in 395 was bidden to stay
military proceedings against Alaric by Arcadius, instigated
by his adviser Rufinus; and that in the second expedition
led by Stilicho to oppose Alaric in the South "the Gothic
enemy was spared in Elis much as he had been spared in
Thessaly." [14] We cannot read with undimmed enjoyment
therefore the exulting cry of triumph:

> With thee, as leader, now erect
> From out the flames Greece raised her weary head;

even though on the second occasion Alaric did retire from
Elis at Stilicho's behest.

The second book tells of the character of Stilicho, in
whom abide Clemency and her sister Faith, with all other
virtues of high renown. And therefore the peoples, Gallic,
Punic, Pannonian and drinkers of the Save, unite to honour
him and give him thanks; the goddesses of the Empire and
Rome herself entreat that he become their consul and lead
his country in the ways of Brutus of old. Their words are
completed for us by a vision of the mighty cave, mother of
time, whence the Sun God bids the golden years come forth
to bless the ruling of the hero. The third book, in the midst
of even more lurid flatteries, is redeemed by passages such
as the well-known words on freedom:

> Falsely he thinks, who under righteous Kings
> Deems men but slaves . . . :

and the equally noted outburst for the glory of Rome, which
shows the poet at his best: [15]

> Among the stars with golden splendour rise
> Her spires in rivalry; her seven cliffs
> Like zones of great Olympus tower; within,

Mother of armour's might and law's restraint,
She rules all races, cradled in her breast
Lay new-born Justice. Sprung from narrow bounds,
Her glory she hath stretched to either pole,
From tiny birthplace she extends her arms
Wide as the sun. Did she not challenge Fate,
When battles countless in one hour she waged,
Took captive Spain, besieged Sicilian towns,
By land the Gaul, by sea Phœnician power
Laid prostrate? From her toils victorious,
And conquered by no wound, did she not rage
With fiercer ardour after Cannæ's field,
And Trebia's stream? Yea, with her land aflame
And foemen at her walls did she not speed
Her soldiers to Hiberian wars afar,
Nor stayed by Ocean's fear, with stroke of oars
Sought Britain's conquest in a world remote?
And who but Rome her vanquished enemies
Hath nurtured tenderly, all human kind
With common name of Mother hath received,
Mother, not tyrant; called men citizens,
Whom she hath caught and bound with loyal chain,
Far distant though they stand? Of her control
And gracious peace it comes that pilgrims now
May find on foreign shores their home, may pass
In safety sure from coast to coast, rejoice
To look on Thule's isle, and far within
The dreaded wilderness may penetrate,
Drink of Orontes' waters, or the Rhone,
Nor ever stray beyond the Motherland.

It has been pointed out that the poem on the Gothic War and on the battle of Pollentia, in which Stilicho and Alaric met in indecisive clash on Easter Day, 402, reveals in the light of after events the fallacy of contemporary pictures of history.[16] Claudian has shown his hero in these pages as the

sole hope of Rome in the dread day of Alaric's first advent
into Italy, and her sole saviour in the hour of her final
triumph and of Alaric's discomfiture. We cannot see here
the future invasions which after this passing hour were yet
to place the City in the hands of Alaric as victor after his
triple siege. In the preface Claudian tells he has received a
statue—not such a marvellous matter among the many
which stood in Rome [17]—and then begins his story of the
panic of Emperor and people when first the news of Alaric's
approach was heard in 401 by the terrified dwellers about
the Court in Milan:

> Seemed not, though once unbending in their strength,
> The towers to weaken then, the brittle walls
> To sink, the ironbound gates to Gothic men
> To open of their will? Nor bulwark nor
> Thick-planted stakes to stay the onward leap
> And rush of horses' flying feet? Now, now,
> We hasten to our ships to seek as home
> Sardinian shores and rocks of Cyrnus drear,
> To save our lives upon the foaming sea.[18]

The same terror was pictured by Paulinus in the eighth of
the poems which he wrote at Nola to celebrate the returning birthdays of his patron Felix; although the times are
full of dread and rumours of wars are in the air, yet he de-
termines to rejoice in the Feast, trusting in the intercession
of his dear Saint.[19] Prudentius likewise told of Alaric's coming in his second book against Symmachus, and glorified
Honorius and Stilicho, who had conquered through the power
of Christ.[20] In Claudian's narrative terrible portents appear
and all is full of dismay; Honorius is imprisoned under siege
at Milan: [21]

> And only Stilicho in our despair
> Divined for us some better thing to come,

> And of our doubtful fate stood forth at once
> The captain and the seer.[22]

It is Stilicho who encourages Honorius and his citizens, who
sails the Larian Lake in mid-winter in a little boat, who
crosses the mountains into Rætia to stay the invasion of
Radagaisus and obtain reinforcements for the Italian army;
Stilicho who returns as suddenly as he went, inspiring with
his confidence troops to flock to him from various quarters
and gladdening the eyes of the crowd in Milan who look for
his approach:

> Who might with truth the Prince's joy
> Describe, the eager welcome of the Court?
> As from the lofty tower we strain our gaze,
> A distant cloud of dust we catch, afraid,
> Uncertain from its shaping whether friends
> Or foes it brings us; anxious silence still
> Keeps poised our judgment, till beneath the whirl
> Of eddying sand flashed Stilicho's high head,
> Familiar gleam of white, like to some star.
> Then glad along the rampart rolls the cry,
> " 'Tis he! he comes!!" [23]

And therefore in the Gothic camp fear replaces buoyant
confidence of victory. A veteran chieftain even counsels retreat while this is yet possible. To him Alaric replies with
scorn. His past deeds of glory, his destiny, the gods themselves, all point for him the road to Rome with the repeated
cry "Penetrabis ad Urbem!", which Claudian contemptu-
ously explains as referring to Alaric's advance to the River
Urbis. In a few words the battle of Pollentia is painted,
ending, as Claudian puts it, in a Roman triumph; and the
ears of the defeated Gothic leader are assailed by the
lamentations of his wife, who has eagerly awaited the spoils

of victory from his hand. Now under Stilicho, as under
Marius, Rome has conquered the barbarians; and in one
day the Roman battle-line has paid in full the losses of
thirty years of ravagings.[24] The moral is clear:

Learn thus, O world insane, to reverence Rome.

Yet all was not so glorious as it sounds. Although the
Romans had the advantage, they gained no complete conquest, and Alaric was allowed to depart with his army un-
pursued. A like clemency was shown him after a second
encounter with Stilicho at Verona in 403, described in the
poem on the Sixth Consulship of Honorius. Here Alaric is
represented indeed as retreating in downcast spirit after his
defeat:

Now humbled by Pollentia's fatal plain,
Though life, as usage bids, was yielded free,
Yet gone were all those many men-at-arms,
And gone his plundered wealth; and he himself
Must needs by order leave the Latin land.
So thus an enemy, and turning back
Upon the topmost point of destiny
Immense, his shameful way he backward traced.[25]

As he comes one of the Naiads sees him and hastens to tell
the joyful news to Father Eridanus, who sits pondering the
issue of these wars and the decrees of Jupiter for Rome.
The tidings impel him to rise in his splendidly wrought
raiment and heap reproaches on the dejected warrior for his
folly in dreaming to bring discomfiture upon the City of the
Gods, undeterred even by the dire example of Phaethon's
fate. With these words the God calls other rivers to rejoice with him over the beaten enemy, and all the spirits of
the countryside unite in thanksgiving. When now the fugitive attempts to escape through the precipitous mountain

passes to Rætia or Gaul, he finds himself hemmed in on all
sides by the penetrating skill of Stilicho and finally imprisoned on one small spot of rising ground. Food is wanting, pestilence is rife; his soldiers hurl taunts at him, their
desertions multiply daily and whole divisions slip away from
his command; his words of rebuke and entreaty are of no
avail. Then at last does he despair:

> Ah me! with what beguiling wraps me round
> The ever fateful Stilicho! He feigns
> To spare me, yet his warriors' zeal the while
> Renews, availing over Padus' stream
> To start fresh conflict. O more cruel this pact
> Than bitter yoke! Then died the Gothic might,
> Then, only then, I struck my bond with Death.
> More fierce than weapons mercy storms our race,
> Mars lurks more grievous under Peace disguised,
> And I am captured, I too in my turn,
> By cunning all mine own. What comforter,
> What counsel shall I find to cheer my heart?
> Men fear me more as comrade than as foe.
>
> .   .   .   .
>
> Why then the hateful light of day drag on?
> Where now the fragments of my wreck conceal?
> What fields discover wherein Stilicho,
> And Italy's too-powerful name no more
> Shall ring about mine ears? [26]

Once again Stilicho allowed his rival to escape, and gave
reason to his enemies to bring charge against him of treachery. This matter of Stilicho's repeated leniency toward
Alaric is a vexed one, viewed variously by writers both
ancient and modern. Claudian himself takes much trouble
in defending his hero:

Nay, other reasons gave his mercy birth.
He thought, O Rome, on thee, thy welfare bade
Him open to his captives flight, lest worse
In thrall should rage their madness, well aware
Of death awaiting; nor, wert thou assailed
By nearer aim, deemed he that vanished race
And name of Gothic men would pay the price.[27]

The despair of Alaric pictured above is invented, we may think, for the same end. Yet modern students of history are inclined to agree so far with this apology as to admit that it was the part of prudence for Stilicho, who had already been compelled to seek reinforcement from Rætia for his army, who was threatened by intrigue in the East and by the danger of Radagaisus, the German barbarian, to try to pacify rather than to drive to desperation this enemy who might have united arms with Radagaisus for the destruction of the Empire. Further, Stilicho was of barbarian blood himself and could not be expected to look with horror upon barbarian enemies as did Apollinaris Sidonius and his aristocratic friends of a later day in Gaul. And thirdly, Alaric was to prove useful, Stilicho hoped, in aiding him to capture part of Illyricum from the Empire of the East.[28]

The remainder of the poem is taken up with Rome's reproaches to Honorius that the City is deserted by her rulers. Only thrice within a hundred years has an Emperor been received within her walls, and each time because of civil tumult. The point of this reproach lay in the fact that the Roman populace was granted special indulgences by the Empire in consideration of the ruler's residence in their midst; a well-fed and well-entertained body of citizens might indeed be trusted to show their loyalty to the Court, the removal of which might lead to the withdrawal of material privileges and the establishing of Constantinople as a more favoured imperial capital than the Eternal City herself.[29] Honorius answers, of course, in Claudian's panegyric that his absence has been more than compensated by the presence of his general. Finally, however, the prayer is granted, and all ends happily with the triumphant entry of the Emperor and Stilicho side by side into a Rome enlarged and beautified, her new walls built to resist the terror of the Gothic invasion. Games are held, and the year of Honorius' Sixth Consulship is sent rejoicing on its way.

Much has been written on Claudian's ethics as historian. The fact that he is the only writer who tells in detail some of the history of his time gives to his work an importance often sadly out of harmony with the judgment it reveals; for his worship of his patrons and unrelaxing condemnation of their enemies drive investigators constantly to compare his account with the far less vivid and, in cases, fragmentary writings of Churchmen, Greek historians, and chroniclers. It is difficult, moreover, to judge of Claudian's reliability amid the differing views of other men. For, if Claudian was over-partial to Stilicho, other Latin writers of the fifth century were not; Rutilius Namatianus the poet and Orosius the historian waxed vehement in bitterness of attack upon him. Our special Greek authority, Zosimus, even differs in tone according to his differing source; in following Eunapius, who was a pagan, and lived in the East where Stilicho was declared a public enemy, Zosimus looks on the Vandal leader of Rome with hostile eye; in following Olympiodorus, who is friendly to Stilicho, he adopts likewise a kindly attitude.[30] Unfortunately the works of Eunapius and of Olympiodorus do not help us as they might in a less interrupted state. We may admit indeed with his critics that Claudian errs in various ways: by omission, by misinterpretation, by exaggeration. On the other hand, we may also agree with his defenders that his lesser untruths must lie on a sound basis of fact because he was encompassed by so great a crowd of witnesses, his characters were so well-known, the events of which he told were so recent in men's minds, his poems boldly offered to criticism in recitation at the great festivals and imperial gatherings of Rome. If we take into careful account the writer's own personal prejudices and ambitions and remember that he was working for the Empire of the West, always more or less engaged in rivalry and strife of Church and State with the East, we shall not go far astray under his hand.

Certain of the minor poems which have been attributed to these years are worthy of notice. Especially delightful is No. 20, on the old man of Verona who had never passed beyond the fields encircling his town—that town which had seen, with what dismay!, its peace so rudely disturbed by the clashing forces of Roman defenders and the assailants of the year 403: [31]

> O happy he who lives in fields his own,
> > Whom the same homestead sees both young and old,
> Who leans on staff where once as child he played,
> > And in one cottage counts his years unrolled;
> Whom fortune has not dragged in varied maze,
> > Nor has he drunk a wanderer's stream alone,
> Nor feared the trader's storms nor bugle's call,
> > Nor yet in market-place loud strife has known.
> Untaught in worldly things, to city strange,
> > His joy he holds beneath these freer skies;
> By harvests, not by consuls, reckons time,
> > By fruits the autumn, spring by flowers, descries.

The same field hides the suns, the same reveals,
    By his own world this farmer measures day;
His tiny seedling now a mighty oak,
    His woods he watches with himself grow gray.
More distant yet than swarthy India lies
    Verona for him at his very door;
Benacus' waters might, for all he knows,
    Be beating ever on the Red Sea's shore.
Yet in his strength untamed and stalwart form
    Three generations sees this sage uncouth;
Let others wander even to furthest Spain,
    More part have they of travel, he of truth.

The *Praise of Serena*, No. 30 of the *Carmina Minora*, tells in its unfinished length of some two hundred hexameter verses of the charm of this niece of Theodosius the Great, with whom neither Claudia nor Penelope may compete; of the affection of the Emperor for her when a little child and her power over him as she grew older and lived in his palace as his adopted daughter. When stress of public care bore hard upon the Chief and he returned home in stern or wrathful mood, when sons fled before their father's face and his wife herself feared his angry presence, Serena alone could soften and heal with persuasive words.[32] Later comes the story of her marriage with Stilicho and her happy wedded life, unmarred by foreboding of tragedies to come. Another poem in elegiacs briefly thanks Serena for her help in furthering the marriage of the poet with a lady of North Africa. He has journeyed thither to celebrate his wedding, and prays her to wish for him a safe return.

So much for things secular. The spirit and the form of Claudian's poetry have been clearly portrayed in the judgment of critics like Mackail and Glover.[33] With their help we may realize the purity and abounding richness of his language, the dignity and deep rhythm of his majestic verse, the wide range of the epithets and pictures with which his imagination lights up his tale. With them again we may feel his lack of intimate correspondence with the warm realities of life, whether it be that his precise Alexandrian classicism was untinged by the romantic feeling of the dawning Middle Ages, whether it be that his conventional expressions of belief, his faith in Empire rather than in any God, could give no comfort in an age that needed so sorely the inspiration of a wholly alive and certain religious creed. And perhaps here a word may find place on the poet's stand-point in religion. For his adherence, at least in conventional manner, to the faith of his pagan fathers there is ample argument from evidence both from without and from within his work. Augustine wrote of him that he ascribed to God the victory of the Emperor Theodosius, in spite of the fact that the poet was a "stranger to the name of Christ": [34] a statement followed up by Augustine's disciple Orosius in the description of Claudian as "an excellent poet in truth, but a most obstinate heathen." [35] The writings themselves are saturated with pagan colour, full of pagan mythology, and constant in their reference to the gods of old. Boissier remarks that Claudian, although sharing with Prudentius and Orosius their intense love for the City of their forebears in its hour of menace, could yet excel them in patriotism because he had never forsaken its creed, and that he won thus the hearts of Roman Senators by his glorifying of pagan Rome.[36] Expressions proper to a pagan pen meet the eye throughout the poet's work: Theodosius dwells in glory, a new star among the constellations on high; Stilicho prays for aid to Mars; Alaric is rebuked for his assault upon the "City of the Gods." [37] More significant are the two passages in praise of Victory. In one of these, amid the description of the triumphant entry of Honorius and

Stilicho into Rome, at the end of the poem on the Emperor's
Sixth Consulship, Claudian writes:

> In her own temple stands swift Victory,
> Guard of the Roman name; with ample wing
> She fosters holy shrines where statesmen throng.
> Unwearied comrade of thy camp, at length
> She joys in union, and for evermore
> Gives thee to Rome, to thee herself entrusts.[38]

The lately restored goddess, it would seem, was honoured in
the triumph of the Christian Emperor.[39] Equally striking in
Claudian's poetry is the absence of Christian phrase and
word.[40] Twice an attack on Christian practice may be suspected, though in general the poet abstains from blame as
from praise. The first instance appears in a reference to the
sending of Eutropius, afterward High Chamberlain in the
Eastern Court, by Theodosius the Great to enquire of the
Thebaid monk John what fortune might attend the campaign against Eugenius in 394. Claudian writes scornfully
of the hated rival of Stilicho:

> No more for thee false visions sees the Nile,
> Nor, piteous creature, watch thy seers for thee; [41]

and describes the oracle obtained by him as "Egyptian
dreams." [42] The second assault is descried in the irreverent
references to Christian Saints in the fiftieth of the lesser
poems—*In Iacobum*—dated 401:

> By pyre of Paul, by hoary Peter's shrine,
> Harm not my verse, Sir Jacob, I entreat.
> So for thy breastplate thee may Thomas shield,
> As comrade warring go Bartholomew;
> So help thee Saints that Alps no Goths invade,
> So blest Susanna be to thee defence;

So, if he boldly swim the Ister cold,
Thy foe be drowned like Pharaoh's wingèd steeds;
So vengeful missile smite the Gothic troops,
And Roman legions favouring Thekla guide;
So may thy guest in dying give thee praise,
And may tip-tilted pitchers quench thy thirst;
So ne'er may foeman's blood defile thy hand,
Harm not my verse, Sir Jacob, I beseech.[48]

It would seem that the evidence fully justified scholars in acclaiming Claudian as the last of Rome's great pagan poets. But this judgment has been contested by the existence— amply supported by MS. tradition of the best kind—among the *Carmina Minora* of a poem fully, if conventionally, Christian in expression. It is entitled *De Salvatore*, and belongs naturally to the time following the accession of Honorius in 395:

CHRIST, Lord of all, of this returning age
Creator, Voice and Consciousness of God,
Whom from his Mind mysterious poured on high
The Father sent, and gave to share his throne;
Who of our life the disobedient deeds
Didst conquer, patient of this body's dress,
Of intercourse with men, of human name;
Who, God revealed, in secret didst increase
A virgin's womb, that with amazement knew,
A Maiden Mother, in her Son her Lord;
Who made the heavens, yet hid in mortal heart,
Who wrought this world, yet shared our human race,
Beneath one breast concealed embraced all things
Created far and wide; whom neither earth
Nor sea nor sky can hold, yet now lay bound
In tiny flesh. Nay! thou a felon's name
And bonds didst undergo to rescue us
From peril, banishing from out our midst

> Death by thy death; then borne on clouds above
> Didst seek thy Father's joy from cleansèd earth.
>> Keep thou our ruler, that with holy days
>> He may observe the round of feast and fast.[44]

These lines have caused scholars of the authority of Birt, Vollmer, Bardenhewer, and Rolfe [45] to believe that Claudian professed externally some sharing in the Christian creed, though scrupulously maintaining in his writings the forms of the pagan faith. Style and metre both confirm the Claudian authorship and forbid ascription to another pen, such as that of Claudianus Mamertus or of Damasus the Pope; other poets of undoubted Christian profession, such as Ausonius, Dracontius, and Sidonius, used freely details of pagan mythology; while Christian poets of recognized standing, Merobaudes and Sedulius, imitated this poem in question and thus seem to show that they respected its author, who was moreover himself well acquainted with Christian literature. The statement of Augustine, further, may be understood as applying to Claudian's political poems in the sense that he abstained from introducing Christian matter into them; [46] Augustine may not have seen *De Salvatore*, one of the shortest of the poet's compositions; Orosius naturally followed his master's lead. Lastly, a man truthfully characterized as a "most obstinate pagan" would not be very suitable for appointment as tribune under a Christian government,[47] while the poem *In Iacobum* and the scornful description of Thebaid oracles point rather to impatience with certain forms of pious cult than to any real aversion to the Christian Faith in itself. Such are the arguments for an inclination on Claudian's part toward Christianity. It is not claimed that he was baptized in that Faith, and indeed many so-called Christians in the fourth century lived all their lives without baptism or submitted only on the eve

of death.[48]   The thought does not seem unreasonable that
the poet, while giving formal allegiance in his verse to the
religious tradition of his forefathers and rendering foremost
glory thereto in his tribute to its external embodiment in the
City of ancient Rome, could yet find it possible at the will
of his Emperor and of his patron Stilicho, marked himself
by his tolerance of both Christian and pagan in turn, to add
the Christian Lord to the company of the old gods; and to
utter in courtly style upon some occasion of request conventional expression of deference to this new God among
gods, appearing late in time to knowledge of men—to this
new God, who might haply bring succour to the modern
world as the more familiar dwellers in Olympus had done,
he declared, so marvellously in the days of old.[49]

The question, however, is still in doubt, and Claudian remains the great witness to the glory of pagan Rome at the
opening of this fifth century.   But if he might conceivably
be thought to entertain friendliness to the Christian creed,
no one may hold this of Claudius Rutilius Namatianus,
whose description in elegiac verse of his return from Rome,
his adopted country, to his home in Gaul shows no sympathy
but rather bitterness towards its faith.   Born of high station
in Transalpine Gaul, at Toulouse, probably, or Poitiers, he
was taken in early youth to Italy by his father Lachanius,
who as *consularis* administered the region of Tuscany and,
it seems, was dignified in Rome by the offices of *comes
sacrarum largitionum, quæstor,* and *præfectus urbis.*   In
the capital city Rutilius himself also attained high rank, and
fulfilled the duties of *magister officiorum* and of prefect in
his turn.   The year of his prefecture, which he held for
only about eight months, was 414, and in September, 416, he
left Italy on his journey homewards.   We do not know
certainly what prompted this return; he himself tells us that

pity for the afflicted state of Gaul called him back. That country was indeed for the time at peace by covenant of the Visigoths with Honorius and by their promise of departure for the harrying of other invaders in Spain, although we can realize only too well in what state the tide of invasion had left it. Another and perhaps more potent reason for his return may be seen in his resolute adherence to a pagan belief in a city officially Christian.

The history of the tradition of his poem is one of chance. The manuscript lay hidden till 1493 when Giorgio Merula despatched his secretary Giorgio Galbiato to Bobbio for research in connection with Merula's proposed narrative of the Visconti. In the monastery Galbiato accidentally discovered a number of Latin works previously forgotten, among them this *De Suo Reditu* of Rutilius. The *editio princeps* was not issued till 1520, when it appeared at Bologna, the work of J. B. Pius, consisting of one book of 644 lines and the fragment of a second. It opens with the mournful decision to say farewell to Rome and with the story of Gaul's unhappy fate at the hands of the barbarian invaders of 406 and the following years:

> But now my fate is cut from these dear moorings,
> With me, their son, my native pastures plead;
> Unsightly they may seem through war's long conflicts,
> Yet, shorn of beauty, deeper pity need.
> Contempt of tranquil folk is no great sinning,
> But common troubles seek for each man's care;
> Our ready tears we owe to homes ancestral,
> Nor vain the service rendered to their prayer.
> No longer may we shun that wide destruction,
> That sorrow's measure by our sloth refilled;
> Haste we in fire's cruel wastes and ravaged acres
> New homes, if only shepherds' cots, to build.

Could but the springs themselves send forth their voices,
　　Could trees and orchards speak for us their need,
With just complaint how would they urge the tardy,
　　How to my longings add swift sailing's speed! [50]

But Italy had suffered also from the repeated invasions of
Alaric; the horror of the threefold siege and the capture of
the City were still fresh in men's minds.　And therefore
Rutilius purposes to travel home by sea rather than by land.
Before he goes he offers a last tribute to this chief City of
the Empire, Mother and Mistress of far-flung lands:

Hearken, O Queen of all thy world most fair,
　　O Rome caught up to heights of starry sky!
Hear, Mother of men, yea, Mother thou of Gods,
　　Within thy temples Heaven itself draws nigh.

Our praise be thine for ever, if Fate will,
　　In safety none can mindless be of thee,
Let cursed oblivion sooner hide the sun
　　Than to our hearts be lost thy majesty.

For like the Sun's bright rays thine equal gifts
　　Are strewn where'er the Ocean flood recedes;
Doth not the Sun-God, Phœbus, Lord of all,
　　From Rome arisen hide in Rome his steeds?

Thee neither Libya's flaming coast could stay,
　　Nor Ursa daunt thee with her armour cold;
Doth Nature's vigour reach to North and South?
　　So far the earth hath felt thy spirit bold.

One thou hast made for all, one Fatherland,
　　Fierce lords learn kindness from thy flag unfurled,
With conquered men thou sharest thine own rule,
　　One City made from what was once the world. [51]

Even from her troubles Rome shall draw future glory:

> And as new strength the down-turned torch regains,
>> From lowly fortune thou dost rise to great;
> To Roman ages pass on living laws,
>> Alone fear not the spinning-wheel of Fate.

> Though ten times sixteen and a thousand past
>> And this the ninth year now is speeding by;
> Time yet remaining runs thy race unstayed,
>> While earth shall stand, while stars abide on high.[52]

From this last passage we draw evidence for the date of the journey of Rutilius; 1169 A.U.C. = 416 A.D.[53] The chant of praise ends with a prayer that the writer's travel may be prosperous in reward for faithful service.

When however the last farewells to friends have been spoken, and in the paler sun of autumn Rutilius seeks at length the ship on the Tiber's right-hand course, the stormy setting of the Pleiads delay him there for thrice five days, gazing from his exile back to the City and catching from the Circus the shouts which hail the September Games. Then the moon changes, and the ship departs, keeping for safety close to shore, past Alsium (Palo) and Pyrgi (Santa Severa) and Cære (Cervetri) to harbour at Centumcellæ (Civita Vecchia). There a visit is made to the hot springs of the Bull, three miles distant, which in loyal pride he compares with the spring of Helicon, also caused by the blow of a hoof. At dawn the journey continues past the distant house-tops of marshy Graviscæ and the ruined walls of Cosa (Ansedonia), whose citizens, as Rutilius relates with apology for such jesting in his serious tale, were compelled by mice to desert their homes. Camp is struck this second day at Portus Herculis (Porto Ercole), and the evening hours are beguiled by stories, first of the wicked deeds of Marcus

Æmilius Lepidus, who fled thence to Sardinia after his attack on Sulla's legal reforms in 78 B.C., and then of the evil tradition of later members of that clan. The third day carries the voyagers with wide circuit past Mons Argentarius (Monte Argentario) to the sight of the distant wooded hills of the island Igilium (Giglio), which earns high praise for shelter extended to fugitives from Rome at the time of Alaric's attack. On the banks of the River Umbro (Ombrone) Rutilius wishes to land, but is compelled to travel on by his eager sailors. Soon, deserted by wind and daylight, they are forced to encamp and bivouac in improvised tents made by oars and poles from the ship.

Next day the journey proceeds by slow labour of rowing. Elba is passed, rich in ore, and iron receives commendation to the detriment of corrupting gold. At noon the tired sailors are obliged to rest in Faleria (Falese) where, as it chances, a festival of Osiris is in progress. The scenery of wood and water is delightful, but the churlish behaviour of the Jewish innkeeper gives occasion for a diatribe against the practices of his faith:

> For in that place was host a plaintive Jew,
>   A creature with no joy in human fare,
> Who damage done to shrubs and seaweed bills,
>   Demanding pay for even water there.
>
> Affronts we render due to his vile race,
>   Which circumcision's baser use delights.
> Sheer folly; sabbaths cold make glad its heart,
>   Colder that heart than its own pious rites.
>
> It wastes through shameful sloth each Sabbath day,
>   As in soft image of a weary God;
> The winding path of this mad people's lies
>   Not many a child, I think, in faith has trod.

> And would Judæa had not been oppressed
>   By Pompey's battles and by Titus' power!
> More widely creeps infection when well pruned,
>   Before the vanquished now the victors cower.[54]

Although the North wind is against them, they depart that place and reach the ruins of Populonia with its fort. The fifth day takes them past the Corsican mountains rising dim in the dawn, and Capraria, inhabited by monks, whose mode of life is strongly condemned:

> Capraria rises as our journey speeds,
>   An isle unkempt, of men who flee the light—
> Monastic in Greek term they call themselves,
>   For that they live alone beyond men's sight.
>
> They fear the gifts of Fortune, dread their loss.
>   Who would be wretched lest he wretched be?
> What madness this of foolish, erring minds
>   Which dreading evil must from blessings flee? [55]

The narrow channel leading to Volaterrana Vada is next described, and near this town, detained by rough weather, the traveller enjoys a visit to his friend Albinus, who had followed him as prefect of the City in 414 and might but for loyalty have been elected in his stead. Albinus takes him to view the saltpans in the neighbourhood, and Rutilius gives some account of their use. A cry of joy marks his meeting with Victorinus, whom the capture of Toulouse by Athaulf had driven to settle in Tuscan territory. When the journey is at length resumed, the sight of the island of Gorgon (Gorgona) gives him a shudder, for a young acquaintance of his has retired thither to lead the ascetic life of solitude:

> In midmost sea the wave-washed Gorgon's isle
>   By Corsica and Pisa's shore doth loom;

Its cliffs I shun, recalling recent loss:
Here lies a citizen in living tomb.

Just now a youth, my friend, of noble birth,
Of no less goodly state in wealth and wife,
Impelled by madness left mankind and lands,
And fondly gave to exile's shame his life.

He fancies sordid living feeds the soul,
More stern than wrathful Gods himself he finds;
Does not such sect more harm than Circe's draughts?
They altered bodies, now men change their minds.[56]

The Portus Pisanus arouses admiration by its breakwater of floating seaweed. Near it Rutilius stays awhile to visit the Villa Triturrita and Pisæ, where dwells his friend, Protadius. In the marketplace of Pisæ he rejoices to see the statue raised in honour of his father by the grateful Tuscans. Stress of weather again holds him at Triturrita, and the first book closes with an account of the enjoyment of country sports amid the violence of stormy sky and sea.

Of the second book we have only 68 lines, though from the extended introduction it has been inferred that Rutilius planned to write at some length. The fragment is, however, notable for the fierce attack upon Stilicho, who had been put to death eight years before, in 408; the bitter accusations resemble those hurled by Claudian at Rufinus.[57] For, not content with betraying his country to the Goths, Stilicho dared, writes Rutilius in a charge not found elsewhere, to burn the Sibylline Books, and outdid other traitors and murderers in his guilt. Even Nero must yield to him in evil doing; for Nero smote indeed his own mother, but Stilicho has smitten his motherland. After this outburst a few more lines bring the traveller to Luna, where his narrative suddenly breaks off.

If from this outline we turn to read the work as a whole, we find reflected in simplicity of writing a man of simple and attractive character. Trained and educated as his station required, he was at the same time a lover of plain words, fervent alike in his loyalty to country and to friend, as in his hatred of traitor and contempt for those whom he could not respect. The parts of the poem which have chiefly aroused interest are the tribute to Rome and the three attacks, upon Stilicho, upon the Jews, and upon the monastic life. Three at least of the passages concerned have been variously interpreted. Was Rutilius merely a "cold declaimer," as Gibbon judged him,[58] foolishly lauding a city whose glory had long ago passed away? Or was he happily blind to this passing in his unwavering faith in the Rome of older days? One prefers to read his words in this light. They help thus to explain his bitterness against Stilicho, even fallen and dead, in that, according to his view, Stilicho had compromised and parleyed with the Gothic enemies of the City instead of fighting them to the end as Rome had always fought those who dared oppose her. Whether Stilicho was justified in his cautious policy or partly responsible in his middle course for Rome's future disaster is a question on which, as we have remarked, writers differ.[59] For Rutilius, indeed, the effects of Gothic ravaging were evident both to ear and eye, not only in Rome, but in Gaul, and, we may believe, in that part of Gaul especially which was native to him, the district around Toulouse. Moreover, Stilicho was half a barbarian himself, deserving of suspicion for this very cause, and by no means worthy to be counted among the nobles and officials whom Rutilius naturally regarded as his own proper and loyal class. Thirdly, the man who, he believed, had burned the Sibylline Books, whose wife profaned the necklace of Rhea, Mother of the Gods, in her temple itself, could not but be hateful to the Roman who had the old faith at heart.[60]

More determined discussion has centred round the invective against the Jews and the question whether Rutilius intended in attacking them to attack the Christians also. On the one hand, there is the opinion that Rutilius, face to face with the passing of the pagan worship of his fathers, yet not daring to attack openly the official religion of the Empire, was assailing it secretly in the persons of the Jews and of the Christian devotees of the monastic life.[61] On the other, we may admit, as seems more probable, that his attitude toward Christians living in the world, among whom he and his friends had held high office, was characterized in general by nothing worse than indifference or silent contempt, and that Christians themselves might be found in plenty who had no love for monks and solitaries.[62]

Controversy marks to a lesser degree opinion on the merits of Rutilius as a writer. In spite of Gibbon's sweeping statement that his poetry as such is "mean and creeping, destitute of strength and devoid of harmony," other critics give him place among authors of the second rank, especially when viewed in the light of his contemporaries and successors. His tale carries us pleasantly along in its realistic description of the Maremma, interweaving details of geography and history, incidents of travel, personal feelings, whether joyous or bitter. Pichon has happily remarked that Rutilius differs from Ausonius and Claudian in lacking the professional zeal for learning expressed in allusion and literary reminiscence, that he reveals himself an educated amateur in his verse.[63] Imitations of earlier authors are found in number, more particularly of Vergil and Ovid, but they are not disagreeably laboured; the digressions which constantly stay the advance fit in well with the details of the route, and the writer pursues his way in leisure of body and mind after a manner that may perhaps humbly suggest the "Journey to Brundisium," to which it, of course, owed much. The metre is mainly correct and fluent, and, though care for rhetorical effect is certainly marked, as we must expect, it does not disgust or even weary the reader by its over-insistent voice.

But Rutilius in his faith in the Eternal City knew and feared little the troubles which lay in wait. We have seen that upon the ravagings of Vandals and Visigoths in Gaul and Spain followed the unsettled time after Honorius' death of the usurpation of John, supported by Aetius; and that this soldier and statesman, Aetius, born in Silistria of a Scythian father and an Italian mother, played the leading part in the government of the Empire as chief minister of Galla Placidia and her son Valentinian the third during the thirty years that followed the punishing of the pretender in 425. It is true that under Aetius Africa was lost to Rome through the opportunity granted to Gaiseric by Boniface, true that in his time the invader Attila all but entered Rome; yet it was Aetius who in the days of his friendship with the Huns pacified Gaul repeatedly by their aid and held back both Goths and Huns in later years from the imperial gates. Question there may be of his own genius, or mere good fortune in his allies, yet the well-known answer made to Valentinian after his fatal assault on his supporter cannot lack its significance: "Whether the deed had been wrought honourably or otherwise, it was not possible to tell. But this was most certain, that the king had cut off his right hand with his left." [64]

And so he, too, like Stilicho, found a poet in his own century to sing his praise. In one of the less important works of Apollinaris Sidonius we find mention among various

writers of one who left his home in Spain to settle amid
"the thirst of marshy Ravenna" and was subsequently honoured by a statue in the Forum of Trajan.[65] Sirmond, followed by later authorities,[66] thinks we may see here a reference to Merobaudes, a native of Spain, described to us in a
record of the fifth century chronicler Hydatius and in an
inscription dated 435,[67] as soldier, poet, and senator under
Theodosius and Valentinian. Until the nineteenth century
the only work assigned to him was of religious content, a
poem *De Christo*,[68] but he may now be ranked more properly
among secular writers on the ground of the researches of
Niebuhr. In 1823 this scholar wrote his conclusion that certain fragments of Latin poetry which he had lately discovered in the monastery of St. Gall must be attributed to
Merobaudes, basing his argument upon the similarity of language found in the inscription mentioned above and in the
preface to one of the works he had found.[69] Niebuhr's claim
has been supported by later study; and we now know Merobaudes chiefly from these writings as panegyrist of Aetius.

The fragments in Vollmer's edition include those of two
panegyrics, one in prose and another in verse, and of four
shorter poems. Vollmer refers the prose *laudatio* [70] to the
second consulship of Aetius in 437, held shortly after he
had obliged Placidia to admit him to supreme favour through
the power of his friends the Huns, and had gained in Gaul
his notable success against the Goths. The hero is represented as combining all endurance of body with brilliant
qualities of spirit; his bed is the bare rock, his armour is
clothing unto him rather than protection, his nights are spent
in watches, his days in toil; he is swift in counsel, stern yet
mild, of quickly passing anger, of long lasting affection.[71]
The two hundred hexameter verses which still remain of the
second panegyric celebrate the third consulship of Aetius in

446. Peace has come to the world through his labours; Gaiseric, the Vandal King, has sought friendship with Rome in ending of his menace to Africa and marriage for his son Huneric with Eudocia, elder daughter of Valentinian and his wife Eudoxia.

The remnants of the four *Carmina* give us altogether less than a hundred lines. The first two are in elegiac metre and describe the baptism of Placidia, younger daughter of the same parents; she became afterwards wife of Olybrius, Emperor of the West for a short while in 472. The ceremony is pictured as taking place in one of the rooms of the Imperial Palace at Ravenna; its walls are adorned with mosaics, in the midst of which the Emperor, triumphant over the usurper John, shines as a star of high heaven with the wife he brought from the Eastern court and with others of his family. The font is fashioned with figures of the hart in memory of the Psalmist's words. The third poem, also in elegiacs, tells of some woodland retreat; the fourth, in hendecasyllabics, was written in honour of the second birthday of Aetius' younger son, Gaudentius. The child was of goodly heritage, we are told, but happier than his father in that he had so far escaped the fate of hostage.

In general the verses of Merobaudes show traces of the influence of Claudian and were themselves imitated by later writers, as by Dracontius. But they are of concern to us for no reason save that of their connection with history. Much the same, only with incomparably greater measure of interest, might be said of that far more important personage of the latter half of the fifth century, Sollius Apollinaris Sidonius. As politician, country nobleman, and finally bishop, he has left us in his *Letters*, full of rhetoric and most difficult reading as they are, one of the most valuable sources for our information on life and its history in Gaul and Rome during the closing acts of the tragedy of the West.[72] Lyons saw his birth in a family of official rank and high cultivation; he was well acquainted with the leading families of Gaul, married the daughter of Avitus, afterward Emperor of Rome, and enjoyed friendship with Theodoric the second, King of the Visigoths. Reference has already been made to his labours as panegyrist of three Emperors of Rome: of Avitus, his own father-in-law, and of Majorian, nominee of Ricimer, the "King-maker" of the fifth century, and of Anthemius, raised to the Western throne by Leo, Emperor of the East. But the poetry of Sidonius can claim little merit as literature. After his visits to Rome for political purposes and a year endured with little joy as prefect of the City, he dwelt in retirement on his estate Avitacum in the territory of Auvergne. From this quiet spot issued a stream of letters on all kinds of subjects, matters of politics in Rome and Gaul, matters of literary and cultural interest, matters of daily routine and amusement. His vivid picture of tranquil and leisurely enjoyment of all things delicate and beautiful, with its avoidance of the noisy, the unpleasant, the coarse, shows him to us as feudal lord of his family of retainers, as head of his charming household, as hospitable friend and host, discussing the day's occupation in sport or study, the newest books, the latest news from Rome or the frontier, while still the rising tide of barbarian invasion advanced ever further on its way to engulf his home.

Nevertheless, in this retreat Sidonius soon heard a call to think on higher matters; for about 471 at the age of some forty years he was elected to the Bishopric of Clermont, passing presumably *per saltum* through the lower orders of the ministry.[73] His position in the world and his learning and wealth naturally made him of special value as Chief

Pastor in those troubled days of Church and country, beset in one and the same race by enemies to the Faith and invaders of the soil. And now at last the constantly increasing menace of Euric, successor of the second Theodoric in the Visigothic Kingship, centred even in Auvergne, in the diocese of Sidonius. There for some strenuous years he and his flock defended with splendid courage their city of Clermont, besieged by the Gothic assault. Everything that prayer and parley and power of arms could do on behalf of the city was done. The Emperor of this time, Julius Nepos, tried to stay the cession of Auvergne by peaceful settlement, and four Bishops of Gaul were appointed to hold conference with the Goths for this end. But all was of no avail, and Sidonius poured out in a letter to one of the four, Græcus, Bishop of Marseilles, the anguish of his soul at seeing himself and his people thus forced after all their devoted suffering to become subjects of a barbarian and alien king. His own devotion indeed led to special punishment, and he was imprisoned for a while in a castle near Narbonne. Eventually he regained freedom at the intercession of a friend in Euric's court, and returned to minister to his diocese, to write many more letters for his fellow-bishops, for his priests and workers, for his friends of various kind, to compose verses and to elaborate religious treatises, now lost, till he died in his own see some ten years before the end of the century in which he had played so varied a part.

The *Letters* were published in nine books during his own life-time. Not only for their picture of contemporary history are they of deep interest, but for the persons to whom they are written and of whom they tell. In their pages we may read of the barbarians and their looks and ways, of Theodoric the Goth and Sigismer the Frank,[74] of the visit of

Sidonius to Rome just when Ricimer was marrying the daughter of Anthemius, of doings and sufferings during the great siege of Clermont, of the Bishop's captivity under Euric.[75] There are many details of private concern: a charming view of the estate at Avitacum, which reminds one of Pliny's letter on his villa, the story of a friendly visit in its neighbourhood, the narrative of incidental happenings in the country at home.[76] Much space is naturally given to things connected with the Church, whether literary or administrative or spiritual. Claudianus Mamertus receives high commendation for his book *On the Nature of the Soul*, written to condemn the teaching of Faustus, Bishop of Riez; a poem celebrates the shrine built by Bishop Perpetuus in honour of Saint Martin of Tours; descriptions show us various functions, of a bishop's electing and its attendant wrangles, of a peaceful religious festivity and its merriment.[77] Deeper moments reveal the Bishop's own religious faith and its practice both for himself and his flock, as when he tells that in the midst of the terror of barbaric invasion the people of Auvergne put not their trust in walls or barricades, but in the "Rogations" first set forth by Mamertus of Vienne.[78] Great names appear in the list of the later correspondents: the four Bishops of the commission from Gaul to Euric, Leontius of Arles, Græcus of Marseilles, Faustus of Riez, Basilius of Aix; moreover, the Bishop and Saint of Reims, Remigius, who afterward baptized Clovis of the Franks; also Lupus, Bishop and Saint of Troyes, at one time Abbot of the monastery at Lerins.[79] And interspersed amid all subjects of whatever kind are light verses, or epitaphs on relative or friend, which show the man of literary bent side by side with the politician and the bishop whom the Church at a later day also canonized for his holy words and works. It is this blending of the world of battles and of books, of people and of prayer in the life of Sidonius that makes his written records of so great value still to the student of the history both secular and ecclesiastic of this time.

CHAPTER III

THE POETS OF BIBLICAL HISTORY

It is rather strange to pass from this field of assault and invasion, of barbarian menace and fear of Church and State, to the quiet backwaters in which during these troubled years lovers of Holy Writ found leisure for expounding its story, that they might use in the service of religion the fruits of their study of the word both of God and of man. In his remarks on the schools of Gaul Mayor praises the "wiser, more truly catholic teachers, such as Sulpicius Severus . . . , Claudius Marius Victor, Hilary, Alcimus Avitus, and . . . Cyprian, who, while borrowing from the Roman models their language, their taste and examples of primitive virtue, endeavour to create a reformed literature, not ashamed to draw its inspiration and topics from Hebrew and Christian tradition."[1] We have here therefore a line of writers who sought to teach Divine truths with the help of classical models in hope of attracting men of literary training.

The medium is usually verse, but we may perhaps notice fitly in this place the prose *Chronica* of Sulpicius Severus, that friend of Paulinus of Nola and ardent disciple and biographer of St. Martin of Tours, whom Scaliger called "ecclesiasticorum purissimus scriptor" and Barth the "Christian Sallust."[2] Thirteen letters written to him by Paulinus between 394 and 404, with the brief account of Gennadius, are our chief external sources of knowledge concerning his history.[3] From them we learn that he was born in Aquitaine of goodly race, attained celebrity as a rising lawyer in Bordeaux, and married a wife, also of aristocratic family, and of substantial wealth; that after her death he forsook the world and its promise by counsel of Saint Martin, and lived in retirement near Toulouse, first at Eluso (Elsonne), and afterward at Primuliac, following a strict rule of ascetic life and prayer. Gennadius tells us further that he was ordained priest, that "in his old age he fell into the error of the Pelagians and, acknowledging the sin of chattering talk, kept silence till his death that he might atone for his fault." [4]

In a preface to the *Chronica*, which was composed about 403,[5] he states that many have asked him to write a brief summary of Holy Scripture, which he has accordingly done in two short books, taking care, however, to be as comprehensive as he is brief. We learn, moreover, that he has also used Gentile historians for the completing of his narrative, for the informing of the unlearned and the conviction of men of culture, but that this account is not meant to stay his readers from seeking these matters at their source. His promise to be comprehensive is conscientiously fulfilled, with some interesting exceptions. Starting from the Creation, some eighty short chapters give the events of the Old Testament and Apocryphal Books, dealing strictly with historical matter and omitting the substance of Leviticus and the words of the Prophets. True to his legal training, however, Sulpicius does not neglect to record succinctly from the Old Latin version the substance of the Law of Exodus XXI, XXII, and XXIII in language adapted to Roman ears.[6]

This agrees with his aim throughout. For his style is modelled on Sallust, on Tacitus, of whose work he indeed makes use as source, and on Velleius Paterculus; and so cunningly, as Bernays has remarked, that he has fashioned for himself a manner which reflects his patterns but does not yield their actual words.[7] All is presented to us in periods which are a delight to read for their simple clearness, especially when contrasted with the terrible constructions of the "pedestrian prose" of Apollinaris and Avitus. Repeated reminders are given by the writer of his zeal for brevity; but this does not prevent him from digressing when he tells that the Levites received no portion that they might the more freely serve God (*Joshua* cc. XIII and XIV). Such a fact is commended to the clergy of the Church in his day, whose minds are poisoned by greed of possessions, who, even if they do not engage in actual traffic, yet sit still waiting for gifts "while they put forth, as it were, their sanctity for sale." We shall meet further diatribe against the clerics of Gaul when we come to Sulpicius' story of holy Martin. There is much talk of dates; discordant records of chronology are excused as "coming about with consent of God or through fault of long-past ages."

This businesslike précis of Biblical narrative is based on some Old Latin translation of the Hebrew text, with now and then a diversion belonging to the Septuagint; [8] there are also five references to the *Chronicles* of Eusebius. Occasionally we find an individual touch. The people of Israel were rescued from tyranny by Deborah: "So little hope was found in their leaders that they were defended by a woman's aid." She is, however, a type of Mother Church in delivering men from oppression. Jephthah's daughter also showed courage passing the fashion of women: "With constancy strange in her sex she refused not to die." One wonders whether Sulpicius forgot those brave companions of Jerome, his contemporary. Very possibly he visited them, if the sojourn with the Doctor attributed to Postumian, one of the "characters" in the *Dialogues* of Sulpicius, written about the same time as the *Chronica*, was in fact his own experience (*Dial.* I, 8 f.). A sense of reverence will not allow the

writer to include in this brief summary the matter of the
Gospels and the Acts of the Apostles. We have a bare mention of the birth and crucifixion of Christ, and then proceed
to the reign of Nero, who was so evil that "many have believed that he was to come again before the coming of the
Antichrist." To this belief Sulpicius returns in the second
of the *Dialogues,* where it rests on the testimony of holy
Martin himself. Nero, declares the Saint to Sulpicius, will
come to rule over ten subject Kings in the West and to com-
pel men to worship idols; Antichrist will rule the East with
Jerusalem as his chief city, until finally he subdue Nero and
reign supreme before the advent of Christ. And more.
Antichrist, according to the Saint, was already born, and
when of ripe age would assume his power. Sulpicius notes in
his narrative that eight years have now passed since Martin
thus declared. Great reason is there indeed for present fear!

In the relation of Rome's imperial history the account of
Helena's finding of the Cross is of interest, though lovers
of Sir Thomas Browne will remember his doubt of its detail. Sulpicius reproduces it here (II, 33 f.) from a letter
which Paulinus of Nola had sent him.[9] We are told that this
mother of the Emperor Constantine overthrew the idols and
temples she found in Jerusalem, and set up basilicas in the
places where the Lord suffered and rose from death and
ascended to Heaven. But therein was seen a marvel, that in
the place of his ascension no paving could be laid! For the
stones were straightway rejected by earth and flew up from
the ground in the faces of those working, and the imprint of
the Lord's feet ever remains clearly to be seen. When on
the place of the Passion three Crosses had been brought
forth with toil from their imbedding in the earth, there was
questioning of which one had wrought salvation, and it was
decided to lay on each the body of a man who recently had

died. At this very moment a funeral passed by. The test was made: "After two crosses had been applied with no result, the body was touched by the gibbet of Christ. Then, wondrous to tell, while all were amazed, the dead man was hurled forward and stood upright among those who watched. And thus the Cross was found of men and hallowed with fitting ritual."

With this the chronicle leaves Biblical story; but it may be worth while to follow Sulpicius through the further portion of the work, of greater concern to us in its dealing with the religious troubles that beset his own day. After describing in some detail the mischievous doings of the Arians, he tells of pursuit of the Gnostic error—"superstitio exitiabilis," as he calls it, in which Priscillian and his disciples were involved in Spain. There is a vigorous picture of this man who first as layman and after as Bishop led so many to follow his attractive cult of freedom to be attained by intellectual search and bodily abstinence: "Noble of family, passing rich, keen, restless, of eloquent speech and learned by much study, prompt in discussion and debate, happy would he have been, had he not corrupted a splendid intellect by evil enthusiasm; much good was found in him of mind and body; long could he fast and bear hunger and thirst, in no way avaricious and most sparing of possessions. Yet of right foolish spirit withal was he, and puffed up unduly by knowledge of worldly things; nay, it was believed that from his youth he practised magic arts" (II, 46). His skill in persuasion and pleasant address won many to his fellowship. Especially women of unstable loyalty and mind that craved novel diversion sought him in crowds, attracted, too, by his winsome humility.

As his critics have observed, Sulpicius maintains studied fairness in his narrative of the unhappy Priscillianist con-

troversy (II, 46 ff).[10]   He tells that Idacius, Bishop of
Merida, when the teaching of Priscillian had been reported
to him, added fuel to the flame by his indiscreet exasperating
of the offenders; that, when Priscillian for the furthering of
his cause had been consecrated Bishop of Avila by certain
of the episcopate who sympathized with his views, then
Idacius and also Ithacius, Bishop of Ossonoba, unwisely approached secular authority and obtained from the Emperor
Gratian decree for their banishment. Whereupon Priscillian
and his episcopal friends made a triumphant progress
through Aquitania, "magnificently received by the ignorant
and scattering the seeds of their treachery," and there was
ugly talk of immoral living.   In Rome they were repelled by
Pope Damasus, and by Ambrose in Milan; but from Gratian, by bribery of his *magister officiorum,* they obtained the
cancelling of their exile and returned to Spain and their re-
spective sees.   And now things were going in their favour
and badly for Ithacius, who lacked not will but power for
their undoing, when Maximus of Spain usurped the imperial power of Gratian and marched victoriously into
Trèves in 383.   In him Ithacius found attentive hearing, and
the offenders were summoned for trial before a Synod of
Bishops at Bordeaux.   But Priscillian appealed for trial by
the new ruler and the Bishops allowed his appeal, although,
as Sulpicius observes, they had no right to admit such
proven deeds of ill for trial before the Emperor.

The brief statement of the trial gives occasion for a few
words concerning the prosecutors, the Bishops Idacius and
Ithacius, "whose zeal for convicting heretics I would not
blame had they not striven with more desire for conquest
than was fitting." "And," continues Sulpicius, "to my mind
both accused and accusers are equally displeasing." There
follows a scathing indictment of Ithacius, who regarded all

good followers of abstinence and studious life as disciples of Priscillian, and even dared—wretched creature!—to hurl openly slander of heresy at the blessed Martin himself. For Martin, at that time staying in Trèves, was ceaselessly requiring him to forego his accusation, and praying Maximus to keep his hand from shedding the blood of the unfortunate. "Sufficient is it," declared the Saint, "that the heretics by sentence of Bishops should be banished from their sees; a crime grievous and unheard it is that a secular judge should try the Church's cause." And thus as long as Martin tarried at Trèves, the trial was postponed; and when he departed he obtained a promise from Maximus that no violence should be shown the prisoners. For this reason truly has one of his critics remarked: "It is no light praise to have protested against the first capital punishment for heresy." [11] But when he had disappeared, Priscillian was judged guilty of evil teaching and conduct and put to death, though Ithacius at the last moment withdrew from his charge in fear for his episcopal seat. A number of Priscillian's disciples also met punishment of death and exile. Sulpicius ends by remarking that "thus men most unworthy of the light of day in fearful warning were slain or banished," although "the heresy of Priscillian was not only not checked by the execution of its author but strengthened and propagated; since men held him a saint while he yet lived, but after his death revered him as martyr and deemed it a binding oath to swear by his name."

We cannot here discuss the theological views of Priscillian, a very interesting question, on which light has been cast by recent discovery,[12] but must turn to poetic versions of Biblical narrative. And first to the work of Claudius Marius Victor, the *Alethia*, of which three books survive, containing, with an introductory *Precatio*, about two

thousand hexameter lines. Our knowledge of the author is
not certain, as most of it is based upon a statement by Gennadius [*de vir. ill.*, c. lxi(lx)] that a rhetor of Marseilles,
Victorinus (*v. l.* Victorius) by name, published a commentary on Genesis in four books; that he treated his material
with pious and Christian feeling, but that his opinions were
of little weight, as was natural in a reader of secular literature, unguided and untrained in the study of Holy Writ;
that he died during the rule of Theodosius and Valentinian
(the third). If, with Schenkl and Bardenhewer,[13] we accept
this statement as referring to the author of the *Alethia*, we
learn, of course, that he died some time between 425 and
450. The reference in Gennadius to four books is explained
variously by the incomplete state of the manuscript as we
have it, or by the deed of the poet in leaving his work unfinished, or by the reckoning of the *Precatio* as a separate
part.

This introduction is devoted to the praise of God; and
as we approach its end we discern a pedagogical leaning:

> Grant knowledge to my prayer,
> While tender minds and hearts I seek to mould
> For virtue's path of truth in childish years,
> To teach what Moses' roll reveals of law,
> How rose the firmament, whence came the world.[14]

There is also a prayer that faults of style and metre may
not impede the instruction:

> But if from metre's law my page shall err,
> Shall err in faulty speech and doubtful sense,
> Though here and there shall run unguarded lines—
> Let not truth's measure suffer loss therein,
> By JESUS CHRIST . . .[15]

The first book gives the story of Creation and follows closely the opening chapter of Genesis. The Spirit broods upon the face of the waters, light flashes forth, the firmament is created and the Earth, the Sun, and the Stars:

> The seeds of day first planted now
> Spread out from rosy sparks their blood-red locks;
> The moon, night's glory, burned with her own light,
> Or with his mass conflicting, poured her rays
> Struck by the coming sun, and far below
> Hung subject on her lower path; the stars,
> Painting the firmament with varied zones,
> Shot forth their differing hues, celestial flowers;
> In glorious darkness fairer shone the Heavens
> And held deep Night amazed.[16]

What, however, avails the creation of the world to God if there be not some one to admire and possess the same? He therefore decides to fashion Man in the Divine image, and, as thus fashioned, Man shall enjoy created things at his own free will. In emphasis on human free will Victor has been accused of inclining to the teaching of Pelagius, whose alternate acquittal at Diospolis and condemnation at Carthage and Mileve had stirred the world of theologians not long before this time. Man was formed full of intelligence, discerning with clear sight his work of adoration of the Lord.[17] Immortality was his dower, and righteousness and freedom from care; moreover, the very command given him to abstain from eating of the fruit of the Tree was an opportunity granted him of advancing in merit and gaining yet further reward.[18] The description of the dwelling-place given to Adam by God is vividly drawn. In the calm sunlight of eternal spring it stood, enriched with harvest of fruit-trees and all things joyous to sight and taste and smell.

The earth was radiant with starry blossoms of various colours ever fresh.   Such sweetness filled the air as never the Mede or the Persian could boast, yielded in one perfect essence from all herbs that anywhere are found, with music on every side:

> A gentle wind awakes the woodland glade
> And in one nectar blends its fragrance fair;
> Then service new fulfilling, from each tree
> Calls forth her mingled voice. Thus trembling each
> And slowly moved in dulcet overture
> With quivering foliage stirs; in union all
> The forest sings to God its hymn, and soft
> Re-echoes whispered harmony.[19]

Eve is then created after the fashion in Biblical story, and all is happiness for a while.   In their Godlike state the pair need not sustenance of food, nor defence against fleshly tribulation:

> With soul divine inspired they needed naught
> Of this world's wealth, nor subject to disease
> Bore they their bodies prone to appetite.
> Food was but pleasure; what our needs demand
> Was not then life's support, in their own strength
> Their souls immortal lived.[20]

Into this Paradise comes the serpent tempting the woman. His words "Ye shall be as Gods" for the first time in Man's life make mention of more than One God.[21]   The sin of Adam and Eve takes little space, but their misery after its accomplishing is well pictured as Victor reproaches them. God in truth is everywhere and their only hope of refuge is in him:

> Ille potest Dominum fugiens evadere summum,
> Qui fugit ad Dominum . . .[22]

The Fall in Victor's theology seems to be due to weakness of the pair, which causes them to yield to the tempting of the serpent and brings death to the body as penalty for themselves and their descendants. Yet this weakness does not excuse Cain for his far more grievous offence, through which new guilt and new punishment have been brought into the world.[23] In the *Precatio* even good is attributed to the Fall. For first no one, the writer declares, possesses free will unless he possess the right to perish through error if he so desire; and no one would have proved that this right had been given Man unless sin had been committed.[24] Secondly, it was the Fall that occasioned the victory of Christ over sin and death, and it is a greater thing to conquer death than to know naught of dying.[25]

When sentence has been passed upon the serpent, upon terrified Eve and upon Adam, husband and wife are driven out from Paradise by the winds (an original touch) ignorant of all save sorrow. At this point, the beginning of the second book, the writer admits that he is drawing upon his imagination.[26] The depression of the exiles is here described as they view lofty cliffs and wild forest and bristling thorns around them, as the thought of their former home rises more glorious than ever before in memory. But at last, after yielding in his need and helplessness to a moment of despair, Adam regains courage and supplicates Almighty God for aid that he may know how to begin to subdue this savage land and to provide food for himself and Eve in their outcast state. The spirit with which Adam counsels his repentant wife in Milton's poem is also seen in the prayer which Victor has conceived for him: [27]

> Most Mighty Father, who pervadest all,
> To thee with trembling heart and prayer we flee;
> Hear those whom thou dost ever see and hear. . . .

When with just punishment I was condemned,
So sore my fault, so struck with grief my mind
Itself disdained, that thou, most clement judge,
I thought hadst set me to avenge my crime.
Wherefore my cause I tears and groans denied,
For that I seemed deserving of no grace,
And finding comfort in my punishment
Will hold this very thing among thy gifts,
A grace of mercy condemnation hold,
No grievous lot. In thy still majesty
Hear us, who nothing disobedient seek,
Nor yet do tearful wait till of thy love
Thou shalt thy servants grant remission kind,
But bid thy sentence hold its power unstayed.[28]

At this moment the serpent is spied hastening to conceal itself in fear of their wrath, and Eve urges her husband to kill the cause of their troubles with a well-aimed stone. As they then ply the creature with missiles, one of these strikes a spark from the bare flint and opens their eyes to a thing hitherto undreamed:

And soon in flaming tresses spread the fire
Extending widely, bright in smoke displayed.
Their steps affrighted then swift refuge sought.
Yet panic holds them and a curious care
Reveals in human weakness, that they wait
To see that fearful sight, and safe removed
On ridge of barren earth spellbound behold
The falling clusters of dense forest growth,
The clouds of ashes and day's light obscured,
The earth all glowing and a radiance strange
Below the sun.[29]

The conflagration now mounts high, now sinks deep within the earth, till she opens her veins and pours forth molten metals in streams, which cool after a while and present formless shapes. Adam and Eve through the mercy of God perceive in this happening his help extended to them and proceed to test the various kinds of ore. Gold is found to be too soft, silver better, bronze still better, but steel best of all. A digression follows on the proper limitation of seeking after knowledge. Would that man had been content to know what God gave him to know and had not soiled his mind by unbidden search!

We need not trace in detail the treatment of Biblical narrative as it continues here, but may perhaps pause a moment at the death of Noë. After this event his descendants lost the power of righteous knowledge granted to men while they lived pure lives in worship of God, and were moved by vain ambition to inquire into the future by study of the stars and by false divination. Then arose magic arts, and at last Nimrod the evil hunter, a giant in mind and body, crowned this wickedness by paying cult to an image of the son of whom he had been bereaved by death. From his example followed the vice of offering supplication to shades of the dead, as, says Victor, the Alans do; men even held as gods their own departed parents and their kings, while Satan elicited omens from fire and hot water and caves. Themis first deceived men, and afterwards a like leading astray was true of Apollo, who once dwelt in Gaul but now has gone to vex German tribes. In the days after Noë men were not content with the short span of life allowed them and made foolish complaint:

> How wretched is our fate in swift decay!
> While years ten hundred lived our forefathers,
> Scarce thrice a hundred lasts our weary life,
> Ere banished from our land our nameless limbs
> Unknown and naked give we to some tomb.
> Up then, O comrades, while our band is strong,

Create from deeds a fame that shall abide,
Forever rest with us nor know stern end.
A city let us build and in its name
Raise up a tower on high; until the stars
That deck the sky and great Olympus' vault
Be torn asunder, and our children deem
That we, when we have left this earth, have made
Our journey unto Heaven.[30]

So is wrought the confusion of Babel. The third book ends with the destruction of Sodom. Lot flees, his wife perishes, the city is consumed in flames; but the mercy of God exchanges fire for flood, a symbol of grace to come in the waters of regeneration which shall prevail against Gehenna's fire by the washing away of human sin.

At times we catch glimpses of poetic power in the work, and, as has been remarked, imagination is not wanting. The influence of Vergil is, of course, very strong, as everywhere in this age; Schenkl notes more than 120 examples of imitation in the two thousand lines extant. The metre is correctly devised, though rhyme is found in abundant measure, as we should also expect in these declining days.

The dubious "Hilary" and Cyprian of Gaul need not occupy us long. The former was the author of a work called *Metrum in Genesim* consisting of 204 hexameter lines, inclusive of six addressed *Ad Leonem Papam* at whose behest the task was undertaken. In manuscript tradition the work was attributed to Hilary, the great Bishop of Poitiers in the fourth century; editors have assigned it to Hilary, Bishop of Arles in the fifth century, among whose *opuscula dubia* Migne includes it.[31] Rudolf Peiper, in adding it to his edition of Cyprian of Gaul, refuses to identify this Hilary with either of the two Bishops, but thinks he may have belonged to the time and country of these writers. The material treated extends from the Creation, told in some detail, to the time after the Flood, but the story of the Fall and subsequent events embraces only some 45 lines. The writer addresses himself constantly to God the Father and uses the Bible story as a thread round which he may weave his matter reminiscent of Ovid and Horace and Vergil. The work of Cyprian of Gaul is of interest as giving light regarding the old Latin version of Scripture in vogue before the version of Saint Jerome.[32] His editor, Peiper, places him in the early years of the fifth century on the ground that Claudius Marius Victor read his work and that he himself used Claudian.[33] The narrative, which bears the name of *Heptateuch,* has been the subject of much scholarly labour since 1560, when the first 165 lines of the *Genesis* were published by the printer Morel from a manuscript of the Library of the Abbaye de Saint-Victor at Paris. Additions were made to this by the Benedictine scholar Martène in 1733, and by Cardinal Pitra, who in 1852 completed the *Genesis* and in 1888 added the other books which make up our whole.[34] We have now therefore an account by Cyprian of the first five books of the Bible, also of Joshua and Judges, with a very few lines from sections now lost dealing with other books. The metre is usually hexameter, though occasionally the Phalæcean is substituted, as in the song of praise of the Israelites after the drowning of Egypt in the Red Sea. The literary value of the narrative is negligible, as it lacks both originality and poetic grace.

By far the most interesting of the metrical versions of the Creation and of the history of Israel in this time is that given by the Bishop of Vienne in Dauphigny, Alcimus Ecdicius Avitus.[35] He was born in Vienne at a date not exactly known, of a family distinguished in state affairs and politics, such as in the troubled times of this century repeatedly gave to the Church for her Bishops men who could stand high among strangers and foes of alien creed. His father had been Bishop of Vienne before him, and his brother Apollinaris held the see of Valence on the Rhone. From his own writing we learn that his mother, a woman of saintly character, was named Audentia, and that he had a sister, Fuscina, in Religion. After becoming Bishop of Vienne in 494 he acted as counsellor and correspondent of Gundobad, nephew of Ricimer and ruler of the kingdom of Burgundy in which the see of Avitus was placed, and endeavoured without success to convert the king from Arianism to the Catholic Faith. But Gundobad feared the Arians too greatly. We have still fragments of a Dialogue with the King, or, as it was called, *Books Against the Arians*. Gundobad died in 516, and his successor on the throne, Sigismund, became an adherent of Catholicism under the direction of the Bishop. The Bollandist *Life* tells that, once a rebel against the Bishop's authority, he was brought to repentance through the miraculous healing of his sickness by means of the Bishop's cloak, begged of Avitus by the queen and laid over his sick-bed.[35] Other works that show the zeal of Avitus for the Church, of which he was the most noted leader in the Southern Gaul of his day, are two books against the Eutychian heresy, letters to Gundobad and other people, homilies, and, most important from the literary point of view, six books of *Poems*. His prose is a torture to read, for it suffers much from the prevailing sins of artificiality and rhetoric; his poetry on the other hand is simple, and, though hampered by unnecessary and wearying digressions, shows in parts a real gift of insight into character and poetic imagery. The five former books, dealing with the Biblical tradition, were probably composed at the end of the fifth century; for in the preface, addressed to his brother Apol-

linaris, he states that his poems, which Apollinaris had desired him to publish, had been scattered "in that notorious
crisis of panic," a reference to the siege of Vienne at Gundobad's hands in 500. Some books, however, had been found
subsequently in a friend's house. In a letter (dated 507)
to the Bishop Apollinaris, son of the Bishop of Clermont,[36]
he refers to word received from this Apollinaris expressing
approval of the "little books in metre on the events of
spiritual history, my recreation in the intervals of serious
and more necessary writing."

The first three parts deal with the Fall, and, as Ebert
remarked,[37] form a well-ordered whole; for the writer pre-
pares the catastrophe, then describes it, and finally gives
the consequences, in the successive divisions. He is not
careful to follow minutely the Bible narrative, but allows his
imagination free play; even the order of Creation differs
from that of the Biblical Genesis. Some thirty lines are
given to the forming of the world and its lower inhabitants
in Book I, entitled *On the Beginning of the World,* while
about seventy describe the nascence of Man, including a
very dull and detailed account of the formation of the
various parts of his anatomy. The rib which shall be fashioned into the body of Eve is taken from Adam's left side,
and her forming represents mystically to the poet the birth
of the Church, the Bride of Christ, from the pierced side of
the Lord upon the Cross.

For the Bishop Avitus, as for Victor and Dracontius, the
narrative of the Creation and Fall was literally true; his
theology followed in detail the teaching of Augustine.
Adam was created in the image of the Lord, endowed with
high honour and Godlike mind of fair beauty; his it was to
give law and name to all creatures, to mark the stars, the
constellations and the paths of heaven, to conquer the fierce

sea, yoke beasts to the plough, and by his intellect possess
all things within his vision; to God should he raise his eyes
in constant quest, and plant his steps firmly by the help of
skilled prudence and the light of reason.   Absolute purity
was also his in this dowry of righteousness.   United by God
with Eve in the joys of marriage for the begetting of a race
that should be without end, with spirit ever contemplating
the glorious life of Angels, he was to be spotless as the redeemed hereafter, who shall have no part in fleshly union
and hot passion of sex.   And to fulfil his happiness a fair
place was given for his indwelling, so fair that after his banishment it passed to Angels for delight.   There no changes
of climate vexed the body, no seasons were found; there was
no need of rain, for dew fell in abundance; no winds raged
and blustered, no clouds dulled the sky; all was light and
calm.   Pangs of hunger distressed him not, nor had he need
of food for the sustaining of life; no pain had he, but innocent pleasure in the gifts of God, and of death he was to
have no knowledge for evermore.   It is in the narrative of
this state of happiness of Adam and Eve and of its passing
through the Fall that Avitus shows his power both of word
and art during the course of the second book, *On Original
Sin*.   The story reminds the pagan of the peace of the
Golden Age and its Christian author of the peace of the
world to come:

> Meanwhile, all ignorant of future fall,
> A tranquil joy they find in liberty,
> And blest abundance of that spot; to whom
> The ready earth gives food, the bushes rich
> From yielding turf hold sustenance of fruit
> Both fair and constant; and if bowed with weight
> The fertile branches bend ripe burdens low,
> To blossom swells straightway the empty shoot

With promise of new bud. Should slumber sweet
Be grateful for a season, on soft mead
And broidered lawns they lie, while for delight
The sacred grove bears store of every kind,
And riches new in plenty. Thus they feast,
Whom hunger cannot drive. . . .
Their bodies naked see nor suffer shame,
No evil thinks their untaught innocence.[38]

Satan is then described and his transformation from an angel of light to a monster. As such he seeks consolation in beguiling Man to a fate similar to his own:

O grief, that things of clay should swiftly rise,
A hateful race increase through our descent!
Once great was I in virtue, now refused,
To exile thrown, while mire Angelic state
Puts on, and earth ascends to Heaven to reign,
Of common mould, ennobled by my loss.
Yet all hath not been lost me; still my power
Doth hold its own with skill immense to hurt.
Nor will I linger; now with argument
Persuasive will I haste, while new this life
Of blessedness, while yet no artifice
Their simple hearts protects against my shafts.
Yet better snare them now alone, before
They bring forth children for undying time.
Nothing immortal must this world produce,
The fountain-head must die, its conquered source
Shall to this race be seed of death. Let all
Be struck in one; from dead root springs no tree.
Thus to my ruin rests some comfort still.
If I can never pass Heaven's portals closed,
Then be they closed to man. Lighter my fall,
If these new creatures perish in like case.[39]

The imitation in form of the *Æneid* and the likeness in matter to *Paradise Lost* strike the reader at once. As Milton in graphic detail enlarged upon the Bible story of the devil in serpent's guise, so did Avitus long before him in words culled from Vergil. Thus arrayed Satan addresses Eve with seductive speech; and in the dialogue between tempter and tempted, while tracing the gradual yielding to persuasion, Avitus shows a vivid skill in psychological narrative. Both he and Milton represent choice of the easier feminine prey, to whom the serpent of Avitus begins thus softly and in simple words:

> O, this world's glory, happy maid most fair,
> Whose radiant form thy shamefast blush adorns,
> Parent of men to come, whom mighty earth
> Awaits as Mother: thou in whom thy Man
> First joy and solace found assured, nor deems
> Apart from thee he yet could live, thy Head,
> Yet rightly subject to thy love, himself
> Thy husband dear, to whom in treaty's bond
> His children thou shalt yield; right worthy here
> Your seat in height of Paradise, to you
> Meek service renders in subjection's fear
> All this world's life; all creatures born in sky
> Or earth or ocean's whirling depths combine
> To fill your needs, nor aught doth Nature hold
> From your full sway. Nor envy I in truth,
> But wondering revere. Yet of your grace
> One thing I fain would know, wherefore your hands,
> Free though they be, one Tree surpassing sweet
> Will never touch? who gives such stern command?
> Who grudges you these gifts and in rich feast
> Bids fasting intervene? [40]

Eve replies that only indeed from this one Tree is their approach withheld; to touch this God has warned them,

would be death. But will the serpent with his learning
please explain to her what death is? For she and her husband are ignorant. The answer comes prompt and vigorous:

> An empty name of terror thou dost dread,
> In woman's wise. No pain of speedy death
> Doth threaten; nay, the Father's jealousy
> Willed not for you an equal lot, nor gave
> That you should share his secret knowledge high.
> What profit painted fetters, world's domain,
> For minds in wretched prison blindly pent?
> The body's senses and wide-open eyes
> Their nature gives to brutes, one sun alike
> To all is servant, beast as man hath sight.
> Take then my counsel and in higher things
> Plant thou thy mind, raise up thy thought to Heaven.
> For this same fruit forbidden, which from fear
> Thou touchest not, shall knowledge give of all
> Thy Father's hidden store. Stay not thine hand,
> Nor bridle pleasure long by law confined.
> For once upon thy lips that taste divine,
> Thy cleansèd eyes in thine own sight shall see
> Thee equal to the gods, all things discern,
> Unjust from holy, false from true divide.[41]

And now with crafty touch Avitus shows Satan narrowly
watching his victim, and when he sees her inclined to yield,
he repeats his tempting words, while he detaches one of the
apples from the Tree, distils over it a fair fragrance, and
enhances its beauty of form. Eve takes the deadly gift and
turns it over uncertainly in her hands. Now she smells it,
now puts it tentatively to her lips:

> How often then, raised to her lips, once more
> By conscience pricked she drew that fruit away!
> Her hand, unsteady from its burden grave
> Of evil daring, fled from sin's dread deed.

Yet gladly would she be as God, still keeps
Ambition's poisoned drug its creeping path.
Now love commands her mind, then fear; now pride
Would banish thought of law, then law returns.
Thus seethes in stern engagement dubious strife
In her divided heart. Nor does the serpent cease
Meantime to urge his guile; before her doubt
He holds on high the fruit and mourns delay,
Persuading to its fall the soul now poised
On edge of doom.[42]

At length she yields, while the devil looks on with carefully concealed joy. Adam now chances to return from a walk; his wife runs to meet him and offers him part of the apple saved for him. It took more than eighty lines to accomplish the fall of Eve; the fate of Adam is sealed in twenty-five. For Eve knows how to persuade:

And thus began her words; for half-consumed
She kept that fatal fruit of misery:
"Take, husband dear, and taste this quickening food
Which like unto Almighty God himself
May haply make thee, peer of Angels high.
Nor yet unknowing these my words; for now
Right skilled am I since first my taste within
My body penetrated, breaking faith
With peril bold. O trust me readily!
How shameful that a manly mind should shrink
When I, a woman, dare. Wouldst thou have feared
To lead the way? Then follow, raise thy heart!
Why look aside? why hinder joyous prayers,
Why steal the time from long and happy days?" [43]

The Eve of Milton also pleads her newly-won knowledge.[44] No feminine fear here deters Adam; Avitus does not show us the Adam of *Paradise Lost,* beset by fear of separation

from his wife; and here he promptly devours the half. Thus
are his eyes likewise opened unto death.

The stress laid upon the struggle of Eve enhances the
greatness of the Fall; and its fatal nature is emphasized in
repeated words . . . *ignorans ludit de morte futura* (II,
216) . . . *pomum letale* (II, 214) . . . *capitur mors horrida pastu* (II, 232). For the first time death and the conflict with evil are born into the world. Not weakness
merely, but deliberate and deadly sin have caused this undoing:

> Erubuit propriæ iam mens sibi conscia culpæ
> Pugnavitque suis carnis lex indita membris.[45]

As a result human nature is infected henceforth with hereditary taint—*vitium,* the technical word. The views of Avitus
on this subject are clearly expressed in the lines which open
the work:

> All divers labours vexing mortal men,
> Whence lives foredoomed to death take their brief day:
> That human ways are fouled even at their source,
> Oppressed by deeds primordial, not their own;
> That (though our own ill deeds bring added guilt)
> From olden days we err with loss of grace,
> I trace to thee, first parent; by death's seed
> Thou for thy sons didst vital germ destroy.
> And yet though Christ himself has done away
> The evil plague in Adam's stricken race,
> Now through our father's fault who debt of death
> First gave us, pestilence and grievous pain,
> Still lives in dying flesh the scar of sin.

The fatal inheritance brought by the Fall could not be told
by a hundred tongues or a voice of iron. Neither the bard
of Mantua nor of Mæonia would avail to gauge its measure

—sin, disease, and disaster; in time of war, panic, bloodshed, plunder; in time of peace, if perchance war fail for a
space, envy, anger, strife between brothers. There is no evil
to which from the time of Eve the natural world is not
prone.[46]   And not only do men inherit evil tendency, but
actual guilt from this first Fall. So Avitus writes to his
sister in Religion that she sorrow not because she may not
bear children after the flesh:

> Not thine the evil, nor the sentence dire
> Which smote our mother, and Death's mother, Eve,
> Bearing her children dead in living sin.[47]

Only Christ the Maker can repair the "fallen mass, the shat-
tered vessels" of humanity.[48]   The means of making anew is
Holy Baptism; and here Avitus accepts the terrible doctrine
of Augustine regarding the certain damnation of infants
dying unbaptized.   In congratulating his sister on her unwedded state he reminds her of the sorrows that may be the
lot of parents, and ends with this fearsome climax:

> And worse than all perchance, if lacking yet
> The Heavenly laver, greedy death thy child
> Should seize so tender, reared for Hell's despite;
> Thus then no more his mother's progeny,
> Son of perdition would he be. Forlorn
> His parents sore would grieve their babe saw day,
> Begotten but for flames.[49]

Returning to our text, we find that Satan now lays aside
his mask and openly exults in his victory. God, he declares,
no longer holds right of sway over his creatures. Let him
indeed keep the forms he created. The greater part, the
Man informed by knowledge, is now of the devil's ownership.

In the third book, *On the Sentence of God,* the Lord delivers judgment. As the guilty pair hear his voice they would gladly die, though as yet they understand not the various forms of death. God asks of Adam, "Where art thou?", and Adam replies with complaining excuse: "Too easily did I believe, but thou didst teach me to believe, in giving wedlock, in weaving me sweet bonds. Oh, would that life which once in happy loneliness ran strong in me were now mine own alone, that never it had felt the pact of wife nor been subdued to evil comradeship!" [50] Milton pictures Adam addressing this reproach to Eve herself as he bitterly regards their misery before God's advent is perceived.[51] Sentence is passed, and husband and wife are driven from Paradise into a region deprived of sunlight, in which the stars hung in far heaven mourn such fate. So shall the spirits of men after their passage from earth long for space wherein to redeem the past.

The fourth and the fifth book relate each a separate incident, the Flood and the passage of the Red Sea. The nature of Man before the Flood is likened variously to a plain grown wild by neglect and overrun by brambles and barren trees under which wild beasts find secure shelter; or to a little stream, tiny at its birth, which gathering strength in absorbing other waters rushes at last victor of all it meets on its furious journey oceanward. When Man had at length attained a span of nine hundred years, neither terror of death nor of sin remained to him. Giants were born of strange union, whence sprang the lying stories, current among the Greeks, of creatures half-man, half-dragon, and of monsters who hurled stones toward heaven and piled mountain on mountain. And now the Angel who was in later days the Angel of the Annunciation and of the Coming of John the Baptist visited Noë with command to build the Ark; to its forming Ossa and Pelion and even Atlas contributed their share, while standers-by made merry. "How could so great a mass be brought to the river? Scarce could Euphrates or the Nile enclose it in their banks." Then entered in chosen ones of all creatures, and human beings, all one family; for sin had not yet subjected one unto another. There is a vigorous picture of the Flood, of waters descending from heaven and springing from earth to meet in one raging storm of conflict. Rivers leap back from the sea, pursued by its stream in their flight; in terror men seek to gain towers and roofs, whence the mounting wave sucks them down. Others climb mountain-sides; yet others essay in vain to swim the torrent, while more are overwhelmed by falling masonry. The cry of perishing man and beast rises to Heaven amid the general voice of panic.

The last book lays stress on mystical interpretation. It tells of the oppressing of the Children of Israel, of the plea of Moses for their liberation and the proud answer of the Pharaoh chastised by the scourge of the Ten Plagues. There is some graphic description, as in the second visitation:

> Scarce cleansed from blood throughout its course, the stream
> In hideous croakings buried Egypt's towns,
> Filling their chambers, streets, their tables, shrines,
> Till royal purple feels unnumbered leaps
> And groans to underlie, not men, but frogs.[52]

At length the Chosen People march out in battle array, and the work ends with the backward rushing of waters and the fate of the Egyptian Prince.[53]

It is difficult to approve of the addition to this story of a sixth book in the shape of a "consolation" for the unmarried life, addressed to that nun, the Bishop's sister Fuscina, though it throws some light on the education of women of the time. For the lady was of no mean learning, not only acquainted with Holy Writ, but with sacred poetry, and could herself indite the same. The unworthy belittling of the wedded state introduced as part of this brotherly and episcopal counsel and comforting has justly called forth upon Avitus the censure of his readers.

Let us pass on to him whom Peter Eyssenbergk called "Christianissimus poeta,"[54] Sedulius, described by Bardenhewer as the best known Christian poet of the fifth century.[55] From the sixth century onwards his *Paschal Song* was widely read, and in the Middle Ages it attained far-reaching note. Neither the year of his birth nor that of his death is known to us; Gennadius, so far as we can tell, did not mention him. The little information we have regarding his life comes mostly from a notice appended to ancient and good manuscripts of his work.[56] It tells that as a layman he studied philosophy in Italy, that afterwards he taught the principles of metre, and that he wrote his books in Achaia in the time of the second Theodosius and of Valentinian the third. We may think, then, that he was a native of Italy, possibly of Rome, to which city Aldhelm assigned him.[57] Isidore of Seville (*de vir. ill.*, 20) described him as priest. We read that his *Paschale Carmen* was favoured by the *Decretum Gelasianum de libris recipiendis,* and that an edition was prepared by Turcius Rufius Asterius, consul in 494.

The five books which compose the work are introduced by a letter to Macedonius, his friend, spiritual guide, and patron, in which he explains his reasons for writing. God has called him from using his talent in secular studies to devote his power to Divine service; he writes in verse in the endeavour to make his words more attractive. The name *Paschal Song* is given to the work because Christ our Pass-

over was sacrificed for us. At the end of this preface appear
the names of divers of his associates in religion. Among
these after the manner of Jerome he reveres women as well
as men, and sings enthusiastically the praise of Syncletice, a
woman of manly intellect, who but for her sex might even
teach dogma of Holy Writ, and of her sister Perpetua, tender in years, but aged in upright life.

The story begins with Enoch; then come Sarra and her
late bearing, Abraham and his sacrifice, Lot and the fate of
his wife. This receives the comment which is typical of the
mystical spirit of the whole work:

> A pillar then of salt transfixed she stayed,
> For punishment converted; for that none,
> Who fleeth not this base world's evil lot,
> But looketh backward, shall salvation gain.
> Nor ought the ploughman plying worthy task
> To cast his eyes behind him.[58]

As Moses led the Israelites over the Red Sea, so Christ
leads his people to baptism with voice sounding over the
waters; so was he manna and drink to them in the wilderness. The folly of worship of idols is rebuked even with
ridicule when we reach the Book of Daniel:

> Some worship cabbages; in gardens rich
> Parched deities they tend with water; thus
> They seem to cultivate transplanted gods.[59]

Having now told of the Old Testament history:

> sancti coniuncto Spiritus actu
> Quæ Genitor socia Nati virtute peregit,

Sedulius will now turn to the New Covenant:

> sancti coniuncto Spiritus actu
> Quæ Natus socia Patris virtute peregit.

This leads directly to condemnation of the errors of Arius and Sabellius:

> Again: "My Father and Myself are One."
> That "One" should Arius learn; Sabellius
> "We are" should straight acknowledge. He the Faith
> Of Three rejecteth, Arius scorns the One.[60]

In the second book the New redeems the Old by the atoning of the "second Eve":

> That, just as from sharp thorns springs the soft rose,
> All innocent, passing its parent's flower;
> So Mary from the holy stem of Eve
> The sin of Maid of old, a Maiden new,
> Might expiate.[61]

From this point we follow the story of the Birth and Life of Christ, for the most part after the record of Saint Matthew. The lines on the Holy Maid and Mother, beginning *Salve, sancta Parens,* are well-known, for they are still used as Introit in the Mass of her Feasts. The Wise Men offer their gifts of sacred symbol, and the narrative reaches in due course the Call of the Twelve. From this point to the end of the book original matter is introduced in an interpretation of the Lord's Prayer, explained petition by petition.

The third book tells of the Miracles, still following Saint Matthew; in the fourth the way is prepared for the Passion. All four Gospels are drawn upon for its story in Book Five, wherein Christ reigns from the Tree, King of all:

> If any know not that the very Form
> Of this the Cross must honoured be, which bore
> Our Lord rejoicing, under meaning deep
> It gathers all four regions of the earth.
> For from his Head there shines the glowing East,
> His sacred Feet are washed by Western star,

His right Hand holds the North, mid-pole his left;
And thus all Nature from his members lives,
And Christ embraces in his rule the world.[62]

The Resurrection is then described, and the narrative of the
Ascension brings the work to an end.   In all it gives some
1770 hexameter lines of simple texture, easy to read, full of
the phrases of Vergil and, in lesser measure, recalling other
classic poets, yet showing independence of spirit in its treatment.   One instance will illustrate the mystical interpretation of miracle—in the story of St. John IX, I ff.:

Then passing on he sees a man born blind
Sit by the way, who, sprung from natal womb
Ill-fated, unto light in darkness came.
Then he, Man's Author and Creation's Source,
Not suffering that the work should show defect,
Upon his eyelids passes native clay,
From seed of old supplies his human need.
Nor yet received he sight, ere, to the Lord
Obedient, at Siloam's pool he stooped
And saved by liniment of kindred clay
In water clear had washed his eyes.   Then soon
They glow with life and merit unknown day
To contemplate at last.   Learn, all mankind,
What mystic miracles may teach our minds.
For we are blind, the sons of wretched Eve,
And carry darkness, born in error long.
But when God deigned to take our mortal form
Of human covering, from a Maid became
Earth our salvation; washed by holy font
It opens to us rays of nascent light.[63]

It may have been the digressions from Holy Scripture
that moved Macedonius to direct the composing of a second
version in prose, a task which Sedulius obediently fulfilled

and called *Paschale Opus*. Critics agree in seeing a distinct change for the worse in its turgid and rhetorical sentences.[64]

There remain yet two "Hymns," of which only the second deserves the name. This contains the famous verses of which the Church still makes use. At Lauds of Christmas Day she sings the lines beginning *A solis ortus cardine;* and at Vespers of the Epiphany the lines 29 ff., which are also known in the version of Luther—"Was fürcht'st du, Feind Herodes, sehr"—and in the English translation—"Why, impious Herod, vainly fear?" [65] The hymn from which these passages are taken is of the type called *abecedarius*, that is, a form in which every strophe begins with a letter of the alphabet from A to Z; the strophes consist each of four iambic dimeters. The first "Hymn" is really a poem of fifty-five elegiac distichs, connected by epanalepsis; the content passes very briefly in review events of the Old Testament, giving to these a parallel in the work of Christ for men. Its literary merit does not encourage quotation.

The last of our Biblical poets brings us back for a moment into the sphere of secular history. It will be remembered that under the regency of Galla Placidia the Vandals made inroad into Africa, either invited by Count Boniface in his unequal conflict with the government at home, or taking advantage of this distraction in time of revolution and religious strife; [66] in 442 they had settled down by treaty upon the richest regions of Northern Africa as permanent possessors. We have seen also that in the time of Aetius, the great minister of Galla Placidia and Valentinian, was planned a marriage-bond between the son of Gaiseric, Huneric by name, and Eudocia, daughter of Valentinian, a plan which was, however, long delayed in fulfilment. The peace between Rome and Carthage was not broken till after Valentinian had been murdered by plot of Petronius Maximus and Maximus had won for himself the Western throne in 455; whereupon Gaiseric, making excuse that Maximus had forced the widow of Valentinian, Eudoxia, to become his bride, and, it may be, induced by appeal from the lady for support, made attack upon the city of Rome, seizing vast spoils and carrying into captivity the ex-Empress Eudoxia and her daughters. It was now that the marriage between Huneric and his father's prisoner, the Princess Eudocia, was at length celebrated. Famine followed the capture of Rome through possession of the Mediterranean by the Vandal fleet; and the terrific task of endeavouring to overcome the ever-present menace of these barbarians led to the downfall of the two emperors who followed Maximus, Avitus and Majorian. Under the succeeding emperors of the West, Severus (461-465) and Anthemius (467-472), Vandal attacks continued, though in 468 Leo, Emperor of the East, had made a mighty effort to crush the common enemy in a naval expedition. Peace was made at last in 474 between Roman Empire and Vandal Kingdom by Zeno, Leo's successor in Constantinople from 474 till 491; it lasted almost sixty years, till in 533 Justinian brought the African dominion under his own sway. In 477 the great warrior Gaiseric had died, and was followed on the Vandal throne in that year by Huneric his son. The rest of the fifth century saw two other Vandal Kings in Carthage, Gunthamund, who succeeded Huneric in 484, and Thrasamund, Gunthamund's brother, who assumed the rule in 496.

Under these Vandal sovereigns Roman Africa gave some evidence of literary life, in the poems collected toward the end of their sway and now forming the Latin Anthology of the Salmasian Codex; in the extraordinary composition, if this were written under rule of Gaiseric, of Martianus Capella; and in the poetry of Blossius Æmilius Dracontius, first (unless we include Commodian) of Africa's Christian poets,[67] who chose the story of Creation for his theme and therefore concerns us here. He was born of aristocratic lineage, whence he inherited the title, *vir clarissimus,* which he mentions at the end of one of his shorter poems (*Romulea* V); in the same place he tells us that he acted as advocate in the court of law of the proconsul of Carthage, Pacedeius. Two of his shorter poems are dedicated to a certain Felician, who seems to have been of note as teacher in Carthage and under whom he studied grammar and rhetoric. He had already attained distinction in his legal career when he incurred the wrath of the reigning monarch, Gunthamund, because of a poem, now lost, which he had composed in honour of a foreign lord; very probably, though not certainly, this was Zeno, the Byzantine Emperor of that date. Such laudation of a foreigner was too much for Gunthamund's jealous sense of right, possibly inflamed, as the poet declares, by treacherous representation; and the writer was cast into prison, where he endured great misery of body and mind. But his trouble proved a blessing. Already the author of some minor and insignificant verse, he now sought to turn the heart of the irate sovereign by a poem of about three hundred lines of elegiac metre, which he named *Satisfactio.* It met with no success, however, and he repeated his appeal in another far more ambitious work in three books, *De Laudibus Dei.* The fate of this poem is doubtful, but the writer eventually won his freedom through the intervention of powerful friends. There is also evidence pointing to his composition of a poem in honour of King Thrasamund.[68]

The "subscriptio" given at the end of the former work runs: "Explicit Satisfactio Dracontii ad Gunthamundum Regem Guandalorum dum esset in vinculis." An invocation addressed to God Everlasting and Almighty forms the opening. He, according to the theology of Dracontius as herein expressed, is responsible for both good and evil among men:

> The minds of men thou leadest where thou wilt
> And by thy bidding guidest intellects;
> Thine anger makes them to oppose thy will,
> Thy mildness to them righteous deeds directs.
>
> Whatever men may do both good and ill,
> All from God's wrath or favour takes its start;
> Thy words give proof of this, to Moses said
> When thou didst harden Pharaoh's stubborn heart.

Therefore God himself is held by Dracontius to have impelled him by Divine anger to the misery of sin:

> My heart then God, when that my conscience sinned
> In time unseemly, drove to lawless things;
> That I—who might my leaders' deeds declare,
> Triumphant warfare of the Asding Kings,
>
> Whence mine had been reward and wholesome praise
> With bounty great in this my sovereign's face—
> Should prizes scorn, of kindly Lords say naught,
> Should sudden seek this certain dire disgrace.[69]

From the very beginning God mingled good and bad in the world:

> My fault is grave indeed, yet grace may crave
> In that no man was ever free from sin;
> For God's Almighty power that made the world
> Could banish sorrow, make all glad within.
>
> Yet differing and discordant things he joined
> And evil mixed with good, and good with ill;
> So elements of various sorts he blent,
> The damp with dry, the fire with cold and chill.[70]

"May God therefore pardon my sin, and after God, my sovereign Gunthamund!" It is indeed to sin that Man owes his knowledge of God's mercy:

> If in our human race there were no sin,
>> Why call God Love if he forgot not blame?
> But since he giveth grace, remitting sin,
>> Through work of love he holds his gracious Name.[71]

Moreover, the sinner has been punished sufficiently by bonds and blows and starvation in captivity.[72]

The second attempt to win forgiveness, the *De Laudibus Dei,* opens with the glory of Creation. The description of the fair beauty of Paradise may be compared with that of Avitus:

> A place there is diffusing rivers four,
> With flowers ambrosial decked; where jewelled turf,
> Where fragrant herbs abound that never fade,
> The fairest garden in this world of God.
> There fruit knows naught of season, but the year,
> There ever blossoms earth's eternal spring.
> Fair vesture clothes the trees, a goodly band;
> With leaves and sturdy branches well entwined
> A dense-grown wall arises; from each tree
> Depends its store, or lies in meadows strewn.
> In sun's hot rays it burneth not, by blasts
> Is never shaken, nor doth whirlwind rage
> With fierce-conspiring gales; no ice can quell,
> No hailstorm strike, nor under hoary frost
> Grow white the fields. But there are breezes calm,
> Rising from softer gust by gleaming springs.
> Each tree is lightly stirred; by this mild breath
> From moving leaves the tranquil shadow strays. . . .[73]

The fourth day saw the creation of the sun and the moon, the sun to flood all things with its joyous health-giving

radiance, the moon to despoil darkness and bring forth
again the trembling dawn.   The fish and the birds were
fashioned on the fifth day, as many fish as there are waves
in the sea, and birds pouring out sweet melody:

> Praising, I think, the Lord who gave them birth.[74]

As Man, once formed, first draws the breath of life, he
looks around him marvelling:

> On all his eyes he cast; and wondered there
> At place so lovely, at those rivers four
> From clear springs flowing with resounding course
> Amid the forest glades and grassy plains.
> Then wonders at himself; what Man may be?
> For what created? innocently seeks,
> Yet hath not whom to ask; what merit his,
> What gave to him this world, this kindly home,
> This kingdom fair with flowers?   And patient beasts
> Far off he sees in meadows; silently
> He asks himself the meaning of these things.[75]

In *Paradise Lost* Adam tells the same story to Raphael, and
later on tells God that only solitude mars his joy.   A like
loneliness is described by Dracontius:

> Nam consorte carens cum quo conferret egebat.

And so God pities him, and in his pity plans for his
creature the gift of harmony in wedded life.   Eve is formed
and appears before Adam's eyes at his awakening from sleep
in all her beauty; to her and to her husband God gives all
he has fashioned for their happiness, save the one Tree.
There follows a description of their first experience of sunset
and sunrise.   Born of earth, they think not to see the wonderful radiance again when once it has departed, and con-
sole their fear of darkness with the light of moon and stars

in the clear heavens. But with the morning joy comes anew. In innocence even as the creatures of the forest they are happy among the flowers,[76] no birds, no beasts intrude upon their privacy.[77] Alone the scaly serpent, fount of all evil, with honeyed poison bubbling beneath his fangs, can creep within their bower for their undoing:

> Seeking device to capture honesty,
> Simplicity to ruin, that belief
> May fall, not through its fault but misery.[78]

The Fall, therefore, in the narrative of Dracontius is due to the weakness of Adam and Eve. It results indeed in an inheritance of physical death for their descendants:

> Supplicium infelix, quo mors datur atque negatur:

for death is relief from ills as well as punishment. Yet when Dracontius is not immediately crying in fervid prayer for restoration to favour, his theology emphasizes rather Man's freedom to be righteous if he will: [79]

> In ignorance the snake doth strike, but we,
> Unrighteous crowd, we know, but culpably
> We scorn to follow justice.[80]

With the judgment passed on the pair of Eden, meting out thus both life and death, the most interesting part of this book is told, and we find a long digression on the power of the Spirit of life, born and reborn in Nature and in Man. "As God brings down the oppressor and comforts the afflicted, so may Gunthamund help the writer in his sorrow for his fault."

Before we leave these fifth century versions of the story of the Fall, a word may be in place with regard to the nature of the Tree of the knowledge of Good and Evil as therein described. For the Biblical *lignum* the word *arbor* is freely used, and *pomum* in its general sense of "fruit" without specification as to kind of fruit. Thus may we interpret the word in the writings of Avitus, of Victor, and of Cyprian of Gaul,[81] as well as in the *Pange lingua* of Venantius Fortunatus, composed toward the end of the sixth century.[82] There is, however, another word, *malum*, which is used in classical Latin to signify "any tree-fruit fleshy on the outside, and having a kernel within," and is regularly translated in our dictionaries as "apple." This word occurs in the narrative of Avitus and may have helped in the interpretation of "that crude apple that diverted Eve." [83] The Devil disguised as serpent plucks the "apple" to tempt the woman:

> Unum de cunctis letali ex arbore malum
> Detrahit et suavi pulchrum perfundit odore.[84]

The word is also used twice by Cyprian of Gaul, in whose story the "Thunderer" commands the two:

> Ne trepidate simul licitos præcerpere fructus,
> Quos nemus intonsum ramo frondente creavit,
> Solliciti, ne forte malum noxale legatis;

and the serpent tempts Eve:

> Dic mihi, cur metuas felicia germina mali?
> Numquid poma Deus non omnia nata sacravit?

a passage which brings out well the general use of "poma." [85]

The second book of the *Praises of God* treats of the glory of the Holy Trinity, of the Incarnation, with vehement attack against the Arian heresy, of the miracles of New and of Old Testament. All creation joins in worship in this beautiful hymn:

Thee Cherubim and Seraphim adore
Their God and Lord; and all the Angel Choir,
The soldier ranks with hymn beseech, and Thrones
With lowly song incessant make their prayer.
Thee stars and signs and planets magnify,
Confessing thee Creator; thunder's bolt
And lightning worship thee, the whirlwinds fear,
The storm of hail thy power acknowledges.
At thee the fields of ice, and tempests quake,
Of thee do all things tell in every breath,
Rain, flood, and sea, and snow, and summer's heat.
To thee earth lifts her voice, to thee the air,
The waters o'er the firmament's high vault;
The streams revere thee, spring and marsh and pool
Praise thee with their own psalm; swift-changing clouds,
The dawn's clear light, darkness of Night profound,
Fair seasons adoration yield each tide,
Spring, summer, fall and winter, every year.[86]

But from these high levels we quickly descend. It is
not to the point to describe in detail the course of this
book, spoiled by excessive and wearisome repetition and
ill-arranged matter, as is also the third, which contains illustrations of good and evil life drawn from Scripture, and,
for the benefit of pagans, from the stories of Greeks and
Romans, both men and women. Daniel and Hercules, St.
Peter and Salmoneus, Codrus, Regulus, Judith, Semiramis,
Dido and Lucretia, are all, with others, brought into a run-
ning commentary.

In addition to these two poems of Christian character
there are ten of an entirely secular nature, the *Romulea*,
or "Roman" compositions. The first, a youthful work, is
dedicated to Felician. Therein the master is praised:

Who Afric's banished learning hast restored,
Who teachest foreigners with sons of Rome.

The second goes on to tell the story of Hylas in dull fashion; the third is again a preface addressed to Felician, introducing in No. 4 Hercules contending with the dragon. This also calls for no comment. The fifth is a rhetorical *controversia,* the sixth and seventh are wedding songs, the eighth gives a long account—more than 650 lines—of the Rape of Helen, the ninth shows us Achilles deliberating over the body of Hector, and the tenth tells the story of Medea. Lastly there is the *Tragedy of Orestes.* Nearly a thousand lines in length, it reminds one of Seneca in its horrid un-Greek dwelling on the scene of destruction for gruesome effect.

The merit of Dracontius as poet rests upon his account of Creation, called by Eugenius of Toledo the *Hexaemeron.* In his story of Adam and Eve we find lines of real poetic interest, though the whole does not equal the narrative as given by Avitus.[87]   In addition to the numerous digressions which spoil the unity and mar the interest of his work, critics point out many errors against the rules of prosody. There are the usual imitations of poets classical and Christian. In later days Dracontius was read in Spain by Isidore of Seville, in addition to Eugenius, in Gaul by Venantius Fortunatus, and in England by Aldhelm and by Bede.

An important question arises here: Did Milton consciously or unconsciously draw upon these authors in *Paradise Lost?* We have seen that a number of parallels have been traced; and indeed in the additions, Latin and English, to the Biblical narrative resemblances may be clearly observed. The motive of revenge for his fallen estate and jealousy of newly-created Man which inspires Satan in Cædmon and Milton we have also noted in Avitus; in all three poets Satan himself replaces the serpent, though, whereas in Avitus and in Cædmon he assumes a serpent's form, in Milton, we remember, he enters the body of the serpent while it sleeps. In all three poets Satan in this shape coils himself around a tree—in Avitus a tree without special name, in Cædmon the Tree of Death, in Milton the Tree of Life. In Avitus and in Milton Satan deliberately assails the woman first, fearing the stronger nature of the man; in Cædmon he only approaches Eve after receiving repulse on her husband's part; both Avitus and Milton carefully show Eve alone at the time of temptation. In Cædmon indeed Satan declares himself the messenger of God, a rôle which casts an entirely different light upon her fall. In both Avitus and Cædmon Eve takes the fruit from the hand of Satan; and in Milton Satan assures her that he himself has plucked and eaten of the produce of the Tree. With Dracontius, further, Milton shares the picture of Adam's marvel in his first beholding of Paradise, and of his imperfect happiness in his lonely state without a human sharer of his joy.[88]

Yet in regard to the influence of the Latin narratives students of literature have not spoken with certain voice, with the exception of George Sigerson, who unfortunately confuses Sedulius with an Irish poet of the ninth century, Sedulius Scottus; and thus in his work the good accomplished by translations from these comparatively little known writers and a most interesting store of parallels with *Paradise Lost* and *Paradise Regained* is joined with much mistaken criticism. Henry Osborn Taylor speaks of Avitus, "precursor of Milton, who appears to have used the Latin poet"; Parizel in his book on Avitus is inclined to believe that Milton was influenced by him, following the parallels adduced by Guizot, who pronounces with regard to the work of Avitus on Creation in his Lectures on the History of Civilization in France: "Ce n'est point par le sujet et le nom seuls, Messieurs, que cet ouvrage rappelle celui de

Milton; les ressemblances sont frappantes dans quelques parties de la conception générale et dans quelques-uns des plus importants détails. Ce n'est pas à dire que Milton ait eu connaissance des poëmes de Saint Avite: rien sans doute ne prouve le contraire; ils avaient été publiés au commencement du XVIe siècle, et l'érudition à la fois classique et théologique de Milton était grande."

That, I suppose, is where the question may best be left. As Sir Walter Raleigh observed in writing of the erudition of *Paradise Lost:* "It is partly this wealth of implicit lore, still more, perhaps, the subtly reminiscent character of much of his diction, that justifies Mr. Pattison in the remark that 'an appreciation of Milton is the last reward of consummated scholarship.' " [89]

CHAPTER IV

HISTORICAL EVENTS IN CHRISTIAN POETRY

It will be noticed that the scene of the composition of the Biblical narratives described in the last chapter has been in large part Gaul. And yet the literature of Gaul, even on its poetical side, was by no means in these days the reflection in general of peace and undisturbed cogitating on things spiritual or intellectual. Indeed, of all the countries which suffered at the hands of barbarians in the fifth century, the distresses of Gaul especially seem to have called forth pity and indignation from Christian writers no less than from the pagan Rutilius. Their work is chiefly of interest for its illumination of this age, with its grievous record of pestilence, famine, slaughter, and oppression of all kinds. And first, a cry of suffering through plague reaches us in a simple story dated by scholars toward the end of the fourth or in the beginning of the fifth century, when the author commonly known as Severus Sanctus Endelechius wrote his poem *On the Death of the Oxen*. Our knowledge concerning him is more or less uncertain, but it is thought that he was identical with a rhetorician mentioned in the subscription to a manuscript (*Cod. Laur.* 68, 2) of Apuleius as giving lectures on oratory in the Forum Martis in Rome in the year 395. He may also have been the "Christianus vir, amicus meus Endelechius" of whom Paulinus of Nola wrote (*Ep.* 28, 6) as having incited him to write his panegyric on the Emperor Theodosius, a work composed in 394. The manuscript from which the *editio princeps* was printed is lost,[1] but the title in that edition appeared as "Here begins the poem of Severus Sanctus, that is, of Endelechius the Rhetor, concerning the Death of the Oxen." From the author's name as here given it has been suggested that he assumed the two former parts after his conversion to Christianity.[2]

The poem consists of thirty-three asclepiad strophes, composed with metrical care and fluent simplicity of language; the form is cast in a conversation between three neatherds, whose names, Ægon, Bucolus, Tityrus, show Vergilian influence. At the opening Ægon asks Bucolus why he wanders alone and weeps with downcast eyes? Speech is good for sorrow; let him declare forthwith his hurt to a friend. This sympathy elicits a mournful tale of fatal pestilence that has crept unawares upon the cattle of Bucolus and destroyed the herds that once filled valleys and mountain-ridges with their number. Ægon recognizes the scourge that has swept over Europe, following its noxious course from Pannonian and Illyrian fields to Italy.[3] Further questioning calls out more detailed description of the terrible swiftness of the disease; for the cattle fell in their traces, and the flocks died before even their sickness was known. Oxen, ewes, calves, the proud father of the herd himself—as many as the falling leaves in autumn or the snowflakes in winter were the victims in their multitude. But why, wonders Ægon, has the herd of Tityrus escaped? And Bucolus, catching sight of their owner, asks him what god has saved his cattle from the general disaster? Tityrus triumphantly proclaims that he has marked them with the Sign of the Cross:

> Mark which men hallow, of God's crucifixion,
> Who in great cities God alone is worshipped,
> Christ, everlasting glory of the Father,
> Only-begotten.

This Sign in centre of the forehead printed,
Of all my oxen was the sure salvation;
Thus God most truly by this Name all-powerful
      Saviour is blessed.

Straight the dire sickness fled from out my sheep-folds,
All ill escaping. Thou too, an thou willest,
Mayest pray this Lord God; faith alone thou needest
      To aid thy seeking.

No blood our altars sacrificial steepeth,
Nor kill we victims for disease's healing;
Only by simple spirit's purifying
      Cometh a blessing.[4]

Straightway Bucolus gives in his allegiance to the true
Faith, and Ægon desires to join them in their pilgrimage;
for a Sign that can conquer disease in the herds must also
be of aid to man.

We come now to actual references to war and barbarian
ravages. In his edition of the *Alethia* published at Lyons
in 1536, Gagny included an additional 110 lines of hexameter verse, which he assigned to Claudius Marius Victor, adding them to his work as a fourth book with the inscription *Ad Salmonem.* Later scholarship decided, first,
probably from this inscription, that we have here a Letter to
Salmon,[5] then that we have, not a letter but a dialogue,[6]
and, lastly, that the poem is not by Victor, but by some
author unknown to us; conjecture has suggested Paulinus,
Bishop of Béziers c. 400-419.[7] The scene of this simple
and unaffected little poem, which bears in manuscript the
title *S. Paulini Epigramma,* is a monastery. Two of the
characters of the dialogue are a monk of its community and
a former pupil of his in religion,[8] Salmon by name, who has

returned from his present home, some city near the river
Tecum (Tech) in Gallia Narbonensis, according to Schenkl's
theory, to visit his instructor of former years. The beginning is lost. In the opening lines of the extant fragment the
monk asks Salmon whether he has come to seek spiritual
solace of the Abbot or to enjoy a friendly talk? Since he
wishes to talk, they settle themselves comfortably in the
house in which a certain Thesbon, who also takes part in
the conversation, receives brethren in need of rest and refreshment. Salmon, in answer to inquiry, now describes the
state of his country after the ravagings of the barbarians:

> And truly plague within and deep-laid war
> Long time have harried us with arms' dense cloud,
> So far the fiercer as more secretly
> The foe lurks in retreat. And yet if aught
> Of devastation hath Sarmatian worked,
> If aught hath Vandal burned or Alan swift
> Hath carried off in rape, though feeble hope
> Be ours and sick endeavour, still we strive
> In fashion of some sort to mend our lot
> To pattern of old days.[9]

In these lines Schenkl sees a reference to the devastating of
Southern Gaul by the Vandals and Alans. The attempts at
reconstruction mentioned lead him to suppose that some interval of precarious peace is in course, possibly that brought
about by Constantine, and he dates the work accordingly at
the beginning of 408.

But, continues the visitor, morals have in no way bene-
fited by this trouble; for men still persist in evil as before:

> Not swords, not pangs of hunger, not disease,
> Have worked our ruin; we, we once did live,
> Who now and always in our sins remain,

> Forever fault unending. Who till night
> Would feast of old, yet drunken joins alike
> The sunrise to the lamps; adulterer
> Was Pedius, in darkest leprosy
> Still fast abiding. Envied Polio?
> Still envies he; and Albus, once of all
> Rich prizes hungry seeker, doth he less
> In this world's downfall for ambition toil? [10]

Even those who cannot be convicted as open and notorious evildoers are misled by the attraction of vain and secular learning and seek to discover the secret things only known of God.

"Ah, yes," breaks in Thesbon, "but these are masculine failings. No great trouble has fallen upon you if your women sin not grievously," a reply which opens the lips of Salmon in really fervid outburst. Day is not long enough, he declares, to voice the sins of the women of his country, for which men, as the guardians and controllers of women, are themselves to blame. Gaudy attire, silks, precious stones, even paint and powder, mar feminine virtue. Vain also is their talk. The precepts of Paul and Solomon are set aside, and they revel in Dido and Corinna. What wonder that sufferings have come upon the world? However, it must be conceded, argues the monk, that there are yet many good folk in the Church. This Salmon admits as the one comfort in life. But now the sun is setting. It is time for worship, and further talk must be postponed till the morrow.

More evidence of this kind is found in Dill's well-known book on the last century of the Western Empire: "The poems entitled *Ad Uxorem* and *De Providentia Divina*, which used to be wrongly attributed to S. Prosper, and the *Commonitorium* of S. Orientius are, as it were, the solitary

voices which come to us from the dim mass of the generation who witnessed the Suevic and Vandal invasions. In
phrases often almost identical they describe the suffering
and terror of the time." [11]   We read once again in these
poems of the early years of the century distressed by barbarian havoc in Gaul.   The work *On the Divine Providence*
was assigned to Prosper of Aquitaine for reasons of manuscript, and quoted as his in the ninth century by Hincmar of
Reims; it resembles his writing in style, language and
metre.   So much scholars grant; but on the other side it is
argued that the mention of ten years of plundering by
the Goths and Vandals points to its composition about 415,
a time when Prosper would seem to have been too young to
produce the theological reflections of its content.   It has
also been thought that the "semi-Pelagian" tone of its utter-
ance of free will is not suited to the pen of Prosper, that
zealous follower of St. Augustine.   Ebert suggested that the
writer might have been a cleric from his use of the word
"fratres" for his readers, and possibly a dweller in South
Gaul from his mention of olive-trees, though the latter in-
ference seems scarcely compelling.

The "Carmen," as the title describes it, begins with
ninety-six lines of elegiac verse.   Grief has caused silence
in the poet, who now, however, opens his complaint:

> Right happy he to whom by gift of God
>   Befalleth lot of freedom in these days!
> Whom ruin striketh not through neighbour's plight,
>   Whom neither flames nor water's flood dismays.
>
> But we in so great storm of miseries
>   In helpless mass are driven on to die;
> Our thoughts behold our burning fatherland,
>   And all things wasting ever meet the eye.[12]

In this trouble the writer, as a Christian, has been attacked by "javelins of tongues," shooting out reproaches: "For what reason," says the doubter, "have so many cities perished? Do you believe that things are really governed by the will of God?" The situation is indeed hard:

> Though ocean's flood had swept the fields of Gaul,
>   Yet greater wastes this dreary ravage sees,
> When flocks are wanting, seeds of harvest gone,
>   When place is lost for vines and olive-trees;
>
> When force has raped our dwellings, fire and storm
>   (Though sadder sight the few that empty stand),
> Scarce bearable our scourge; for these ten years
>   The prey of Goths and Vandals lies our land.[13]

"Neither fortresses nor towns nor lofty mountains have been able to withstand barbaric fury," continues the reproaching voice of the enemy. "We have endured the uttermost. I will not complain of common folk slain without distinction or of nobles dead in the strife; their sins may have merited this fate. But what of innocent boys and girls whose short life has given no occasion for sin? What of the temples of God and the sacred vessels? Neither virgins nor holy religious have been spared; anchorites and priests have suffered even as the wicked. The rule of God has not brought forth justice either in times of old nor in the present."

And so the poet goes to work to combat these errors, and for this end exchanges the pentameter for the heroic measure, "lest his discourse suffer from unequal lines." All men, he declares in his answer, have always perceived the existence of God; consciousness of him as Creator is innate in everyone. He created all according to his will, whatever is in heaven or earth or sea, animate or inanimate. Wisely did he create; even the resistance of creatures to one another is beneficial. One man's poison is another man's meat; what harms now may at another time be helpful, and everything in Nature has its use through the gift of Christ. The Fall brought death to man's body and the flaw of evil to his soul; yet in Christ he finds new life and victory. If man refuses salvation it will be through his own fault:

"Why lack I good?" "Thy fault." "Why sin?" "Thy wish."
"Why will I things of evil, good abhor?"
"Know, thou art free, canst right discern from wrong,
But choosest lower things, in folly blind.
I err, sayest thou, yet would I might not err.
A twofold choice then thine; for either thou
Dost long to flee from life or reason yield.
Doth he not err who strays from righteous paths,
Yet to the road returns if Christ be Guide?
But he whom no straight way receiveth, he
Can never err; who stands not, fears no fall." [14]

Those, then, who attribute their sin to the influence of their natal stars are a prey to the devil; even so men of old reverenced the sun, the moon and the star Rempham. But Joshua and Elijah controlled the heavens; these therefore obey and do not rule. If man's fate were fixed by the stars, he might sin at will if his destiny were favourable; in vain, if it were of evil omen, would he attempt a virtuous life. Finally, this doctrine of the stars either leaves man at the mercy of innumerable gods, or teaches that no god takes heed for him. This last error is also that of the Epicureans, who say that God does not rule the world because the good suffer and the bad prosper. But God's rule is shown in the regular workings of nature and of natural law. And who has not sinned and does not deserve punishment? If God gave all their due and meted out straightway to the wicked their punishment and to the good their final reward, they would disappear from earth and earthly life would cease. Now the mercy of God gives the guilty the chance of recovery—till the end, when the obstinately sinful shall indeed meet their doom. Misfortunes, like blessings, fall on good and bad; though instances as those of Rahab, Daniel, the Three Children, St. Peter in Chains, show that God does spare those who serve him. Yet to the good misfortunes are not evil; sometimes they give occasion of vicarious suffering:

> The just must suffer for the unjust man;
> Thus, while the innocent are sorely tried,
> Yet win they mercy for such evil folk,
> By pattern of their virtue turned to grace.[15]

A Husband's Poem to his Wife was also published with Prosper's writings and is still attributed to him by scholars for reasons of style and metre, though Manitius admits its lively spirit does not altogether savour of his manner.[16] There is external evidence also for his authorship; for Bede (Keil, *Gr. Lat.*, VII, 257, 21) mentions an exhortation of Prosper Tiro to his wife. The little composition is a welcome change from the dull hexameters of the preceding one; in quick earnest lines which show a very human spirit the author calls his wife to ascend with him to higher things in matters spiritual. There follows another realistic picture of the sufferings of Gaul during these years 405-416, written in elegiac couplets which are used for most of the 122 lines of the poem. All is coming to its last end; even were longer life granted yet man is mortal and but a stranger for a little space on this earth:

> Exigui vitam temporis hospes ago.

Let the wife therefore help and comfort her husband in united labour.

The author of the poem called *Commonitorium*[17] is thought to be the Saint Orientius, Bishop of Auch in Gers of Aquitaine (Augusta Ausciorum), of whom the Bollandist *Life*[18] states that in his old age he went on an embassy for aid of Theodoric the first to the camp of the Roman general Aetius and Litorius, his subordinate, when they menaced the territory of Theodoric in 439. The description of ravaged Gaul given by Orientius tallies with those given in the poems just now considered,[19] and his strictures against the prevailing lack of moral behaviour recall the bitter words of Salvian and of the author of the "Epigram."[20] His poem certainly does not show originality, and would appear to many people only "pious and dull";[21] yet Robinson Ellis could place it "on the highest level of early Christian poetry," remarking, in a criticism which examination of the work indeed justifies, that "the want of novelty in the subject matter is compensated by the dexterity of the treatment."[22] We are concerned here with a pastoral letter, written in two books and somewhat more than a thousand elegiac lines. The verse flows smoothly enough and the style and language make easy reading. There is indeed nothing unfamiliar in this kindly admonition, which may be summed in a word: "Life in the present world was given to us that we might prepare for the next; let us love God, the giver of all good things, and man, our fellow-creature; let us resist evil, for we shall rise again with these bodies, exactly the same as now we own them, to meet our due reward whether of dire punishment or of supreme joy." The Bishop knows the toil is hard, and sympathizes keenly with the tempted in the words of Dido and of Saint Paul. In lines which seem to run spontaneously from his pen he counsels his readers: "Flee from false beauty, from envy, avarice, and falsehood; give of your substance to the needy, give a cup of cold water if you cannot give hot, and if you have nothing of material gift, then bestow your prayers." [28]

We come now to our last writer on this subject, Paulinus of Pella. And here we note at once that if Orientius and the "Husband" and the despairing priest of these last pages tell us nothing new save of ravaged districts and morals, at least they give us little trouble in the reading; for which the student of their work may well feel a moment of gratitude when he turns to the terrible concoctions of this old gentleman, more interesting as they are in their description of little private details. A further glimpse of invasions and their consequences is given in his *Thanksgiving to God and Description of my life* (*Eucharisticos Deo sub ephemeridis meæ textu*), which "curious little poem," as Boissier remarked, "shows us the trials of a man of wealth during the first half of the century." [24] It is an entirely amateur production, the autobiography of the writer, undertaken in his eighty-fourth year not for his own glory nor for the notice of scholars, but as an act of gratitude for Divine mercies. We learn from its crabbed lines that the author was born at Pella in Macedonia during the prefecture of his father, and was taken before he was nine months old to Carthage on his father's appointment as pro-consul of Africa. Before he reached the end of his third year he was again on his travels, this time to Bordeaux, the native city of his forebears. He made there the acquaintance of his grandfather, consul in that year. Scholarship has identified this grandfather with the poet Ausonius and his son Hesperius as father of our writer. [25] In Bordeaux his education was carried on under the vigilant eye of pious parents; he studied Greek literature and afterwards the *Æneid*, though he found Latin hard after his custom of talking Greek with the servants of his house. These studies were interrupted in his sixteenth year by an attack of quartan fever, after which the doctors prescribed a period of holiday and indulgence in sport, in which his devoted father eagerly joined.

All his thoughts were now centred on his hunting and his games; his horses, he tells us, had to be adorned in fine array, his own attire of the most expensive kind, fragrant with costly essence, the balls for his games obtained from Rome. And further than this went his dissipations at this time of his youth, although with a strange complacency he congratulates himself even at this later date on a discrimination which seems to have gone far for the condoning of lax virtue in the morals of the day:

> Yet in so far as wanton freedom might
> With cautious moderation be restrained,
> Lest on my faults I pile some deeper charge,
> Desire by law I bounded; this I ruled:
> No maid unwilling or of alien rights
> Would I approach, yea, for sweet chastity
> To none of free-born state would yield, although
> Of free-will offered me; content to find
> My pleasure in the slaves of this our house,
> Preferring thus of fault to be accused,
> Not serious sin, for mine own honour's sake.[26]

Such was our writer's life till his twentieth year, when he unwillingly yielded to pressure laid on him by his parents and married a wife belonging to an ancient house, who brought him an estate much the worse for neglect. To the care of this property he then devoted himself and his household with such zeal and success that he was soon able to pay off debts and lay by a sufficiency for comfortable leisure. Then followed once more a life given up to selfish ease, eager for nothing but bodily enjoyment without ambition or care for the outside world. It reminds one at once of the similar round of petty self-centred occupations in which Sidonius and his literary friends indulged their cultured bent, though Paulinus does not even have the merit of this culture. This was his lofty aim:

> That mine might be a house of spacious halls,
> For varied seasons apt; and there withal
> A board abounding, servants—young—in crowds,
> Much furniture for every pleasure's need,
> And silver, costly more than cumbersome,
> With workmen skilled in divers arts to fill
> My orders with despatch. Then stables, too,
> All full of well-bred horses, and for drives
> Some carriages both safe and seemly. Yet,
> Not for augmenting of this store so much
> As for its beauty would I care, not keen
> On wealth's increasing, on official state,
> But rather truly haunter of delights,
> If I might these at little cost procure
> With reputation unimpaired, that no
> Black mark of profligacy stain my name.[27]

We are not to forget, of course, that Paulinus is here accusing himself in somewhat the fashion of Augustine before him and that he finds fault in his old age with his idle youth. When thirty years of life had gone, his luxurious peace was interrupted by his father's death and by the inroad of the Goths into Gaul. As this was undoubtedly the invasion of 406, we find here evidence for the birth of Paulinus, dated on this ground in 376, and for the composition of the work in 459. Troubles now followed quickly, both private and public. His brother disputed the father's last will against the interests of their mother, and both he and his mother were despoiled of their property by the Goths who burned Bordeaux in 415 before their departure from Gaul.[28] The two migrated to the neighbouring town of Vasatæ (Bazas) in which forefathers of Paulinus had dwelt, only to run into danger through a rising of slaves against those of noble birth. The city was in the throes of blockade by Goths and Alans in this year, and Paulinus conceived the idea of escaping from the town by the help of the king of the Alans, who had long been on friendly terms with him and was engaged in the siege rather by the will of his Gothic allies than of his own desire. After some negotiations Paulinus succeeded in bringing over the Alan king and all his army to alliance with the government of Honorius; whereupon the Goths, finding themselves deserted by their partners in the siege, broke it up and departed. The writer now continues by telling that he thought it better to leave the land of his fathers for the East, where his mother, evidently a Greek woman of wealth, had extensive possessions; but his wife firmly intervened. A similar consideration for his family stayed also his desire to become a monk, an aim fostered by a revival of religious zeal in his forty-fifth year.

The rest of these jolting hexameters tell the tale of lonely later years. One by one the members of Paulinus' family departed this life; of his two sons one, a priest, thus left him, the other gave him no help. So he lived in poverty in Marseilles, yet not so poor that Horace's wish did not befall him, a home with a little bit of garden and its fruit. Yet here once more came failure, and he returned "exul, inops, cælebs" to Bordeaux, to be supported by others until an honest Gothic stranger bought his house at a generous price and enabled him to support himself.[29]

The note of the title of the work is maintained throughout by repeated acknowledgment of the mercies of God, and the whole impresses one as springing from a genuine feeling of piety on the part of a zealous layman in literary art. Imitation of Vergil is found in abundance; Brandes cites more than eighty instances.[30] The influence of Ausonius has also left its mark, as is natural, but of the work of other writers there is little trace. Paulinus does not appear before us as a scholar, but as a private citizen of ample means leading the life common to many in this day and, rather fortunately for history's enlightenment, possessed of a well-aimed *cacoethes scribendi*.[31]

CHAPTER V

CHRISTIAN PROSE: JEROME AND AUGUSTINE

While the poets of Gaul tell of the miseries in their land consequent on barbarian inroads, writers of prose bear witness not only to this same material trouble in Gaul and Italy, but also to the spiritual havoc wrought by adherents of schism or error of belief in far-off countries of the world. Yet here we are not merely concerned with destruction; but rather with the great constructive work wrought for the Church by the two mighty Doctors of this century and their disciples, whether this work was bound up with the abiding life of the soul or with the passing affairs of the history of their time. First of the two let us look for a moment at Saint Jerome, now permanently established in the East after his migrations of earlier date. From the five years of sojourn in the desert country of Chalcis he had passed to Antioch, to Constantinople, and to Rome. In Rome he had carried on study of the Scriptures and had preached the life of self-denial, especially to the high-born lady Paula and her relatives and friends, among whom Pammachius the senator and the lady Marcella were to prove singularly devoted to the cause and its preacher in time to come. But the Imperial City did not love ascetic practices or criticism of its ways; and in 386, having just passed the age of forty, Jerome retired across the sea to Bethlehem, followed shortly afterward by the intensely eager Paula and her daughter Eustochium. On them, each in her turn, devolved the supervision of the community of women Religious who gathered in the city, as their own director ordered that of the men.

Here until 419 [1] he was engaged in writing amid manifold distractions and griefs of body and spirit that multitude of letters and those treatises and studies of the Scriptures which still remain to us from his pen. At the beginning of the fifth century much had been accomplished; to the revision of the Psalms and of the New Testament begun under Pope Damasus in Rome he had added the finishing touches, had written Commentaries, lives of hermits, a book *de viris illustribus ecclesiasticis,* and, above all, had advanced far in his work, finally completed soon after Paula's death in 404, on his new rendering of the Old Testament.   This, when united with his rendering of the New Testament from the Greek, was known as the commonly accepted or Vulgate version in later days; for his revision of the Old Testament he had set himself the Herculean task of examining the Septuagint and the three other Greek versions contained in Origen's *Hexapla* in the light of the original Hebrew text.

It is in the *Letters* that we find much of the human interest of these last twenty years of his life, when rumours from without added to trials within overshadowed his days. There are indeed brighter moments, as when he feels that the victory of Christianity has now come. In 403 he writes of the dirt and squalor of Imperial Rome: "The Golden Capitol is shabby; all the temples at Rome are covered with soot and cobwebs. The City is shaken from its foundations, and a flood of people are rushing before the half-ruined shrines to the tombs of the martyrs." [2] Sihler has an interesting comparison of these words with the glowing description of Claudian,[3] written about the same time, and reminds us that in part Jerome's wish was father to the

thought; that his triumphant panegyric on Christian Rome
is not in keeping with the state of things that evoked Augustine's *City of God:* "Even in the City the heathen are
left in solitude; the former Gods of the nations have found
their dwelling with the owls and birds of night in the
lonely house-tops." [4]   But of a truth there is more sorrow
than triumph in these personal records, and we see a picture as time goes on of a troubled man, older than his years,
still persisting with indomitable spirit through hostility of
barbarians and heretics within his adopted home, tidings
of disaster from abroad, bereavement, sickness, physical and
spiritual distress.   Thus he describes tersely his varied vexa-
tions in a letter, dated 405, to Theophilus, that Bishop of
Alexandria whose friend and fellow-convert he had become
in campaign against Origenistic heresy: "A sudden invasion
of the Isaurians; devastation of Phœnicia and Galilee; terror in Palestine, especially in Jerusalem; no building of
books, nay, but of walls.   Add to this a hard winter and
hunger unbearable, the more so for us, on whom has been
laid the charge of many brethren." [5]   References to the fury
of the enemy in Gaul and Italy are repeated.   Rusticus, a
gentleman of Gaul, is bidden if possible to follow his wife's
example and seek the Holy Land; but, "if the remnants of
your possessions detain you, that forsooth you may gaze
upon the deaths of friends and citizens, the destruction of
cities and dwellings, at least amid the evils of captivity and
the savage faces of the enemy and the utter shipwreck of
your province, cling firmly to the plank of penitence. . . ." [6]
Ageruchia, who also lives in Gaul, is entreated not to give
herself again to wedlock in the miseries of the time: "Who
will believe it?   What histories will find fitting words to
describe it?   That Rome within her own bosom should be
fighting not for her glory but for her safety!   No, and not

even fighting, but ransoming her life at the price of gold and all her furniture! Not through the fault of princes has this befallen, for they are truly of deepest piety; but through the crime of a half-barbarian traitor, who with our own wealth has armed our enemies against us." [7]

So does the partial critic laud the worthless emperors, and rashly condemn Stilicho's effort to restrain the barbarian hordes. The occupation of Rome by Alaric calls forth a cry of despair: "A dread rumour is borne from the West, that Rome is besieged and that the safety of citizens is being redeemed by gold. . . . My voice chokes, and sobs stay my words as I try to dictate. The City is taken, which did take captive the whole world!" [8] Later on he laments the spoiling of Rome by the same chieftain and the flight of her citizens: "Oh, shame! the whole world is perishing in ruin, but our sins perish not. The glorious City, head of the Roman Empire, has been consumed in one flaming fire. There is no district which does not hold exiles from Rome! The churches once sacred have fallen in ashes and embers, and yet we are eager for our greed. We live as though we were to die to-morrow, and we build as though we were to live for ever in this age." [9]

The letters tell also of Jerome's circle of acquaintances. In one of these he makes excuse to Theophilus for correspondence delayed by illness and by grief at the death of his great friend and disciple, the widow Paula; [10] another epistle, sent as a *consolatio* to her daughter Eustochium, recounts the praises of Paula in no measured language. Deaf to the entreaties of her daughter Ruffina and her little son Toxotius, she had insisted on following Jerome to the Holy Land; and, established there, presided over her convent till her death. Jerome vividly pictures the scene of departure from Rome, and with evident approval: "She came down to the

harbour accompanied by her brother, her family and relations, and, what is of greater moment, by her children, all
eager by their loyal hearts to outstrip the sweet spirit of
their mother.   And now the sails were stretched, and by the
stroke of oars the ship was gradually drawn out into the
deep.   The little Toxotius held out his hands in entreaty on
the shore; Ruffina, who was now awaiting her marriage, si-
lently with tears besought her mother to remain until the
wedding-day.   Yet with dry eyes she gazed upon Heaven,
conquering her loyalty to her children by her loyalty to God.
She knew herself no more as mother that she might show
herself the hand-maid of Christ." [11]   Such was the ascetic
spirit of the fourth and fifth centuries in its cruder form, a
form only too frequently revealed.   The lady of whom Jerome wrote showed similar determination in her future career.   In spite of her director's counsel she persisted in giving
away all her money and left her daughter to struggle with
manifold debt; when seized with dangerous sickness she refused to obey either him or the doctors or indeed the holy
Bishop Epiphanius in remitting a trifle of her accustomed severity of life.   Not even accounts from home of grave illness
of her children induced her to leave her chosen path.   But
she seems to have been a very capable Superior of her convent, a most earnest student and a follower of the strictest
rule of prayer in spite of a delicate frame.   It cost Jerome
two nights of toil to tell of her deeds of charity, her pil-
grimages to holy people and places, and her self-denying
ordinances.

In like fashion he wrote of the lady Marcella, another
widow, who set an example of secluded religious life in
Rome to many other women.[12]   This practice was new for
women in these days, and Jerome tells that Marcella had
been stimulated by the holiness of Saint Anthony and of the

monks of the Thebaid. She was not so self-determined, it appears, as Paula; her fasting was temperate, and she permitted herself a sip of wine for health's sake, when necessary. The letter ends with the story of her capture by barbarians of Alaric at her house in Rome, a terrifying experience which was undoubtedly responsible for her death shortly afterwards. This great triad—Paula, Eustochium, Marcella—are so often on Jerome's lips that he is compelled to apologize for his championship of their sex: "The unbelieving reader perchance may laugh at me for tarrying to praise mere women." There follows the record of the holy women of the New Testament, and the scoffer is bidden to beware of pride.[13] Indeed, the long line of Commentaries dedicated to one or another woman by Jerome is sufficient proof of their zeal.

One of the most interesting letters contains the well-known instruction addressed to Læta, daughter-in-law of Paula, concerning the training of her infant girl, who bears her grandmother's name.[14] The little one has already been devoted to the virgin life, and Jerome is able to spare time for some nine columns in Migne's text of counsel for her preparation. It sounds rather drastic in these lax days. Her baby hands and lips are to fashion the names of patriarchs and prophets; no baby talk is to be allowed, though she may caress her pagan grandfather and chant Alleluia to him even if he does not approve. Her dress is to remind her of her future profession, and, of course, no ornaments are permitted. Her food, when she has outgrown her tender years, shall be vegetables and bread, with a little fish sometimes, but not too often. Baths are to be forbidden modest maidens; so Jerome afterwards praised her grandmother—*balneas, nisi periclitans, non adiit.* Her mental training shall be in Greek and Latin versions of Holy Writ, and in Fathers

of the Church, Cyprian, Athanasius, Hilary; her spiritual
discipline in the Psalter and Prayer-Book, practised by night
and at the Hours of the day. Her time, writes the Doctor,
will pass quickly in a continual round of reading and prayer,
varied at intervals by the spinning of wool. Poor little girl!
No wonder that the man of zeal foresaw Læta's desperate
question how she might thus train the child amid the distractions of the great City? Well, the best course will be
to send off her infant daughter to the care of her aunt in
Bethlehem, "the little one, whose very crying is a prayer for
you." It was this same Paula on whom afterwards at about
the age of twenty devolved the heavy burden of supervision
of the convent of religious women in Bethlehem upon her
aunt's death. There is also another letter on a child's training to a father, Gaudentius, in which, however, distress at
the trouble of the Empire prevents much detail of direction.[15]

Counsel regarding the monastic life is given to Rusticus,
a young man of Toulouse,[16] and, accompanied with much
ecstatic congratulation, to Demetrias, a noble maiden of the
family of the Anicii, who caused great joy to the faithful by
her decision to take the veil.[17] Julian, of aristocratic birth
and considerable wealth, probably a dweller in Dalmatia,
had previously been bidden to seek the same high calling.[18]
Many letters show the generosity of the zealous scholar in
willingness to help a serious student. He writes some
twenty-four columns of the *Patrologia* to a lady of Gaul,
Hedibia, in answer to twelve questions regarding the practice of religion and the interpretation of the Scriptures; [19]
Algasia, another lady of the same country, receives some
thirty-one columns of instruction on eleven matters of a
similar kind.[20] To Sunnias and Fretela, priests of Gothic
race, who desire light in their study of Jerome's revision of

the Psalter, he expresses his joy: "Who would believe that
the barbaric tongue of Goths would inquire into Hebrew
truth, and that while Greeks sleep, nay, engage in contention, Germany herself would ponder the words of the Holy
Spirit . . . ? Now warlike hearts are changed into Christian mildness, and spears into pruning-hooks." [21] Evildoers
are rebuked and heretics receive vigorous condemnation.
At the prayer of son and brother a letter speeds over to Gaul
reproaching a mother and her daughter, total strangers to
the writer, for their loose and unnatural mode of life; [22]
Avitus is instructed to use caution in study of Origen; [23]
Riparius receives a stream of fiery language against Vigilantius: *O præcidendam linguam a medicis, immo insanum
curandum caput!* [24]

This Vigilantius, a priest of Gaul, had been guilty of
preaching against honour paid to relics, prayers for the dead,
and the observance of nocturnal vigils. A cutting letter had
already reached him from Jerome in 396, rebuking him for
an attack on the Doctor after he had stayed with him and
had applauded his teaching in Bethlehem. His errors met
with further severity in the *Liber contra Vigilantium,* in
which, after receiving the written views of Vigilantius from
Gaul, Jerome poured forth his wrath throughout one night
against this *portentum in terras ultimas deportandum . . .
lingua viperea et morsu sævissimo.*[25] "Many monsters,"
writes the pen of scorn, "have been brought into the world,
Centaurs, Sirens, Cerberus, three-bodied Geryon, and so
forth; only Gaul hitherto has been free from such, a land
of brave and eloquent men. But now suddenly Vigilantius,
or, to give him a truer name, Dormitantius, has arisen to
contend with his foul spirit against the Spirit of Christ, to
approve the marriage of the clergy, in which error—the
shame of it!—he holds even bishops as his accomplices, to

doubt whether the prayers of those departed hence in Christ avail for blessing, to attack pious lighting of candles for dispelling of gloom in our churches, to inveigh against the monastic life.   Shall not the Saints intercede for those who in all the world have believed on their Gospel?   Shall Vigilantius, the living dog, be superior to Paul, the dead lion?   If lay folk and holy women in their ignorance and simplicity honour martyrs somewhat zealously by lighted candles, what harm is done?   Did not Mary find acceptance of her fragrant offering in face of rebuke?"   In truth, it is not only to escape his own weakness but to flee from such as Vigilantius, that haunter of taverns,[26] that Jerome seeks the shelter of monastic life.

It was shortly before this time that he had been engaged in his famous quarrel with Rufinus, the Latin writer of Aquileia, long resident in the convent of the lady Melania on the Mount of Olives.   The details of this bitter division between two men, once loyal friends, are too familiar to need repetition at length here.   The trouble rose from fear of suspicion of taint of Origenistic heresy.   Both men had been accused of favouring this heresy by Aterbius, a zealous hunter of such offence, on his visit to Jerusalem in 392. Jerome vindicated his faith by open statement; Rufinus would have nothing to do with Aterbius and his charges. When the next year the equally zealous Epiphanius, Bishop of Salamis in Cyprus, had visited Jerusalem and found John, its Bishop, dangerously unorthodox, as he judged, and had embodied his suspicions in a letter to John, Jerome's translation of this letter mysteriously fell into critical hands by the agency, as he indignantly conceived, of his former friend.   The bitterness of this period was felt in far keener force when Rufinus, now established in Rome, published a translation of the *De Principiis* of Origen and actually dared to praise Jerome in its preface as one who had both admired Origen and translated his writing—statements indubitably true, but inconvenient in their date of appearance. Jerome was as enthusiastic now in his censure of Origen's errors as he had once been warm in praise of his good work. The preface was sent to Bethlehem by Jerome's friends, Pammachius and Oceanus, with the request that he make for them another translation of the *De Principiis;* for they suspected that many alterations had been made in the version of Rufinus for the defence of Origen.[27] Such translation was promptly made by the scholar at Bethlehem and despatched to the same friends with a letter defending the writer's own position in the past.

This second version was brought to the notice of Pope Anastasius, who, though ignorant in general of the Origenistic storm and its cause, was led by it to condemn the author of the original source as heretic. Whereupon Rufinus, in apprehension lest he too be condemned, issued in 400 the two books of his *Apology* (also known as *Invectives*) against Jerome, accusing Jerome of trying to defame him and of harbouring the errors of Origen. About the same time Rufinus also sent a short statement of his faith for the enlightenment of the Pope. It is fair to Jerome to add that when he published his translation of Origen's *First Principles,* he had likewise written a letter to Rufinus which Jerome's busy friends in Rome kept from reaching its destination. Incomplete information regarding this *Apology* was hastily sent across the water, and, without waiting to receive its full text, Jerome answered in 402 by two books of his own *Apology against Rufinus.* "Why," he asks in his wrath, "was it needful to bring me into question, living in retirement as I am, and separated by so great space of land and sea? To expose me to the ill-will of many men

that he might do me more harm by his praise than he bene-
fited himself by his example?   And now that I have refuted
him who thus lauded me and have turned round my pen
and informed him that I am not what he, my friend, declared me to be, he is said to be furious and to have composed three books against me with Attic grace of style,
accusing me on the same points as those whereon he formerly praised me, and putting to my account impious doctrines in my translation of Origen. . . . Why did I translate
Origen?   Because my friends spoke of false interpretations
and changes in the version of Rufinus; and when I had read
that version and had compared it with the Greek, I did see
that he had changed those words of Origen which Roman
ears could not endure." [28]

When Jerome had finally received from Rufinus himself a
letter and a copy of the text of his *Apology,* a third book
issued from Bethlehem.   Its sordid details of wrangling repeat the spirit of the two former ones, which called forth
sorrow from Augustine.   "I have deeply grieved," wrote the
Bishop of Hippo in the same year, "that so great evil of
strife has arisen between two persons of so dear and intimate acquaintance, bound by a bond of friendship known
exceeding well to almost all the Churches." [29]   Yet midway
in Jerome's fulminations we come upon a passage which
shows him in the more lovable spirit always manifested to
those who were true to the Faith as he held it: "And so
do you not accuse me and I will stay my defence.   For what
edification is it to the hearers that two old men should
wage deadly duel with each other on account of heretics,
especially when they both wish to appear Catholics?   Let
us lay aside this defending of heretics.   There shall be no
contention between us.   With the same fervour with which
we once praised Origen let us now condemn him, condemned

as he is in all the world. Let us join hands, unite our hearts, and follow with eager steps the two *triomphateurs* [30] of East and West. In youth we erred, in age let us amend our doings. If you are my brother, rejoice in my correction. If I am your friend, I ought to be glad in your change of mind. . . . Forgive me that in my earlier years I praised the learning of Origen and his keen study of the Scriptures, before I had fuller knowledge of his heresy; and I will grant indulgence to you that with white hair you wrote an Apology for his books." [31]   It is sad to think that in spite of these laudable words Jerome repeatedly poured scorn on Rufinus after his death in 410.[32]

Not only with the views of Origen is Jerome's name connected during this time as defender of his own faith, but with those of Pelagius and Cælestius and their followers who caused so great ado in Palestine and Africa in the early years of the century. The part played by Jerome in this long-drawn-out contention is, of course, slight when compared with the work of Augustine; yet he was too prominent in matters of the Church to avoid some action. And therefore in 415 he sent forth his defence *Against the Pelagians*. It is cast in the form of a dialogue between Atticus, who represents the orthodox view, and Critobulus the Pelagian. Atticus is naturally concerned with attacking the tenet of Critobulus that man could be without sin indefinitely if he so willed; for, Critobulus maintains, the grace of God given him with free will at his creation is generally sufficient, at least in *posse* if not in *esse*, to accomplish this. In answer Atticus holds that as a matter of fact no man has ever been entirely without sin, for sinlessness is of God, and that man needs therefore the grace of God in constant operation to keep him from constant guilt. Many texts are quoted by Atticus to show the ravage and power of sin to which man is liable. His position differs, however, in this respect from the "Augustinian" creed of predestination in that he states that while God certainly possesses foreknowledge of man's future weal or woe, yet this foreknowledge does not take away man's power of free will in choosing his destiny: "God judgeth things of the present, not of the future. Nor condemneth he from his foreknowledge that man who, he knoweth, shall hereafter displease him. . . ." [33]

The treatise caused keen offence to the Pelagians, of whom there were many in Palestine. At the time of the writing of this dialogue Pelagius was himself in Palestine, where he appeared for judgment before its Bishops at Jerusalem, and, at the end of the year, at Diospolis. Shortly afterwards Pelagians burst upon the monastic houses of Bethlehem, murdered certain of the religious, wrought havoc upon the buildings, and forced Jerome to flee for his life to other shelter at a time only some two years prior to his death. References to these troubles occur in two of the letters written about 417. To Riparius Jerome writes: "It has seemed better to us to change our dwelling than the truth of our faith, to lose the delight of buildings and habitation than to be stained by communion with those to whom we must either straightway yield, or certainly contend daily against them, not with words but swords. How great things we have suffered and how the hand of Christ raised for us has poured out wrath upon the enemy, I think you have learned from the frequent tidings of all men." [34] And to Apronius at the same time: "Our house so far as the wealth of the flesh is concerned has been entirely overthrown by the attacks of the heretics, but through the grace of Christ it is filled with the riches of the Spirit. For it is better to subsist on dry bread than to lose faith." [35]

Distress of one kind or another is also reflected in the

prefaces to the Commentaries on the writings of the Prophets, which were bravely continued during the interruptions of these last years. Among these the one illustrating the words of Amos is dated c. 406; in the preface to the second book there is a pathetic picture of the ills incident to declining age. The Commentary on Isaiah, written 408 to 410, and dedicated to Eustochium, speaks of work rendered difficult by sickness (*Praef. lib.* XIII, *lib.* XIV), and of criticism directed against the writer: "It is really impossible to please everybody," he complains; for though he has collected learned tradition for the choice of his readers, still: "They do not want to know the opinions of the ancients, but mine; and so I am a prey to the tooth of envy" (*Praef. lib.* XI). The work on Ezekiel, written 410 to 415, tells the same tale. Bethlehem is the refuge of the oppressed, both men and women of noble rank and once of goodly wealth, so that Ezekiel has been neglected while Jerome has been trying to convert the words of Scripture into living fact and to study deeds, rather than the text, of holy import (*Praef. lib.* III). The preface to the seventh book gives a picture of the disturbed surroundings amid which he has been endeavouring to write: the crowds of fugitive brethren flocking to this hospitable shelter make peaceful study impossible, and at the approach of winter he steals the longer hours of night for his dictation. Moreover, his eyes are weak through old age, as the eyes of blessed Isaac, and he cannot read the Hebrew characters by lamplight; he can hardly do so in full clearness of day, because they are so small. Greek characters must be read for him by the brethren—*nullique dubium, quod alienis dentibus commoliti cibi vescentibus nauseam faciant.* The last work of all, written between 415 and 420, the Commentary on Jeremiah, attacks Pelagius, as might be expected. He is described, if not by name, yet in unmistakable language which shows that Jerome retained his vigorous spirit to the end. The offender appears as "most dense, and heavy with Irish porridge—one who after the fashion of the poets' fables must be smitten like Cerberus with a spiritual club that he may keep quiet in time everlasting with his master Pluto."

A word may be added concerning the relation of Jerome with Augustine, eight years his junior, and regarded in his hopes as his successor in exposition of sacred truths. The correspondence is somewhat overshadowed by the fact that a letter of Augustine to Jerome, written from Hippo about 394 and expressing doubt as to the planning of Jerome's Latin version of the Old Testament and criticism of his Commentary on the Epistle to the Galatians, was not delivered till some nine years afterwards through carelessness of the priest Profuturus to whom Augustine had entrusted it. In this letter, numbered 28 among Augustine's Epistles, he asked Jerome to indicate in his rendering of the Old Testament differences between this and the Septuagint, *quorum est gravissima auctoritas,* and expressed his grief that Jerome, or any other writer, should have explained the difference in the judgment of St. Peter and of St. Paul as deliberately feigned by them. About 397 Augustine wrote a second letter, which was also delayed in arrival till 403. As Jerome before this date had heard of both letters and of rumours of criticism directed against him, he was naturally eager to see what had been written. To Augustine's protestation that he had composed no "book" against Jerome's work, he answered by a warning not to provoke an old man, to remember that Dares overthrew Entellus, and that Quintus Maximus with endurance wore out Hannibal for all his youthful spirit.[36] It may be noted in passing that such references and quotations from the pagan classics come most readily to Jerome's pen even in these later writings, in spite of his abjuration of heathen works prompted by the famous vision on his bed of fever, told to Eustochium in 384 and conveniently revived by Rufinus in his invective against his former friend.[37]

More letters followed, till Augustine had written six on the matter. In one of these [38] he attempts to reinforce his argument of caution to Jerome by the story of the Bishop of Oea in Tripoli, who in the reading of Jonah IV, 6, from the Lesson in his cathedral had given forth to his people Jerome's *hedera* (ivy) for the *cucurbita* (gourd) of long-established tradition. At this so great outcry was made that the bishop was compelled to alter the reading or find himself without a flock. The tone of Augustine's letters is full of a delicate courtesy which is rather markedly wanting in the rejoinders from Bethlehem. However, at last peace was made and continued. It is pleasant to realize that criticism and delay of correspondence did not prevent in future a deep friendship between the two men of God, based on mutual affection and respect. About 405 Jerome wrote: "But farewell to complaints of this kind; let brotherhood unfeigned unite us; henceforth let us send each other letters filled not with questionings, but with love." [39] And long after he rejoiced that Augustine and he were united in their stand against Pelagian heresy: "Nay, I am resolved to love you, to look up to you, to cherish you, to admire you, and to defend your words as mine own. Of a truth also in the *Dialogue* which I lately put forth, I was mindful of Your Beatitude as was fitting; let us rather strive that this most harmful heresy may be removed from the Churches. . . ." [40] Even more striking are the words written by Jerome to Hippo a year or so before his death: "Always in truth have

I reverenced Your Beatitude with that honour which is
meet, and I have loved the Lord our Saviour abiding in you;
but now, if possible, I add somewhat to that sum and fill up
its perfect measure so that without mention of your name I
let pass no single hour, so firmly have you stood with burning faith against the force of the winds." [41]

If finally we picture Jerome for a moment as his writings
and the researches of scholarship have represented him, it
is a rather pathetic figure which with Augustine dominated
the Christian world of his day. Ever in fear of his own
inner frailty, he fled to the desert and lived there more
safely, as he deemed, in refuge from the common haunts of
men; carrying to so great degree his passion for the ascetic
way that he saw in marriage chiefly the source whence might
spring new sons and daughters of the monastery; ordained
priest, yet refusing to exercise his ministerial office; [42] hating
so intensely the error of those who dared to deviate not only
in creed but in matters of practice from Mother Church that
he could not refrain even from foul and brutal words of rebuke; rushing to his pen in quick alarm lest he himself be
thought defiled with tinge of heresy.[43] Yet these are minor
matters in his case. In Jerome the Church canonized the
scholar of the Bible, the friend of all who honestly sought
interpretation of spiritual things.[44] Countless men and
women craved by visit and by letter his aid for soul and
mind and body. Erasmus in his *Life of Jerome* was scarcely
wrong: "Many were drawn to Syria not so much by reverence for the spot as by their thirst to see Jerome." Orosius,
the historian, whom we shall meet later on in these pages,
was sent on to him from Africa by Augustine. Sulpicius
Severus related the impressions of the great Doctor, gathered, as he says, by his friend Postumian during a stay in
Bethlehem: "The heretics hate him because he is always

attacking them; the clergy hate him, because he rebukes their way of life and their sins.   But all good men admire and love him.   He is read through all the world." [45]   His form is well worthy of his matter.   The praise of Jerome's style none has told more eloquently than Erasmus: "Cicero himself would speak differently were he Jerome."   It is with reluctance that we have finally to remind ourselves that the famous story of the lion belongs rather to the realm of the spirit than of the letter. [46]

From East we turn to West to look briefly at some of the mighty works of Augustine.   For we remember that, if the *Confessions* belong to the fourth century, the *City of God* was inspired by the need of refuting the pagan blasphemies born of Alaric's capture and sack of the Imperial City in 410. The first part of Augustine's life may indeed be said to end shortly before the publishing of the *Confessions* in 400, when he had for thirteen years held fast the faith of Christianity.   When the fifth century opened, he could look back upon his life of study in his birthplace, Thagaste in Northern Africa, and at Carthage; he could remember his teaching of rhetoric there and in Italy, at Rome and at Milan, whither Monnica, as ever bound up in her prayers for her son, had followed him, to die at Ostia as they started to journey home once more.   He could look back upon the long struggle in his soul against the pagan powers of darkness, which had led him from reckless self-indulgence to the awakening, called forth by Cicero's *Hortensius,* of a desire for higher things; thence to the holding of the Manichæan creed, and thence, still seeking unsatisfied, to absorption in Neo-Platonic doctrine, which brought him in his discontent to his final yielding in 387, when the Church won the victory and he was baptized by Ambrose at Milan. Soon after this he had returned to Africa to live three years in monastic retirement at Thagaste before he was compelled by the Catholic populace of Hippo to accept ordination as priest for the assistance of Valerius, Bishop in that town. In 391, then, began for him the second term of life, that of his ministry in Hippo as priest, and later on, as bishop, through the stormy years of conflict with schism and heresy in matters of the Church, and in the end with barbaric force levied against the State. Its story is told shortly in the *Life of Augustine* by Possidius, his intimate friend, as Possidius tells, for nearly forty years, and Bishop of Calama, some forty miles from Hippo. A glance at the *Indiculus* [47] added as an appendix to this *Life* and at the list of works described and tersely commented on by Augustine in the work he called *Retractiones*, written about 427, three years before his death, shows the extraordinary range of his works, with which many and important books have dealt at length. It will be sufficient here to notice some of the writings which reveal him especially in the light of this period's history—sundry of the *Letters* and of the treatises levied against heretics, and the *City of God*.

The letters of the last thirty years of the Bishop's life, 400-430, are some 140 in number, including those written by him in the name of the Church and her Bishops. They run in length from a short note to a whole *liber* embracing nearly forty columns of Migne's text. For one of the extraordinary characteristics of Augustine was his generosity of his time to friends and strangers alike. On the one hand, his burning zeal for the universal Church and individual souls therein or without; on the other, his joy in grappling with knotty points of theological import, made him the willing target of any one who wanted light on what he, or she, was to think or say or do in any time of doubt or depression, as also the ready sympathizer with those who asked him to rejoice in their happiness.   There are letters of spiritual counsel sent to individual enquirers.   He writes to a certain Januarius that he submit his private practice of religion in minor matters to the custom of the Church of the country in which he chance to find himself; [48] he consoles the widow Italica for the loss of her husband; [49] he instructs the widow Proba in the science of Prayer.[50]   To Paulinus of Nola and his wife Therasia he sends advice on life in the world among those who have not yet learned to live by death. It is a life beset by trouble, "one unending temptation," and more grievous than a sojourn in the wilderness; "any faint-heartedness and storm of the desert seems to me less vexatious than the things we suffer or fear in the midst of crowds." [51]   The widow Juliana is warmly congratulated on the taking of the veil by her daughter Demetrias; [52] Felicia, of unwedded state, is given kindly exhortation in her perplexity at the unworthy conduct of some of the supposedly holy clerics, and bidden to write back and say she is relieved in this distress.[53]   A gift of a tunic, once belonging to her deceased brother, is accepted from the maiden Sapida; this is contrary to the Bishop's expressed desire, but he does not want to appear unkind to her in her bereavement and is wearing the said garment even as he writes.[54]   Ecdicia seeks consolation in haste, pouring out lament because her husband has deserted her for evil ways.   But Augustine carefully reads the epistle, questions its bearer, and learns that she has driven the unhappy man from his home and Christian life by her extravagant attempts at virtuous living. Not only through her own wilful resolution did she long years before this time refuse to fulfil her part as wife, which her husband patiently allowed, but now, heedless of their son's future, she has given away all, or nearly all, her possessions to a couple of wandering monks in quest of alms (the Bishop doubts whether men who take so great a sum from a woman unknown to them in her husband's absence really are servants of God!) and has further insisted, contrary to her husband's wish, on irritating strictness in her attire. Sound counsel and severe rebuke meet therefore her prayer for aid. "How," asks Augustine, "is the father to see his son deprived of sustenance when he does not yet know what this son's future career will be, and how much he may need? What more ridiculous than that a wife should show pride in her lowly dress? Far better would it be to conciliate her husband by her fair manners than to annoy him by her black garment, and if she must dress like a nun, at least to ask his consent. For he has not required of her sumptuous attire, merely that she should abstain from appearing as a widow while he still lived. Let Ecdicia haste to repent by submission and prayers for forgiveness that she has caused her husband to revolt in sin." [55]

Yet other letters deal with matters of doctrine and sacred writings. Volusianus, for whose soul the tribune Marcellinus interceded by letter with Augustine,[56] entreated to ponder Holy Scripture and send any difficulties to the Bishop, promptly obeys, and is answered in nine columns of text which a fortunate moment of leisure from engagements has made possible; [57] Evodius, Bishop of Uzala, enquires, among other things, whether the soul be accompanied by a body when it leaves the world at death; [58] a certain Honoratus, not yet baptized, receives instruction regarding the Bible teaching and the doctrine of grace, in a *liber* of thirty-eight columns.[59]

Sometimes indeed the work of correspondence weighs

heavily on the busy prelate. Thus Severus, Bishop of
Mileve, who has written an effusion in ecstatic praise of
Augustine and begs for an answer in return, the longer the
better, is gently rebuked and reminded that Augustine has
other people on his mind: "You see that my duty to you
and to other people comes before my duty to you alone;
and time is lacking, not only for ordinary things but even
for the more important ones." [60]   The priest Deogratias who
has passed on six queries sent him by a pagan seeker—on
the Resurrection, on interpretation of Scripture, on sacri-
fices, on the prophet Jonah—receives his answers, but is
counselled to hasten the conversion of his heathen: "I have
answered the questions as well as I could; but see that
he who asked them become a Christian straightway, lest
while he wait to end his queries on Holy Writ he depart this
life before passing from death unto life." [61]   A pagan before
his baptism may indeed fitly inquire concerning the Resurrection, but concerning Jonah, no!   Once Augustine really
does lose even his inexhaustible patience when confronted
with a gentleman called Dioscorus, who sends to him many
questions concerning Cicero with the request for an early
answer: "You thought it your business," the Bishop writes
in his wrath, "to encompass me suddenly, nay, to overwhelm
me, with a medley of enquiries without number, supposing me
to be free and at leisure.   What leisure have I for you in
your haste and on the eve of a journey as you remark, that I
should be able to untie so many knotty points?   For I
should be perplexed by the very number of questions even if
the knots were easy to unloose. . . . How I wish I could
tear you away from those faddy and frivolous investigations
of yours and crowd you about with my worries, that you
might learn not to be foolishly curious; or, at any rate,
should not dare to ask those to provide food and nourish-

ment for your curiosity whose very chief worry among all
their worries is to check and bridle the curious-minded. . . .
How much better, how much more fruitful, if I am to spend
time and energy in writing to you at all, to spend it in trying
to cut down your vain and deceitful ambitions." After
which Augustine bestows upon the offender some sixteen
columns of instruction and wholesome advice, especially on
the subject of humility, ends with an apology for delay
caused by sickness, and asks earnestly for a reply; *quæ
quomodo acceperis rescripta flagito!* [62]

There are letters in plenty on Church government and
discipline, which, when read with the narrative of Possidius,
throw much light on the history of the Church in Africa of
this day. Since his ordination in 391 as priest-assistant to
Valerius, Bishop of Hippo, Augustine gradually had won
much fame by his holy life and his ability in preaching, so
that Valerius, who was a truly righteous man himself, was
greatly gladdened in heart. He even departed from the practice of the Church in Africa in allowing Augustine, though
he had as yet only attained to the Order of Priest, to instruct
in presence of the Bishop in his cathedral Church, for which,
as Possidius tells us, he was criticized by some of his fellow-
bishops. But Valerius recognized the fact that on account
of his Greek birth he could not pretend to the Latin eloquence of Augustine both in the written and the spoken
word. So greatly did Augustine prevail that Possidius tells
us: "By the grace of God the Catholic Church in Africa
began to raise her head after lying out of the way de-
pressed and oppressed for long time through the growing
power of the heretics and especially of the rebaptizing
school of Donatists, the greater multitude among the Afri-
cans. . . . And thence now throughout the whole body of
Africa the glorious doctrine and most sweet fragrance of

Christ has been spread abroad and made known with the sympathy and joy of the Church of God across the sea." [68] Wherefore Valerius, in his fear lest Augustine might be carried off from Hippo to be consecrated Bishop elsewhere, prayed the Primate of the African Church, the Bishop of Carthage, that on account of his own advanced age and enfeebled health Augustine might become coadjutor in the office of Bishop at Hippo while he himself yet lived. This request was granted and carried into effect in 395 against the protest of Augustine, who was unwilling to disregard the practice of the Church that one bishop alone should hold office in one see. In 396 Valerius died, and Augustine entered into the full responsibility of his charge in Hippo and of his defence of the Church at large against the Donatists and the followers of the Pelagian heresy.

The history of the Donatists is well known. Their schism originated in 311, when a certain party in the African Church refused to accept Cæcilian as Bishop of Carthage on the ground that his consecration at the hands of Felix of Aptunga was not valid—in that Felix was one of the *traditores,* those who had yielded to the enemies of the Church her holy writings under the persecutions of Diocletian, 303-311 A.D. As personal holiness of life, they maintained, was essential in the members of the Church, Felix and any bishops or clergy who belonged to the *traditores* could not validly exercise their ministry; consequently, members of the Catholic Church who joined the "Donatist" party were obliged to submit to baptism a second time. The party chose Majorinus as its own Bishop in opposition to Cæcilian. When he died in 315, Donatus received election, and hereafter the schism over which he presided was known by this title, whether through him or another bishop of similar name. In the numerous letters treating of the Donatists Augustine mournfully dwells on them as without the pale of the Church Catholic, separated by their own will and act in schism, possessed in truth of the sacraments of God, yet deprived of the effectual working of sacramental grace within them by reason of their lack of charity, the quickening life of the Holy Spirit. In 401 he writes to Theodorus: "We reject therefore the evil error of these men; but the goodly name of God which they hold and his sacrament we recognize in them and reverence and embrace. But we grieve for them as out of the way, and long that they find profit in God through the love of Christ; so that the holy sacrament which they have without the Church to their undoing they may possess within the peace of the Church to their salvation." [64]   Some years later he writes to Emeritus, a Donatist Bishop, that the evil life of some members of the Church cannot harm faithful sons of her communion: "It is manifest that a man is not rendered evil because he goes to the altar with a bad companion, even if not unknown to him, provided his companion be not approved by him. . . ." [65] Moreover, the sacraments are not rendered invalid by the sinful life of any priest of the Church administering them, as in vigorous language the Bishop tells Vincentius, "Rogatist" Bishop of Cartennæ in Mauretania: [66] "Between an Apostle and a drunken priest there is much difference; between the baptism of Christ given by the Apostle and the baptism of Christ given by the drunken priest there is no difference." [67]   Likewise he declares, baptism administered by a heretic priest is equally valid.[68]   Again and again he protests against the practice of Donatists of rebaptizing Catholics who joined them in their error. He asks indignantly of Emeritus why he persists in condemning the Christian world unheard and in wishing to rebaptize so many churches of the Lord himself?   For it is the Lord

Christ himself who in every case administers holy sacrament, whatever the character of his representative.[69]

Long before this time the Donatists had been again and again called to account, notably in Rome in 313, at Carthage in 314, when Felix was found guiltless of the charge of "traditor," and at Arles in the same year. Of the repeated occasions on which their cause had been convicted by the Emperor Constantine after appeal to him from the judgment of bishops, Augustine speaks zealously: "I think that the devil himself if he were defeated so many times by the authority of a judge which he had chosen of his own will would not be so shameless as to persist in this cause." [70] Moreover, to schism they added violence and outrage, aided by a band of marauders known by the name of "Circumcellions." In 406 the Catholic clergy of Hippo sent a letter, written by Augustine, to Januarius, Donatist Bishop of Casæ Nigræ in Numidia, denouncing in detail the savage acts of these highwaymen: "Now your adherents do us greater harm. Not only do they smite us with clubs and iron weapons, but they even hurl at us lime and vinegar for the destruction of our eyes with incredible plotting of crime. And more, for the rifling of our houses they have fashioned for themselves mighty and terrible weapons, girded with which they rush to and fro, threatening us and panting out murder, robbery, fire and blindings." [71] Possidius tells us in the *Life* [72] that on one occasion they nearly captured Augustine himself; and Augustine reminds the Donatists in a letter of expostulation written in 409 that Possidius when on an episcopal journey was waylaid by some of their number and nearly burned alive in the refuge to which he had fled.[73]

In 411 matters had reached such a point that Marcellinus, "tribune and notary of the court of the Emperor Honorius," as Possidius narrates,[74] was sent from Rome to preside over a conference held at Carthage for the settling of the conflict between Catholics and Donatists. Among the writings of Augustine may be found the letter of the Catholic bishops to Marcellinus, stating their willingness to enter the conference, and an account of the same by Augustine himself.[75] The Donatists were condemned and were required under pains and penalties to submit to the Catholic obedience.[76] Marcellinus was a Christian and well esteemed by Augustine; but some of the defeated party accused him of favouring his own side in the conference: "There were not wanting men who said that these Donatist bishops had not been permitted to tell all the tale for their views before the authority in charge of the case, since the presiding officer was of the Catholic communion and aided his own Church." So Possidius reports,[77] and defends the Catholic cause by stating that Augustine subsequently held a public debate with the Donatist Bishop Emeritus and bade him maintain his side, but Emeritus could make no valid apology for the faith within him.

When the penalties against the schismatics had been put into operation, Augustine wrote to Marcellinus and to his brother, Apringius, proconsul of Africa, asking for leniency in their interpretation: "Fulfil, O Christian judge," he counsels, "the duty of a loyal father; so let your wrath be kindled against their wickedness that you be mindful of humanity. Do not give play to lust for vengeance in dealing with the crimes of sinners, but to the wounds of sinners apply your zeal for healing." [78] Yet it is none the less true that the policy of Augustine toward such offenders had changed from one of persuasion to coercion. The famous doctrine of *compelle intrare* as interpreted by him in the letter of 408 to Vincentius of Cartennæ, in which he approves the imperial edicts issued against the Donatists, had its fatal effect in the encouragement of persecution in later days.   Here occur the well-known words: "It is better to love with severity than to deceive with leniency." [79]   "How many," writes the Bishop in triumphant rebuke to this erring brother, "believing that it makes no difference in what following a Christian abides, persevered in the following of Donatus, because they were born there, and no one was compelling them to depart thence to the Catholic side!   For all these the terror of those laws by which kings serve the Lord in fear has been of such benefit that some are saying: 'This already had we willed in mind, but thanks be to God, who has now given to us the occasion of putting will into act . . .' ; others: 'This we knew to be true, but were held back by custom; thanks be to God, who has burst asunder our bonds.' " [80]

The lenient interpretation of imperial commands did not save Marcellinus.   A year later he and his brother Apringius were seized and put to death on the charge of implication in the revolt of Count Heraclian, a charge believed at the time to have been zealously supported by Donatists.   So Jerome writes in his *Dialogue against the Pelagians* (iii, 19): "Marcellinus, who afterwards in the outcry against Heraclian was slain, though innocent, by heretics."   Augustine wrote most loyally some time later in praise of his official friend and in grief at his untoward departing.

By this time the Pelagians have also appeared to darken the horizon of the faithful and cast their shadow on the *Letters*.[81]   An early mention of these heretics, who preached the self-sufficiency of man and opposed the teaching, developed by Augustine, of the ever-abiding necessity of the grace of God from birth to death, occurs in a letter to Anastasius.   Here the Bishop speaks of "certain men who arrogate too much to the human will, which they think sufficient unto itself for the fulfilling of the law, when once it has been given, unaided over and above its teaching by any grace of holy inspiration." [82]   Pelagius himself, the monk of British race, whom Augustine with that wonderful courtesy to his opponents which so distinguished him, describes as one of pure life and praiseworthy character,[83] had visited Hippo after leaving Rome in 409 in company with Caelestius, his lawyer friend, but had found the Bishop occupied with the Donatists [84] and had departed to Palestine.   Caelestius was seized by the deacon Paulinus for his erroneous views and condemned at a Council of Carthage in 412.   It was in this year that the first of the great anti-Pelagian treatises of Augustine appeared, *On the merits and forgiveness of sins, and on the baptism of infants*.   In this work, from that noted mis-translation of Romans V, 12 as "in whom" (*in quo* instead of *propter quod*) "all sinned," Augustine traces the doctrine of original sin; for all Adam's descendants are identified with him in the guilt of his fall.[85]   Since, then, this first original sin, without any actual sin on man's part, suffices for the condemnation of all,[86] and is transmitted from generation to generation, by the sharing of all in Adam's guilt through identity with him as the father of all men, even new-born infants are involved in sin necessitating damnation; for infants, as well as those stained by actual sin, must be penitents through their fatal inheritance.[87]   If not, why does the Church prescribe for them the washing of Holy Baptism?—the same question which at this time baffled Caelestius before his judges in Carthage.

All therefore, concludes the Bishop, who obtain not regeneration and washing away of this inherited guilt of sin by means of baptism are doomed to everlasting punishment, though in the case of little children this damnation will be extremely mild.[88]   To the question why this should be,

Augustine replies that the mysteries of God are inscrutable. Why indeed is one infant safely baptized and allowed promptly to die and depart to eternal bliss while another lives on to incur punishment by leading an evil life? Even righteous men, made clean themselves in baptism, beget children defiled and weakened by sin, for generation, though not, as Augustine repeatedly declares elsewhere, *per se* essentially sinful, is accompanied by sinful passions, the inherited taint of evil. If therefore Christian men are eager to help children in physical need, how much more strenuously should they seek out and save them from the parents who neglect their everlasting destiny? [89]

Furthermore, physical infirmity and death of the body result for all men from the Fall: *peccavimus in uno omnes ut moreremur in uno omnes.* Our Lord indeed suffered our physical infirmities (though Augustine cannot imagine that he was subject to the mental infirmity of little babes); but he suffered in the likeness of our flesh as willing to submit to those bodily weaknesses which we deserve through our inherited guilt.[90] Again, to physical infirmity is added infirmity of soul; for even those made pure by baptism remain weakened in soul by this inherited flaw of nature and do not always stand upright. Theoretically, declares Augustine, a man might live without actual sin committed after baptism, by grace of God to whom all things are possible; it is a universal fact, however, that all fail in will to be good. Those then (i.e. the Pelagians) must be opposed who presume so far on the free will of man that they hold we need not throughout our lives Divine help to save us from sinning.[91]

The perplexity of the tribune Marcellinus, to whom this treatise was addressed, needed yet further enlightenment; for he could not understand Augustine's statement that, theoretically speaking, a man could live without sin. The

Bishop therefore addressed to him in the same year another work *On the Spirit and the Letter,* reminding him that the fact that a thing never has happened does not mean that God could not, did he choose, cause it to happen, for all things are possible by the grace of God; only be it acknowledged that this grace is not merely the Pelagian interpretation of it as free will bestowed at creation and aided by instruction in precepts of righteous living.   No.   Rather must we believe that the letter killeth and the Spirit giveth life: "That which the law of works commands with threatening, the law of faith obtains by believing. . . . And therefore by the law of works God says, 'Do that which I command'; by the law of faith we say to God, 'Grant that which thou commandest.' "   It was this far-famed dictum of Augustine, as he tells us in a later work,[92] which originally had raised the spirit of Pelagius in revolt against, as he held, such supine and slothful dependence on the working of God in men for their holy living.   Against that Pelagian spirit Augustine again declares in this book, accounted one of the greatest of his works, that Faith is of God and comes to men of his gift.   Yet why to one and not to another once more must be left in mystery.

In 414 the strife was stimulated by the letter sent by Pelagius to that girl of noble and wealthy family, Demetrias, who so thrilled the nascent asceticism of these days by her renunciation of the world that, according to Jerome's radiant message of congratulation, Italy cast aside her mourning and the crumbling walls of Rome regained their glory of old in joy at the conversion of this child of their race.   Some years later Augustine himself sent word to the mother of Demetrias, warning her against the danger of pride inculcated in a certain book—a book written, as he feared, by Pelagius for this holy maid.[93]   But by this date the Bishop had composed two more treatises, both assigned to the year 415. One of these, *On Nature and on Grace,* was addressed to two young men, Timasius and Jacobus. They had been attracted by the teaching of Pelagius, but, feeling uneasy in mind, they had written to enquire of the truth from Augustine, who here put forward and condemned statements made by Pelagius in his work *Concerning Nature,* forwarded with their letters by these suppliants. Among such errors the Bishop notes the statement that sin has no reality in itself and cannot therefore have harmed our human nature.[94] "How then," asks Augustine, "shall we say, 'Heal my soul, for I have sinned against thee'? Let us not so praise our Creator that we deem unnecessary a Saviour." [95] Moreover, Pelagius stated in his work that sin ought not to be penalized in being made the cause of yet more sins in human nature, increasingly enfeebled by yielding to temptation. But, retorts the Bishop, God does not forsake man unless man refuse him. The healing of mercy and grace is ever at our hand. Further, Pelagius was mistaken in declaring that through the gift bestowed in creation men have actually lived without sin in this world. The other work, *On the Perfection of Man's Righteousness,* addressed to two fellow-bishops, answers a number of dialectic "reasonings" or "dilemmas," composed, it would seem, by the forensic skill of Caelestius or some disciple of his, to show argument for such sinless life.

The year 415 was eventful also for Pelagius, since during its course he was twice tried for heretical belief: in July before the Synod of Jerusalem under John, its Bishop, where he was confronted by Orosius, and it was agreed to refer the matter to Pope Innocent; in December at Diospolis (known in ancient days as Lydda) under the Metropolitan of Palestine, Eulogius, Bishop of Cæsarea, where he was acquitted.

In 417 Augustine received the official record of "acts" of the trial and wrote his *De Gestis Pelagii* to show that the bishops present, though they acquitted Pelagius, did not really approve his beliefs, for they misunderstood his meaning. We learn from this work and from the short paragraph describing it in the *Retractiones* (II, 47), that two bishops, Heros and Lazarus, deposed from their sees in Gaul, and taking refuge in Palestine, had brought forward for accusation of Pelagius a book written by him, from which the questions put to him for examination during the trial were taken. The accusers were not present at the Synod, at which fourteen bishops met for judgment. They, says Augustine in explaining the acquittal, spoke Greek, as did Pelagius, but his book was written in Latin. Moreover, Pelagius spoke in ambiguous language, as in affirming his belief in the necessity of grace, by which he meant natural grace, not the supernatural grace of Catholic doctrine as the bishops supposed; and, further, he mitigated his former statements by alteration, as in saying in this trial that "some men had lived holy and upright lives," whereas before he had declared they lived "without sin." [96]

In the intervening year, 416, at two Councils of African Bishops, held in Carthage and Mileve, Pelagius and Caelestius were condemned for their errors, and official reports of this were forwarded to Pope Innocent; at the same time a private letter was sent to him by five bishops, including Augustine, protesting against the heresy. The three replies of Innocent in 417, assenting to the condemnation on the ground of study of Pelagius' views as expressed in his book, evoked the famous cry of joy from the Bishop of Hippo in a sermon to his people: "For now (the judgments of) two Councils have been forwarded to the Apostolic See; rescripts, moreover, have arrived thence; the case is fin-

ished!" [97]   But in the same year Innocent died, and was succeeded by Zosimus of unhappy memory.   The story of his
acquittal of the two offenders, of the determined opposition
of the African Church in upholding by two Councils, held in
Carthage in 417 and 418, the condemnation expressed by
Innocent, and the obtaining official banishment for both
from Rome by an edict of Honorius in 418, of the consequent retractation and condemnation of both men by
Zosimus in the *Epistola Tractoria* of the same date, is matter
of historical record that need not detain us here.   It
brings us to the second stage of Augustine's fight against
their vain talking, in the withdrawal of Pelagius and Caelestius, and the coming into prominence (in revolt against the
more extreme teaching now developed by the Bishop) of
Julian, Bishop of Eclanum, who with eighteen other bishops
of Italy refused to submit to the requirement of assent to
the *Tractoria*.

The same year 418 saw this development of Augustine's
teaching; for, in addition to two further anti-Pelagian
treatises from his pen, *On the Grace of Christ* and *On Original Sin*, it was remarkable for the celebrated letter of the
Bishop to (Pope) Sixtus, in which he expounded the dread
doctrine of Predestination and reduced man's free will to a
shadow of substance.   Some nine years later we find the
fuller expression of these teachings in four works, of which
two were addressed in 426-427 to Abbot Valentine and his
monks at Adrumetum in Tunis in an endeavour to settle a
dispute between certain who maintained that the grace of
God renders null the free will of man and others who held
that it assists our free action.   This latter view Augustine
approved in an epistle introducing the first of these books,
On Grace and Free Will; yet he proceeded to minimize this
free will in manner perplexing to his readers.   In paragraph

32 he writes: "It is certain that we keep his commandments
if we will; but since the will is prepared by the Lord, we
must seek from him that we may will as much as suffices for
our action.   It is certain that we will when we will; but he
causes us to will what is good."   And in paragraph 41: "If
this Divine Scripture be closely examined, it shows that God
not only renders good instead of evil the wills of man, which
he himself creates and directs, thus rendered good, toward
good actions and eternal life, but that even those wills which
abide by the things of this world are in the power of God;
so that he causes them to be inclined whither he wills when
he wills, either to blessings to be received by some of them
or to punishments to be inflicted on others, as he himself
judges in a judgment, most secret indeed, but undoubtedly
most righteous."   So Absalom chose of his own will the
course that worked him ill; yet he was moved to do so because God had hearkened to his father's prayer that this
might be.   It is not surprising that one of Valentine's monks
(so Augustine tells us [98]) remarked after reading the book
that no man must then be blamed for not fulfilling the commands of God; the only thing to do was to pray for him that
he might obey.   Whereupon the Bishop again set to work
and despatched to the monastery in Northern Africa a
second treatise, *On Rebuke and Grace,* in which he set forth
the definition of grace as that by which alone men are freed
from evil, are enabled to think and will and love and act
aright by knowledge of the truth and by power to realize it
in act.   He then proceeded to develop in more technical
fashion that creed which, clothed in words of heartfelt love
and sympathy, was stimulating his Sunday flock at Hippo.[99]
According to this all mankind form one "mass of perdition,"
doomed to everlasting punishment by reason of their guilt
in Adam, including those who have died in ignorance of the

Gospel and those who have not received of God the grace of perseverance. Yet through the undeserved mercy of God some men are saved from this general condemnation; their number and names were fore-ordained before the foundation of the world. However, as no one knows who is included within this elect body, it belongs to all to strive on his own account, and, when occasion rises, to rebuke with zeal and charity his brother for his fault. To those who are thus destined for salvation grace irresistible is given. They are the children of God and cannot perish; even their sins work in them for promotion of righteousness. The fact that God wills all men to be saved is explained as meaning that he destines certain individuals out of every race for salvation. We, as we do not know their names, must desire this blessed destiny for every man.

The other two treatises of the four mentioned above were directed against the modified form of the error known as semi-Pelagianism, which will be noted in connection with Cassian later on. At this point, with a brief mention of yet two more books written to refute the teachings of the Bishop of Eclanum, one of which was left unfinished by Augustine at his death,[100] we may leave him as champion of the Church against schism and heresy and turn to other sides of his work. The two original rebels against the Catholic doctrine of grace were condemned finally at the third Œcumenical Council of the Church held in Ephesus in 431, and troubled her peace thereafter only in the more restrained teachings of ecclesiastics of Southern Gaul.

When we turn to records of the pastoral labours of Augustine, in addition to those wonderful exhortations, the *Sermons,* addressed to his people at Hippo, two documents stand out as especially interesting. One of these was a letter written about 423 [101] to the nuns of the convent at

Hippo over which Augustine's sister had formerly ruled. In this letter Augustine rebukes them for their desire to remove their present Prioress and gives them sound rules for the conduct of their life. After this manner does he counsel: "Let all things be held in common and let distribution be made to each, not equally, but according to her need; let not those who were poor in the world seek in Religion what they could not have possessed as seculars, or be puffed up at associating now in equality with those once higher in social rank; let not others, again, be proud who have contributed of their wealth to the common fund or despise their sisters of meaner birth. Pray without ceasing; fast with common sense; and let the sick receive special treatment without grudging, for their speedier return to health. Modesty of dress and demeanour is necessary for nuns who walk forth from their convent"; and here the Bishop adds special directions for their behaviour regarding the male sex and the treatment of those who offend in this respect. His practical mind is also markedly shown even in so small a matter as the keeping of garments: "These are to be under the care of one or two Sisters, who shall shake them out lest they suffer from the moth; let no member be offended if she be given from the common store clothing previously worn by another of the nuns. Garments are to visit the laundry at the will of the Prioress, lest too keen a craving for spotless attire draw with it a stain upon the soul." Augustine shares Jerome's terror of the bath! Later on, the admonition rises to higher things: "Let not strife be found in the community. Better is the Sister who is assailed more frequently by anger and more quickly seeks forgiveness than one who is provoked less speedily but is slower to make amends. And let love abide among all, not of the flesh, but of the spirit, with fitting obedience to Mother Superior and to the Warden Priest."

The second of these writings, an account of Augustine's official "acts" in the election of a bishop as his successor on the episcopal throne of Hippo, gives striking evidence of his wisdom.[102]   On the twenty-sixth day of September, 426, just four years before he died, the Bishop summoned an assembly of bishops, priests, and lay-folk in the Church of Peace at Hippo.   There he told the congregation that old age, to which there is no succeeding span of life on earth, had now overtaken him; that after the death of bishops, churches are disturbed by men who seek their own ends or stir up strife; and this his experience was leading him to fear such trouble in his own see.   After citing the example of the church in Mileve, where a similar fear had been dispelled by the appointing of a successor by the Bishop during his own life-time, he continued: "Therefore lest any one complain against me, I declare to you all my will, which I believe to be the will of God; I desire the priest Heraclius as my successor" (*par.* 1).   Acclamation of approving voices followed; again the Bishop spoke, and once more his words were affirmed by shouts of assent.   Six times Augustine spoke, and six times his desire was confirmed, till at the end we read of shouts repeated five times five.

We reach now the tragic circumstances which surrounded the Bishop's death.   Mention has repeatedly been made of Boniface, during whose government in Africa the Vandals descended on that land.[103]   Boniface was known to Augustine, from whose pen we find two letters of private interest written to this Roman "Count."   In 418 he sent him advice as to his mode of life when on campaign, and assured him that military service on behalf of the State is lawful for a

Christian.[104]   In 427, just at the time of the crisis, a letter was despatched of very different tone.[105]   The Count had lately married a second time, and this was sufficient subject for reproach, because after his first wife's death he had expressed a desire to flee the world into the shelter of Religion.   Now not only had he failed of this good purpose, but his second lady belonged to the Arian heretics, and so strongly had this influence prevailed in the once fervently Catholic home of Boniface that his daughter had also submitted to baptism at Arian hands.   No wonder that the Bishop delivered a vigorous onslaught of rebuke!

And then Gaiseric swept down with his hordes upon Africa to the terror of all, so mercilessly did they spoil and ravage.   It was at this point that Augustine wrote his well-remembered letter to Honoratus, Bishop of Thiava in Mauretania,[106] who had enquired of him what course of action was fitting for bishops of the Church in such perilous times.   "Should they follow the command *Cum autem persequentur vos in civitate ista, fugite in aliam?*   Or should they stay with their flocks and await in expectancy of death or destruction?"   The answer of Augustine gave no uncertain counsel: "If ministers of the Church are able to flee without abandoning their people in helpless need, then let them flee, as our Lord and Saint Paul fled from the enemy; if all their people have been slain and taken captive then let them flee; but let them not be as the hireling that cares not for the sheep.   Do not all in time of crisis and panic especially seek comfort of the Church and her Sacraments?   What will the flock do if it has no pastor?"

So Augustine stayed in Hippo and Placidia sent Darius to Africa on a mission of peace.   We have some correspondence which passed between him and the Bishop,[107] including a letter in which Augustine congratulates him on the accomplishment of his quest: "For those who fight, if they are good men, without doubt seek peace, yet so as by blood; but you have been sent that the blood of no man might be sought; and thus to others remains their necessity, to you your happy fortune." [108]   But the truce was soon broken. Gaiseric overcame Boniface, and invested the walls of Hippo. And its Bishop died at the age of seventy-six on the twenty-eighth day of August, 430 A.D., amid the hurtling of weapons in the conflict which a year later was to deliver his city into Vandal hands.

The fruit of Augustine's work and thought is summed up in that masterpiece of his later life, the *City of God,* which, published in instalments during the years 413 to 426, reflects in twofold manner the aim of Augustine in its narrower and wider appeal.   For it was written for the instructing both of Volusianus, that proconsul of Africa for whose soul Marcellinus laboured, now perplexed by the problem of reconciling the spirit of Imperial Rome with the spirit of Christianity, and of the world at large, troubled or exultant according to differing creed by the triumph of the heathen and the sufferings of the people of Christ.   Scholars deeply versed in Augustine's teaching have illustrated for us the mighty treatise into which this apology developed under his hand.   Many have written of the work considered *qua* apology, of that science of history in which it was to inspire future ages of Christian men, of the philosophy and theology and exegesis of which it is full, of its mystic teaching, of the seed it sowed, consciously or unconsciously, for the harvest of ecclesiastical polity in days to come. On these great matters this present description may only lightly touch.[109]

Of the twenty-two books of the work the first five explain in reasoned argument that the heathen gods avail nothing for the happiness of men in this present life. Starting from the burning point of debate, the recent capture of Rome by the Goths, Augustine declares that tragedies have ever followed upon wars. Yet only in Christian days has at last mercy in the victor's hour been given, not alone to the followers of Christ by a Christian foe, but through the power of this creed even to pagans and the enemies of Christ, who now ungratefully slander the source of their deliverance from death.

But not merely are these disasters of war lightened in Christian times; to Christian men they are even fruitful of much good when suffered aright. For what lasting harm is wrought for a true disciple of Christ by torture or famine or lack of burial or captivity or even by foul outrage on pure honour? There is no evil save sin. And therefore none may deal death unto himself even in extremity. Lucretia was wrong; Cato was wrong. Long before the very Name of Christ was known in Rome did troubles visit her; not only external calamities, but stain and pollution of deepest dye, inculcated and encouraged by the impure example of heathen gods who both suffered misery to exist and gave no training in upright manner of life to their worshippers. Of this the outward sign and mark was the vile representation of plays, showing for the debasing of Roman people the crimes of the gods. Verily such deities, Augustine repeatedly avows, are but devils in other shape. "Awake," he calls to Rome in that passionate cry at the end of the second book, "the dawn has come. . . . Seek not false and fallacious gods; yea, cast them from thee in disdain and speed forth to true liberty. No gods are they, but malignant spirits, for whom thine everlasting joy is but punishment." Why then did so long-continued power dwell in Rome, a power itself born neither of these gods nor of Fate but of the One True Lord of all? Surely that this pagan city by its zeal for liberty and strenuous endeavour after fame might incite the people of the City of God to greater toil for the faith that is undying. "What matters it," asks this preacher of no abiding city on earth, "to what race we belong in our brief sojourn among men? Take away their pride and what are all men but men? Shame, then, on those who have so much more glorious an heritage for their feeble efforts toward the attaining thereof." [110]

Yet neither are the pagan gods to be worshipped, as some vainly hold, for joys of their bestowing in the world to come. With this argument Augustine fills the five books which succeed, zealously holding up for condemnation Varro's gods, both of myth as they are portrayed in the theatre, and of the City, as magnified in ritual observance. Finally, he comes to issue with the Platonists, who approach most nearly the Christian faith, and enters upon a long decrying of the "demons" (*daimones*), who dwell in mid-air and act as intercessors between heaven and earth, between gods and men, taking delight in all manner of evil, prey of impure passions, yet seeking that worship from mortals which may be given to God alone. Far differently do the holy angels desire our adoration of their and our Lord, illumined as they are by that Light which lighteth also every one of us who cometh into this world. Neither then the storm-tossed demons of Apuleius nor the theurgy which proud philosophers from their intellectual height prescribe for the spirits of unlearned folk may satisfy the Christian, who seeks his haven of rest of mind and soul in the humility of the Incarnation, a stumbling-block to the Platonic despisers of this flesh.[111]

So far runs the destructive part of the work. With the eleventh book Augustine begins to extend his original plan of refuting the enemies who pour scorn on the Faith in hour of crisis, and to construct his picture of the Two Cities: the earthly one of those who seek their present rest and happiness on this earth and have their reward therein, the celestial one of those who journey on earth but as pilgrims, and seek no end but with God in Heaven after death. Among the angels the two cities already had their beginning, and found already each its member in this world in Abel and his brother and murderer, Cain. But whence came evil amid the angels? From nature or from will? Most assuredly from will. Nature *qua* nature is everywhere good, for it is the creation and the gift of God, and God cannot but be the Author of good, never of evil. The will, therefore, with which the angels were created, with which man was originally endowed, was both free and good, as given of God.

So matter is in no wise evil or the source of evil; the corruption of matter was the effect of sin, not its cause.[112] Evil came into being when this will, hitherto good, turned deliberately and of its own accord from serving and obeying God to working the opposite, which is sin; hence nature was changed and corrupted and the will lost its original perfect freedom in this new bondage unto sin.[113] For a will truly free is a will unhindered by sin in its active working of good, unweakened and uncorrupted by yielding to temptation; and in man perfect freedom, once lost in Adam, can only be slowly gained by grace of God availing for his redemption.[114] Nor yet may man rely on grace without his own effort constantly co-operating therewith; not even habitual use of the Sacraments shall save him if he work not with God.[115]

Why then did the will turn from God? Augustine does not know. Evil is no positive thing, only a negative cause destroying good, a no-thing no more to be understood as a self-existing phenomenon than darkness may be seen or silence may be heard.[116] The birth of the germ of evil that originally caused the will to turn from God cannot be explained; but its nature is pride and self-love, just as love of God is but another name for good will.[117] Yet God by his almighty power can and does overrule evil for good.[118]

The earthly city, therefore, the *civitas impiorum,* is composed of all those among men who are devoted to their own selfish aims in this present life and are not guided and controlled by faith in God and love for his service. The end of such is death, and, unhappily, in Augustine's view, they number the greater part of mankind.[119] Their own peace and comfort is their highest desire, though, as their city was founded by Cain, so too do they fight constantly, brother against brother, and especially against their neighbours of the City of God.[120] They worship many foul and false deities, hoping by this service to attain the good of their greed and lust; and divers of them are willing to pay lip-service to the One True God for this end.[121]

This city of the unrighteous is conceived by Augustine in mystical, not in political fashion. Although its progress is traced by him, as that of the Heavenly City, from the Fall of the Angels to the end of this created world, and includes times of history, yet it is to be identified in its entirety with no political State of this earth.[122] To Augustine pagan states such as the Roman State, which naturally he had ever in mind in this work, are parts of this unrighteous city, in so far as their indwellers serve not God as their true Lord. In itself the State is good by nature as the work of God. Neither the tracing of its origin from the hands of Cain, a murderer and dweller in the company of the unrighteous, avails for Augustine to take away this natural good, nor the declaration made in agreement with Stoic theory, that, although God did not originally intend men to be slaves of their fellow creatures, slavery is in truth the lawful consequence of sin.[123]   A state, indeed, governed and animated throughout in ruler and ruled by the principles of the Christian faith, would be a glory to the world in Augustine's eyes, and would be a true portion of the most glorious City of Heaven.[124]   Even in heathen hands the State possesses, *qua* State, not only divine right, as God's creation,[125] but moral right and good.   Its origin lies in marriage and the family; as the family is to be wisely ruled by its paternal head, so should the State be ruled in peace and concord.[126]   Small states, according to Augustine, would in general be preferable, united with each other as friends and hospitable neighbours; since large states owe their birth to wars of aggression on their fellows.   If, however, the ruler of a state of great extent fulfil his office in obedience to the law of Christ, it were well that his dominion extend far and wide.[127]

But, just as human nature, originally good, was corrupted by evil will, so the human political State, in itself good, has been corrupted by its worship of false demons.   For this worship destroys the law of justice, fundamental, not only for the good, but for the real existence of a community lawfully meriting the name of State.   In Plato's *Republic* justice was required among citizens, in that each one should possess and occupy himself with his own things and rights, without infringing the rights of others.[128]   Cicero, moreover, under the person of Scipio in his *De Republica,* defined a republic as "a body of people bound together by mutual understanding of law and by common interests," and declared that a "res publica," which is identical with "res populi," may be said to exist when just government is found therein; without this just government all idea of a commonwealth vanishes.[129]

According, then, to this definition the Roman State was never a state at all; for Augustine cannot allow the possession of true justice by a state that deprives God, Creator and Lord of all, of his rightful due of worship and adoration. In such a state, as there is no justice, so there is no commonwealth, no republic in the true and absolute sense.[130] Such a state—and this is true in Augustine's theory of all heathen states—is but a robber state, defrauding God of just service.[131] In it all kinds of evil flourish; [132] its end, as a state, as the end of all the community of the unrighteous, of which it forms a part, is everlasting misery.

Yet, although in the absolute and highest sense such an institution is no real state, Augustine is willing to grant to pagan communities a lower concept of commonwealth, a concept shared by the Roman people with those of Athens and Egypt and of other lands controlled by governments great or small in their public affairs. Under this lower interpretation a commonwealth is defined as "a great body of people endowed with reason, united by the harmonious fellowship of the things which they love." Such a people may not unreasonably be named a commonwealth without consideration of the things which it loves in each case, though undoubtedly the more worthy these things shall be, the more worthy the people of this partial concept of a state. Accordingly the ancient Roman people were more deserving of this concept than their descendants.[133]

Contrasted with the city of unbelievers is the most glorious City of the believing, of the members of Christ, who live not by corrupt nature, but by grace, who love not chiefly themselves but God, and rest not in this world's joy. As

the history of the unrighteous community was traced by
Augustine from secular records, so the history of God's
people is traced in the records of the Old Testament from
Abel throughout the chronicle of Israel's children and thence
to the fuller life of the Church of Christ.   But here, again,
the City of the believers is not identical with the visible
Church of God on earth, though it is not easy always to dis-
tinguish in mind the two.   It is, rather, the community of all
who believe in God and make him their chief desire.[134]
Outside the visible membership of the Church, as seen of
men, are those who are predestined to be of the City of God,
while within her fold are now ranked false adherents, leading a double life and trying to serve two masters, who shall
be revealed hereafter as of the unrighteous company of the
devil.   For both wheat and tares are found together in this
present life.[135]

The citizens of God, however, are bidden to use the things
of this world, to enjoy earthly peace, to obey temporal laws
and rulers, provided that they find not their rest in the one,
nor obey the other in aught that contradicts the principles
and ordinances of the Faith as it is in Christ.[136]   And here
rises that vexed question of the view to be inferred from this
great work regarding Augustine's conception of the ideal
relation between the two partial and visible embodiments of
the two cities: namely, the Church and the State.   Was he
engrossed in writing for his own day a mighty apology for
the Faith as a child of his own century, not foreseeing the
passing of Rome's Empire and only too conscious of the still
existing strength of pagan gods and of the power of pagan
culture?   One is inclined to agree with Troeltsch in viewing
the *City of God* in this light.[137]   As he observes, the pessimism of Augustine revealed therein, his pointing to a future
life for joy and happiness, the antagonism pictured between

heathen worship and the Christian creed, speak to us of the ancient civilization, even if near its death, rather than of the Middle Ages, even if near their dawn.   It is, as Troeltsch remarks, undoubtedly true that Constantine and Theodosius had aided the Church, that Honorius had issued edicts against heretics, but rather as individuals than as monarchs officially expected to serve the ecclesiastic cause.   It is also undoubtedly true that Augustine did welcome the extended rule of Christian rulers of great States,[138] that he accepted as from God even the ruling of bad governors in punishment of sin,[139] that he did speak of the Church as the Kingdom of Christ and the City of God, and of her bishops as the rulers of the vision of the Apocalypse, that thereby he did prepare the way for those who read into his text the conceptions of Monarchy and Papacy dominant in the Middle Ages.[140] Yet from Augustine's words may be sought varied and exaggerated explanations for the supporting of a special cause, even as from the Bible itself.   Far more efficacious than any theory laid down in the *City of God,* both for the approving of spiritual dominion and for its enforcing by civil power, was the policy of *compelle intrare* allowed and recommended by Augustine in his bitter zeal for and against the Donatists.

Such zeal was his in practice, and this practice did in truth promote spiritual coercion.   But one likes to believe that Augustine's ideal for the Church was rather that of a community ruled in the spirit of love by law and order of clergy, governed by Councils, authoritative in spiritual matters of faith and doctrine, bidding her children observe secular laws with charity and loyalty so far as these in no wise conflicted with the law of Christ; that his ideal for the State was that of a community, lower in order because temporal in nature, only meriting immortal life by incorporation of its individual members into the body of Christ, ruled according to Christian principles, aiding by its physical power the Church whence it draws its spiritual support, and finding in Christianity neither enmity nor oppression, but help for the fulfilment of its destined end.[141]

Wherein, then, lies the highest attainment of good, the End of the Heavenly City? To various philosophies, observes Augustine, are due varied theories of the *summum bonum* of existence. For the People of God it must be nothing but God himself: God, who is indeed Eternal Life, who combines within himself the ideal of Plotinus, the ideal of the Good, the True, the Beautiful; who is at once the remote, unattainable object of contemplation, transcending all man's power of grasp, and is yet through the Incarnation the innermost dweller within the hearts of his children, warming and illuminating all their life by his presence and his love.[142] In pursuit of realization of this End the children of God's mercy and grace journey in their pilgrimage through this world, so looking unto God in contemplation as never to lose sight of their neighbours' due, so caring for their fellows and themselves as never to forget God.[143]

Yet utter rest in God shall never be attained by those predestined to share it till they win the life of the future. Therein no struggle shall vex them from without or from within, no faults shall need their weary care; but "God shall rule man, and soul shall rule the body, and sweet shall it be to obey, and a happy thing to rule. And this in all men and in each shall be forever with no doubt, and therefore the peace of this blessedness and the blessedness of this peace shall be our highest good. . . . But the lot of those who belong not to this City of God shall be rather everlasting misery, which is also called the second death, because neither the soul which is separated from the life of God may be said to live, nor the body which shall be subject to eternal pains; and thereby this second death shall be the more grievous, for that it cannot be ended by death." [144]   The end is attained at the Last Judgment; and in this description Augustine seeks to explain the eschatological terms of the vision of the Apocalypse.[145]   The first and spiritual resurrection of this life will save the people of God from the second death, of the soul, at the Last Day, as the first death, of the body, shall be ended in the second resurrection, of the flesh, in the world's last time.   For the duration of one thousand years, the term of existence of this world,[146] the devil is bound, and may not use his power in its fulness against those predestined to salvation; yet for short space of time, as of three years and six months, shall he be loosed thereafter, when he shall rage mightily even against the elect to prove their steadfast faith.   And then shall come the great Assize, and the books shall be opened.   Each man shall swiftly see pass before his mind his doings in the flesh for his joy or his dismay, and shall find reward accordingly; when heaven and earth shall be new and there shall be no more sea, by which is symbolized the surging waves and tempests of this restless world of ours; when those not elect by grace of God shall be given to a real and material fire which ever shall burn both soul and body in pain greater or less as the guilt of the lost shall vary, and the redeemed of God's mercy shall dwell in the peace and joy of the eternal Sabbath of the City of Heaven.

CHAPTER VI

CHRISTIAN PROSE: OROSIUS AND SALVIAN

Among all the varied aspects of the *City of God* there is
one on which we may dwell for a moment in its connection
with other writing of this time. This is a view of the work
as containing the first full and convincing statement of the
Christian understanding of history, its aims and science and
recording, destined to found the patristic school of historiog-
raphy, to inspire, through Augustine's disciple, Orosius, a
model for historians and source of historical information
throughout the Middle Ages, and, in less direct fashion, to
influence the writing of history in Christian hands down to
modern times.[1] For Augustine viewed history as a tracing
of things at once general and individual, such as none among
pagan historians had conceived. It was his Christian genius
which gave birth to a new philosophy underlying all historical events, which should make of mortal history one
great record of the career of mankind, sweeping on its way
from creation to its final destiny after this world's passing,
dominated throughout by one omnipresent and almighty
Power overruling all for his own all-wise and beneficent
ends.

It is true that before this fifth century, pagan writers, both
Greek and Latin, had set their hands to the recording of
general Histories. Ephorus had told of the Greeks wheresoever their speech was to be heard, and of the peoples who
influenced their lives, as far as the year 356 B.C.; Polybius
of the peoples who dwelt around the Mediterranean; Pompeius Trogus, in the work afterwards epitomized by Jus-

tinus, of the successive World-Empires culminating in the great power established by Philip and Alexander of Macedon. The aim of these writers, however, was limited. Ephorus wrote a "Universal History," not of all peoples, but only of the Greeks.[2] Polybius declared that he wrote his *Histories* in order to trace the "how and when and wherefore" of the passing of the whole inhabited world under the lordship of Rome.[3] Undoubtedly he dealt in his long work with matters of geography, topography, politics, military science; undoubtedly he sought for causes, criticized other authorities, moralized to excess. He saw, moreover, an overruling agency which brought to pass the supremacy he described, in the work of Tyche, that deity so powerful in Hellenistic days; and he deemed it his special task to trace her influence in the growth of history.[4]

Yet, as Bury has shown, the faith of Polybius in this power of Fortune waned as his thought on men and things continued: "It appears that Polybius, having originally started with the conception of an extra-natural power, directing the world and diverting the course of events from its natural path, was led by wider experience of life and deeper study of history to reduce within narrower and narrower bounds the intervention of this *deus ex machina,* until he finally reached the view that it was superfluous for the pragmatical historian. . . . In his actual treatment and presentation of historical events, the fluctuation in his views on this question probably did not make much difference." [5] If, again, we turn to Trogus, we shall find that his aim in his story of World-Empires was to magnify the fame of Macedon. The prevailing thought in all this pagan work was the struggle on the one hand for freedom, on the other hand for power, the rise of empire after empire to dominate the history of its day. We are here concerned with local temporary acts and circumstances of the past, and are not led by the writer to consider the ultimate destiny of mankind singly and in union.

But now, according to the view briefly set forth in the last chapter, of mankind comprehended in the two cities, that of God and that of the world, history is regarded by Augustine as both universal, for it tells of men united in the fellowships of the service of Christ or of Satan, and as individual, for it traces the progress of every individual in either community toward eternal happiness in Heaven or eternal misery in Hell. In other words, history to the Christian philosopher, as distinct from the Pagan imperialist, is as wide as the world, as narrow as each single soul. We have therefore no static narrative of past facts unrelated to the future, but a record of a march once begun at man's creating, the continuance of which is steadily ever maintained, its goal yet hidden from visible sight. In Augustine's eyes history is ever being made, whether in the struggle upward or in the falling downward of the two cities and of the souls who dwell therein, marked and distinguished by their several manners of life and practice. The end of the life of the elect is blessedness, found in the full revelation of God hereafter. The first stages of this revelation are experienced in the history of Israel, the chosen People of God, till, when the fulness of preparation is accomplished, the Incarnation and the Redemption make possible the perfecting of the progress begun in the earlier days, by the nurturing of this People of God, now enlarged to embrace Gentile as well as Jew, upon the fruits of Redemption, the grace of the Sacraments of Christ.

Not only, moreover, in the general scheme of his view of history does Augustine show himself the philosopher, but in its detail, in his penetrating scrutiny of the "Weltanschauung" of the members of his two cities. And above all, both over those elected to happiness and over the remaining vast number of those unelected and therefore bound for misery, God reigns supreme, using both good and evil, both joy and suffering, to further his will and to work the end he has eternally destined for the creatures he has made.

It follows therefore that in this record of God's dealings with men the reason for happenings of whatever kind is to be sought in his will, and in this alone. Subsidiary questions of influences, motives, causes, results, whether arising from human or natural source, details of science, whether political or physical, questions which bulk so largely in modern discussions of history, fade away into the distance before this supreme fact.

Yet such a view of history as directed by the unceasing guidance of God's providence is not the view of necessary control by physical determinism, the *"nexus* of cause and effect in the endless chain of phenomena" supported by the Stoic theory of the "sympathy" existing between all parts of the universe.[6] Man possesses free will, though he use it for evil; and God, as has been remarked before, can in his wisdom turn even man's evil doings to serve good ends. The great point is that nothing in this philosophy of history can happen by accident.[7] It is true that, as Scholz observes, the doctrine of Predestination which Augustine held, and the foreknowledge of God of all things that shall happen, stay the theory of evolution held by some philosophers, of progress in the sense of development independent of God; but we may retort with Fr. Figgis that this complaint "does not eviscerate history of meaning" and that "any teleological view of human life is open to the same objection."[8] It is also true that in Augustine's concept "history" as we understand it, is only a part of the revelation of God, which began before this world, and shall continue after its ending; moreover, that Augustine is not primarily concerned with "history" at all.   He uses it in its proper place as one span of that mighty bridge which he essays to construct from the past, before history was, to the future when it shall be no more.   His first aim is the defending of the Faith and the edifying of those who have ears to hear, simple or learned, but not the discussing of history *per se,* nor yet the refuting of those who are obstinately blind to the picture he draws.

From this great conception of history we now descend to view its literal application in a work, of dubious merit in itself, but of lasting fame as exemplar to historians in ages to come, serving as convenient collection of material for those who cared not to probe into records of original source.[9] For Augustine felt that his work, considered as defence of Christianity, might make a stronger appeal if its picture of man's steady progress to higher things were to be supported in those pessimistic days by a formidable array of solid facts, by, in Professor Shotwell's description, "a mathematical demonstration of its truth." [10]   Accordingly he instructed a young and ardent disciple, Paulus Orosius by name, to compile a history showing in detail the evils which beset pre-Christian days, for the more effectual silencing of those who complained that with the decay of the worship of many gods the glory of Rome had departed.

Orosius was a priest of Spanish race,[11] who left Europe in 414 and journeyed to Hippo to seek its widely famed Bishop.   Augustine tells of him in a letter to Jerome dated 415: "Now a young man has come to see me here, full of religious fervour, my brother in the peace of the Church, my son in years, in office my fellow-priest.   His name is Orosius, and I find him of keen intellect, of ready speech and burning zeal, longing to prove himself a useful vessel in

the House of the Lord for the refuting of vain and pernicious teachings, which have slaughtered the souls of the
Spaniards in far greater disaster than the havoc wrought on
their bodies by the barbarian sword. For this reason then
he hastened even from the ocean's shore, impelled by what
he had heard of me, that he might learn from me touching
those things whereof he would know." [12]

It seems that Orosius had undertaken the journey for the
sake of consulting Augustine in regard to the errors of the
disciples of Priscillian and Origen; also, perhaps, as a fugitive from barbarian invasion, since he tells in his *Histories* of
hairbreadth escapes.[13] Augustine sent him on to Jerome in
Palestine, where he took active part in the campaign
against the Pelagians, came into conflict with the Bishop
John of Jerusalem as President of the Synod held to try
Pelagius in Jerusalem in 415, and addressed for his own
defence and for the smiting of the Pelagian heresy a *Liber
apologeticus* to the priests of that city in the same year.[14]
Finally he returned to Africa, where he completed in 417 or
418 his best-known work, the seven books of the *Historiæ
adversus Paganos*. The date is ascertained from his statement that he was writing after Augustine had completed ten
books of the *City of God* and by his declaration at the end
that he had continued the narrative till the year 417.[15]

It was, then, while engaged on the *City of God* that
Augustine felt the need of supplementary detail. Forthwith
he bade his disciple, whom he had at his hand at the time,
to inveigh "against the prattling iniquity of those who are
strangers to the City of God . . . who seek not the future,
and are forgetful or ignorant of the past, yet cast infamy
upon the present times as though beyond measure beset with
evil—for this sole reason because men believe in Christ and
worship God rather than idols." Orosius shall therefore de-

scribe briefly from all records of history and annals "whatsoever perilous wars, or foul plagues, or baneful times of famine, or fearsome earthquakes, or extraordinary floods, or dread outbreaks of fire, or fierce thunderbolts, or storms of hail, or even calamities of murder and grievous crime he should discover in the chronicles of ages gone." [16]   And accordingly his purpose, for he delighted in the behest of the great Bishop, was to demonstrate that the former pagan centuries had shown disasters far more grievous than those of the present Christian era, and that men had rather reason for joy in present relief from sorrow.

In this pursuit he proceeds to tell of the past tribulations and sins of mankind from the foundation of the world to the foundation of the City of Rome, thence from the empire of Cæsar and the birth of Christ to the comparatively happy period of his own day; and he starts his task with a detailed geographical description of the site of the great countries with which he will deal.   The tale of trouble then begins with the Fall and the Flood.   After these follow the stories of Ninus and of Semiramis and of the destruction of Sodom and Gomorrah for their wickedness.   "How light is the present visitation of God compared with the fate of these cities!" Next comes a strange medley of Scriptural narrative and Greek legend; all is grist, whether myth or history or tradition, that adds bane and blight to this tragic mill—Joseph and the Famine, Athens and the Flood in time of Deucalion, the ten plagues of Egypt and the drowning in the Red Sea (the traces of the chariot wheels can still be seen on the shore, renewed from time to time by act of God!), the sin of the Danaids, and the horror of the Minotaur.   And many other "facta turpia, fabulæ turpiores" of Greek story Orosius carefully mentions if only to state their omission from his narrative.   Did not the miseries of the siege of Troy outweigh anything the year 417 A.D. could show of trouble? "For indeed let those who have learned of the length of that siege, the cruelty of the fall, the slaughter, the captivity, let them take heed whether they be rightly offended at the state of the present time, when by the mercy of God the enemy who might be pursuing us through all lands in panoply of war is offering hostages for peace, seeking to contend for Rome against other nations." [17] The writer is referring to Wallia, ruler of the Visigoths for some three years between the reigns of Athaulf and Theodoric the first; for Wallia, after the destruction of his ships off Spain, had made peace in 416 with Honorius on the understanding that he should restore Athaulf's captive, the royal Placidia, and make war on behalf of Rome upon the barbarian invaders of the Spanish peninsula.

The second book tells at the outset of the Four Great Kingdoms of the world: Babylon on the East, Carthage on the South, Macedon on the North, Rome on the West. Of these, the first and the last, Babylon and Rome, are compared in history and in fate: "See how like was the rise of Babylon to that of Rome, how like their power, how like their greatness, their times, their blessings and their evils— yet not alike were they in fall and passing. For the one lost her kingdom, the other retains it; the one was bereft by the slaying of her king, the other is happy in her sovereign's safety. And why this? Because there in Babylon's ruler shamefulness of wanton vices was punished, here the most restrained uprightness of Christian religion is preserved in our emperor; there without reverence of religion licence of unbridled excess filled up the measure of greedy lust, here they who showed mercy were Christians, and Christians they to whom mercy was shown, and Christians they for whose memory and in whose memory it was done. Wherefore let men cease to attack religion and to provoke the patience of God." [18]

It is true, as we have seen in the words of Augustine, that restraint was shown by Alaric's command in the sack of Rome; but the fact of the utter worthlessness of Honorius and the general ravaging of Rome for those three days in 410, of which Orosius himself tells us later on,[19] cannot be forgotten; and we are sure that to many these words of consolation must have fallen very flat. A comparison with the taking of Rome by the Gauls in early days tries to point the same moral as before; and, if we care, from the second to the end of the sixth book, we may follow the mournful recital of murder and massacre, of plague, pestilence and famine, of fire, flood, and earthquake, of wars and civil wars, of crime, oppression and lust. Throughout the whole course of the history of Greece and of Republican Rome the horrid repetition goes steadily and deliberately on, dull in the extreme, and black as this zealous disciple could paint it. It is even a relief to come unexpectedly in this tale of horrors upon one or two homely illustrations, which make a strange appearance at the opening of Book IV. "Present troubles," says our preacher, "though tiny, are apt to seem more grievous to us than serious afflictions viewed from the standpoint of the past or of the future. Thus he who is pricked at night-time and forced to maintain unwilling vigil because of fleas, undoubtedly bears this affliction with greater impatience than the remembrance of the burning fever which once kept him awake. Yet who would say that fleas are worse than fevers? A man, on rising from his comfortable bed and perceiving without doors the frost and ice of early morning may reasonably remark, 'It is a cold day.' If however in a panic he should rush back to his room and bury himself in his blankets, crying out that 'never was there such cold, not in the Apennines, no, not when Hannibal was cut off by snow and lost great part of his army,' that man should be dragged out into the market-place and bidden to mark the children sporting in their winter games, that he may learn that of his own sloth comes his trouble, not of truly evil circumstance!"

But quickly after this little interlude the scene of mournful history once more sets in with the complaint that "writers in their zeal for their own glory have forborne to recount too many troubles lest they should give offence to their readers by promoting terror rather than edification; and therefore the troubles of Rome can only be learned through those who praised her citizens. When so many evils have squeezed through the pen of panegyrists how many must have been deliberately repressed!" Between the two Punic Wars came peace—for one year, after 440 years of stress. "As a drop of oil on a mighty flame, did it help to extinguish or to foster the fire?" [20]   Later on,[21] we are told that the City itself was saved from Hannibal by a timely hailstorm, in which Orosius follows Livy's account; such deliverance he triumphantly holds up before the "traducers of the True God," supported in his joy by the reflection that in time of drought whenever prayers are offered for rain by pagans and Christians on alternate days, the rain invariably falls on the day allotted to the Christians. There is a note of pathos to the reader of after years in the incredible boast which follows presently touching the "peace" of the fifth century: [22] "In that restful calm of which our fathers had a slight taste after the rule of Cæsar and the birth of Christ, we now are both born and grow old"; for so soon were to appear the terrors of Vandal and Hun invasions of the Empire.[23] At this point we gain a bit of personal history; for, forced to flee from Spain, Orosius proudly declares that through the unifying power of the Christian religion which makes all men one he was received in Africa as though in his own home; he rejoices that all lands of the Empire lie open to him for his Roman birth, that all the people of God welcome him for his Christian Faith. "One single God," he writes, "by all men is both loved and feared, having established this one single kingdom in these times in which he has willed to become known; the same laws rule everywhere, subject to this one God; wheresoever I go, stranger as I am, I fear no sudden assault as though helpless and forlorn. A Roman among Romans, a Christian among Christians, a man among men, I look for aid from the State in its laws, from one bond of knowledge in the Faith, from nature in union of humanity. In this mortal life I find in all the earth my own fatherland, because that fatherland which I love is on this earth nowhere to be found." [24]

This vision of a universal Empire of secular Rome was shortly to pass; yet in the words of Orosius we may clearly see the world-wide fellowship of the Catholic Church which was to outlive the Empire. And indeed, though Rome might lose her secular seat, though the Empire of which she formed the centre might fall, nevertheless she could fling the power of her glorious tradition about the growing Church for its shelter even in the midst of worldly disasters, untroubled by the struggles of Churchmen that in these days were working turmoil in the East. It was in this fifth century that Leo the Great constantly established himself administrator of matters concerning the various churches, and in letters or sermons urged the primacy of Rome among sees through the commission given to Peter. So Theodoret of Cyrus wrote to Leo in preface to his appeal to Rome: "To your Apostolic seat we hasten that we may receive healing for the ulcers of the churches. For it is meet that you in all things should hold the first place. . . . The Giver of all good gifts has granted to your City abundance thereof. For she is chief and most illustrious of all; she presides over the world and overflows with the multitude of her habitants. Imperial power is hers, and she has given her own name to those under her rule. But above all is she made glorious by her Faith, of which blessed Paul witnesses, crying aloud, 'Your faith is made known in all the world.' " [25]   The tradition of leadership which Rome had so long enjoyed was to prove of incalculable value, even after the waning of her imperial sway, throughout the lands which had once owned her government and through her influence had learned the truth in Christ.[26]

In the sixth book arises a question. If the pagan gods were so great that the prosperity of that Roman Empire which they had founded depended on their favour, and if their service was never so devoutly cherished as in the time of Augustus, why did they not stay the birth of that Christianity which was to lead to their neglecting? They tried to put down the Christian religion by all sorts of repressive measures—and were discomfited; they had to give way though no penal measures were applied. "The cult of idols, as it were, failed and was put to shame of its own accord, and yielded to one most merciful bidding unconstrained by any terror of punishment": [27] an observation which has a strange ring when we remember the enactments of Honorius and Arcadius and Theodosius against pagan practices and worship.[28]   With the birth of Christ the aspect of our narrative changes; as formerly horrors crowded thick and fast upon one another, so now they are to seek. Caligula longed for public calamities, but Christianity proved no favourable atmosphere for such; in the time of Claudius military rebellion was stayed by miracle, and Britain was in great part subdued, whereas none before Julius Cæsar nor after him had dared approach it. Only persecutions of the Christians were followed by misery and penalty, as the Egyptians were visited for oppression of the sons of Israel.

At last the course of Roman history is run. We arrive at the times of Honorius, to which eight chapters are given,[29] and Orosius assumes some importance as one of our few sources for these years. His narrative begins with the rebellion of Gildo the Moor in 397, whom his brother Mascezel was deputed to chastise in Africa. Mascezel took with him monks from the island Capraria, of those same brethren so scorned by Rutilius. Through their prayers he gained a bloodless victory, aided by a vision of Saint Ambrose tapping on the ground thrice, with the words *hic, hic, hic,*—a vision Mascezel interpreted as signifying the place and day of his conflict with his brother. But Mascezel departed from his life of piety. He was guilty of violence against a church and met death by force as punishment.

Stilicho is painted in the most lurid colours of infamy, "yielding up the blood of the whole human race that he might invest one boy" (i.e. his son, Eucherius) "with royal purple." [30] He is accused of favouring Alaric and his Goths in secret treaty, refusing prompt battle that he might reserve them for the vexation and terror of the state, and of arousing to arms the Alans and Vandals that they might shake the banks of the Rhine and smite the Gauls. For the punishment indeed of the impenitent City came upon her the invasion of Alaric, whom, "a Christian and more nearly a Roman, and, as the event showed, mild in time of raid through his fear of God," the Lord mercifully allowed to act as his agent of retribution rather than Radagaisus, "a pagan, a barbarian, and a true Scythian." [31] So Alaric, as Orosius tells, allowed all who would to congregate for safety

in the Churches of St. Peter and of St. Paul, and bade his
soldiers take their fill of booty, but refrain from bloodshed.
Here we meet the story of the Christian woman who brought
forth under compulsion the precious vessels of the Church
before the amazed eyes of a mighty Goth and defied him
to dare to seize them. Such was the reverence of barbarians
that a procession escorted the holy treasures with psalms
and hymns of pagans and Christians to a resting-place of
safety. On the third day of the sack the barbarians withdrew of their own accord. Orosius deems that the conflagration caused by them—*facto quidem aliquantarum œdium
incendio,* as he mildly puts it—cannot be compared with
the Fire of Nero's reign, nor with the taking of the City by
the Gauls. "In fact, you would not know the City had been
seized, did you not observe some ruins still remaining from
the flames! What harm was it that Galla Placidia was captured by Athaulf and taken by him as wife? Did she not
work great good to the City by this powerful alliance?" [32]

Toward the end we catch a pleasant glimpse of this
Gothic chieftain: "I," says Orosius, "have myself heard a
certain man of Narbo, who served with distinction under
Theodosius, and who was a man of repute both as regards
the Church and the world, tell at Bethlehem to the saintly
priest Jerome that he had been an intimate friend of Athaulf
at Narbo. He said that he had learned from Athaulf his
desire to blot out the name of Rome and make of what
had formerly been 'Romania' a State of 'Gothia' in order
that he, Athaulf, might be what Cæsar Augustus had been.
Yet when he had found by long experience that the Goths
could not obey laws in any manner because of their unbridled barbarity, and that a state, if it is to be a state, has
need of laws, he decided to seek glory by the restoring of
the Roman name and prestige rather than by its conquest

through Gothic might." [33]   In this aim he was zealously encouraged by his wife till he met a violent death, and Wallia succeeded to his power.   And so in the eyes of Orosius not all barbarians are utter savages, and the breaking down of the barriers has already begun between those within and those without the pale of citizenship of Rome.[34]

Thus did this apologist fulfil his strange work, observing finally that for one reason might thanks be given for the invasion of Roman lands: "Since even at the cost of our undoing, so great races received the knowledge of the truth to which they could not in any wise have attained save by this fall." [35]

The narrative draws chiefly for its matter upon the Bible, Cæsar, Livy, Florus, Justinus, Eutropius, Jerome's continuation of the *Chronica* of Eusebius, and the *City of God*. Its Latin is clear and forcible without pretension of excellence in style.   The eagerness with which, strange as it may seem, the work was sought in later days as a text-book of history is witnessed by the great number of manuscripts, and in especial by the famous rendering into Anglo-Saxon from King Alfred's hand.[36]

Augustine, then, and his disciple had laboured on the negative side; Augustine "had contended that the calamities of his age were *not* the result of Rome's renunciation of Paganism.   He had not, except casually and incidentally, sought to investigate what was their true cause.   Orosius, while to some extent following his master's lead, had ultimately decided that the state of the Empire was not unsatisfactory and therefore that the enigma did not exist." [37] Let us look now at a third writer, who approaches the subject in a very different state of mind, only too sure that he can supply an answer to those who question him on the tribulations of the world of his day. "For the Roman people," he writes, "is sick and suffering through its own sin, and for its wickedness and vice and crime of every foul nature and degree God is sending punishment. Away then with soft phrases wherewith writers are wont to caress the palate of their public, and let salutary healing rather be administered to those in dire need of remedy!"

So declares Salvian, priest of Marseilles, in the preface to his work *On the Government of God,* published at Marseilles between 439 and 451. The date is established by his mention of the capture of the Roman general Litorius outside Toulouse in 439 [38] and by his naming the Huns as allies of Rome,[39] thus showing that the work was written before Attila's invasion in 451. He was born about 400 and, according to an uncertain tradition, at Trèves,[40] probably of good family; he speaks, in the first of nine letters left to us from his pen, of a relative of his captured at Cologne by barbarian Franks—"once of no little name, neither unknown in family nor to be despised in his home." [41] In a spirit of kindliness he begs help for the young man, whose mother is trying to support herself by her handiwork in her great poverty. The fourth letter is a plea to his parents-in-law, Hypatius and Quieta, converts to Christianity, that they pardon him and his wife, Palladia, of whom he writes as "most beloved and well-esteemed sister," for a vow of self-denial they have agreed to observe; in half-playful, half-serious tone he brings forward their little girl Auspiciola to plead their cause and reconcile the offended elders. Another letter, No. 5, is a *consolatio* to his sister Cattura for her late sickness, "which will profit greatly her soul." Two letters are addressed to Eucherius, Bishop of Lyons from 434 to 449, whose friend he had already been in the famed monastery of Lerins, on the island in the Bay of Cannes. Thither, as is well known, had retired Honoratus of Gaul at the end of the fourth century and had gathered about him many of the great Churchmen of following days. A fellow resident in the monastery, Hilary, afterwards Bishop of Arles, in his *Life of Honoratus* writes of Salvian as an intimate friend of Honoratus; [42] and Eucherius reminds his son Salonius that he had been entrusted for advanced instruction to Salvian, distinguished alike for his eloquence and his knowledge.[43] To the same Salonius, when later in the century he had become Bishop of Geneva, Salvian wrote to explain the publication for reasons of modesty of his work *Ad Ecclesiam* under the assumed name of Timothy. The perusal of these letters, though they are in themselves of slight importance, is worth while for the reason that they show the preacher in a lighter mood, of which the reader of the two works left to us would scarcely deem him capable. One of these, the *Ad Ecclesiam* mentioned above, addresses to the Church in general, Religious, Priests and lay people, burning words of rebuke against the prevailing sin of avarice.

But it is by reason of the other, the work *On the Government of God*, written after Salvian had taken up his dwelling in Marseilles, that his name is still remembered for unsparing denunciation of the evils of society in his age. It consists of eight books, dedicated to Salonius. The first two of these are put forward as an introduction for the thesis which is to follow, as showing by principle of reason and by concrete examples from pagan philosophy and the Bible the belief of men of learning, that God does indeed abide with, govern, and judge his people. At the beginning of Book Three we hear the writer exclaim: "Good! Now the foundations are laid upon the solid ground of divine truth.

Let us then to our question: If everything in the whole world is under the direct care and government and judgment of God, why is the fortune of the barbarians far better than our own? Why do all things give way to unrighteous powers? The answer God only knows. But if you ask me as a man," Salvian continues, "taught by Holy Writ to know somewhat of God's will, in the presence of my fellow Christians I will reply: Not because we of this generation do not keep the Old Covenant and the teachings of the Prophets in their fulness, the strict law of the Gospels and the behests of the Apostles, but because we do not observe even a few of the commandments of God given us therein; not because we do not endure for God what blessed Paul and Christians of olden time endured, for these things are too hard for us; but because we, Christians of the Church, have plunged ourselves into a flood of vice and crime that knows no limit. . . . A grievous and mournful thing will I say: The Church herself, who ought in all things to propitiate God, what doth she but provoke God? Except some certain very few who flee from evils, what else is all the assemblage of Christian men but a sink of iniquity? Verily, how many a one wouldst thou find in the Church who is not a drunkard or an adulterer or an abductor or one of dissolute ways or guilty of robbery or murder? And, what is worse than all, given to almost all these vices without end!" [44]

This scathing indictment Salvian then proceeds to amplify. The only kind of virtue now prevalent is to be less vicious than one's neighbour. Against God do men sin. Churches and altars are held in less reverence than the house of any little local magistrate. Any one who dares to intrude into a magistrate's house without due cause is beaten or reviled; but into the temples, even into the very sanctuary, all the rabble of criminals rush with no pretence of reverence within their hearts, that they may straightway go out to commit the sins they seem outwardly to mourn. Against their fellows do men sin. By self-indulgent vice they sin, by harassing of the helpless and poor. Not only are slaves beaten and evilly entreated, compelled to tell lies through fear, to steal through hunger, and to run away because of their terror of the slave-masters set over them, but the lives of free-born citizens are a misery because of the heavy hand of officials. Taxation demanded by Rome is piled upon the poor, who have no means of redress, by the rich and powerful, who refuse to pay their share: "Who could describe in fitting words that piracy and crime wherein the Roman state is even now dead or of a truth is drawing her last breath even in that part in which she seemeth yet to live, strangled by the bonds of tribute as if by the hands of robbers? Yet are there very many rich men whose lawful dues poor men pay, in other words, whose dues slaughter the poor." [45]

And while the great levy oppression upon the underling, tax-gatherers also play their part lustily in the thorough fleecing of the general populace: "Worse still is it, that very many are prosecuted by the few, for whom public taxation is their own source of booty, who make the claims of the public treasury a means of private gain; and of this not only those in highest place are guilty, but those well nigh of the lowest, not only the officials of the Bench, but even those who look to them for orders. In truth, what—I do not say merely cities—what municipal towns and villages are found where there are not now as many tyrants as there have been curial magistrates?" [46] So great is the distress of the poor, the widow, and the orphan, that many, even those of birth and education, flee for refuge to the protection of barbarians, "for they would rather live free under appearance of captivity than be captives under pretence of liberty." [47] Thus they escape in their despair from the new decrees of taxation sent by Rome. Nothing of such nature is practised among the barbarians, whether Franks or Huns, Vandals or Goths. Moreover, it happens often that the wretched peasants cannot flee to the barbarians for relief, because they feel unable to leave their little properties, their cottages, or their families. In this case there is only one resource left to them. Powerless to pay their quota, they surrender themselves and their belongings under bond to their richer neighbours, and in return for immediate relief from the law, forfeit the inheritance of their sons. Miserable indeed is the lot of these *dediticii,* who have lost their possessions and yet are assessed for taxes. Certain of them in the extremity of hopelessness are even compelled to become *inquilini,* or bond settlers upon the land of the great property owners of the district. "Brought to this strait that, banished not only from their means but even from themselves, parting with themselves and all pertaining to them, they are deprived of ownership of their belongings and lose the right of freedom's dower." [48]

Yet if social conditions are bad, moral conditions are still worse. How shall we speak of the sins of slaves, asks Salvian, to which they are driven by their need and misery, when the rich in private indulge in immoral practices to their content, in public sate their depraved taste by vile spectacles and shows of the amphitheatre and circus, such as one may not even describe without defiling the mind by very thought thereon? . . . *ibi præcipue vitia ubicumque Romani.*[49] Only necessity born of loss of wealth can curtail these orgies, in which heathen deities are reverenced while the Church of God is left empty and neglected. Not even the uttermost ravages of barbarians and the ghastly ruin of captured cities mourning their dead and their desolation can stay the Romans in their mad rush after foul revel and impure lust. Thus four times one of the wealthiest of the towns of Gaul, Trèves, capital of its province, was taken by assault of the enemy; yet no repentance followed these disasters but rather fresh impulse of wickedness. "We are brought into fear of death and we make merry on the brink of fate—*moritur et ridet"*—such are Salvian's words of the Roman people of his day.[50]

It must, of course, be remembered that in this day the barbarians were a familiar sight in Roman territory. By 445 they were settled in Gaul, in Spain, and in Africa. In Gaul, in spite of Salvian's melancholy descriptions of ravage, the Romans had recovered from the shock of possession by enemies and were comparatively tranquil in the face of their continued advance—so we learn from the letters of Sidonius Apollinaris. In Italy the stirring events of 410 had lost their first terror, not to be revived for another five or ten years, till Gaiseric's capture of the City in 455. In Africa the conquest of Carthage in 439 was still recent enough to cause fear in men's memories, but even there the settlement of the Vandals was by this time an accomplished fact.

Thus Salvian could look around and in the light of experience and momentary calm compare the conduct of the Romans with that of their enemies. For this is the culminating stage of his despair of Roman life, that in all things even the barbarians do not as the Romans do. Is it a question of faith in God and reverence for religion? The barbarians are doubtless heretics, he says in his scorn; but they have never been taught, their tradition of holy things is imperfect, and they are at least faithful to such knowledge of God as they deem right and true. But among us, he continues, blasphemy against the Name of God is so common that men vow by its power to accomplish deeds of evil and even hold themselves bound to carry out such impious promises.

The story is well known which he recounts of his own experience of this profanity.[51] On begging a certain important individual not to defraud a poor man, the greedy seeker after riches scowled at Salvian and answered that he could not possibly grant this request; for he was bound by holy law and bidding to carry out his purpose. "When therefore I enquired why this might not be, he gave as his reason words which he held most stringent, impossible of gainsaying: 'I have sworn,' said he, 'by Christ, to take away that man's property. Look you, ought I not to accomplish that which I obliged myself to do in the very Name of Christ?' "

Furthermore we read that the barbarians are upright and pure of life as contrasted with the scandalous vices of the Romans throughout the Empire; and here Salvian leads us through the various provinces that he may show forth this bitter theme in its detail. The Aquitani were settled by act of God in the richest part of Gaul, a land of flowers and fruit, of streams and harvests and plenty, in which their abounding prosperity might surely have called out special thanksgiving and piety of life. Yet we are told: "Nowhere was pleasure more evil, nowhere life more impure, nowhere discipline more corrupt [52] . . . the very barbarians are offended by our vileness." [53]   When the Goths are afraid, they trust in God, but "we," declares Salvian, "in our presumption have put our confidence in our allies, the Huns. . . . Did not the king of the Goths himself, prostrate on mat of haircloth, continue instant in supplication till the very day of the battle, when he rose to war from his knees to fight with confidence in God since he had won victory already by his prayer?" [54]

But should any one object that the Aquitani are singular

in their evil life, Salvian would turn with him to Spain, where more signal proof of Roman iniquity awaits him. For God certainly desired to work reward for barbarian pureness of character and punishment for the Empire's vice when he delivered the Romans over to the Vandals, those "feeblest of enemies," who, however, trusted wisely in the power of the Scriptures. The crowning shame fell when for rebuke of Rome God drove the Vandals across the sea to devastate Africa. Here the preacher draws for us his most lurid description of the utter degradation of Roman Africa and of the city of Carthage at this time: "For just as into the offscouring of a deep ship flow the dregs of all filth, so into their morals have flowed as it were the vices of all the world. In truth, I know no unrighteousness which has not abounded there." [55]   The torrent of language that tells the tale is almost unreadable in its unsparing description of perverseness. It is a relief to reach the Vandal conquerors; in spite of all temptations to succumb to the lure of wickedness surrounding them on their entry into Carthage, they resolutely scorned all share in the same. And if there was this gulf between Roman and Vandal, how much more profoundly were these abandoned profligates separated from the professed devotees of the Christian life? "Not without cause did it befall that within the cities of Africa and especially within the walls of Carthage people as miserable as they were unbelieving could scarce look upon a man clad in monastic habit, pale of face and with hair shorn in tonsure, without abuse and execration; and if ever some servant of God either from the cœnobitic dwellings of Egypt or from the sacred places of Jerusalem or from the holy and venerable retreat of a monk of the desert came to that city to fulfil the Lord's work, he was met by abuse, profanity, and evil words directly he appeared in sight." [56]

The question naturally arises of the degree of truth in this most gloomy picture of Roman life, a question that has necessarily been carefully considered by students of history with regard to so important an authority for social conditions in this time. From the study of other contemporary documents it would seem that Salvian's indictment against the oppression of the poor by the rich and highly placed, against the iniquitous burden of taxation and the corruption of the Roman system of finance, finds serious justification in the edicts of the Theodosian Code. Nevertheless, the utter blackness of his description of the moral life of the day is by no means confirmed in the writings of Ausonius, Symmachus, and Sidonius. The good Bishop of Clermont, as we have seen, did indeed portray his fellow aristocrats living amid the careless ease of their culture and wealth in Southern Gaul, but knew nothing of such a fearful state of wickedness as Salvian painted here. Rather may we think with Dill in this respect that Salvian was driven by the quick passion for higher things possessing his own soul to decry in exaggerated terms the indifference and low standard of his countrymen, a condition so grievous to him as man of God and citizen of that Empire which he saw now fallen from its glorious place.

And truly, as has repeatedly been observed, the thirty years which lay between the writing of Orosius and of Salvian wrought deep distinction in their words.[57] Orosius still confidently believed in Rome triumphant over barbarian power as ever in the past, more happy indeed in this era of Christian rule than under pagan hands. Salvian could see only the degradation of his own people both in external and internal ways, as compared with those better men to whom, albeit of foreign and savage blood, the Lord had entrusted the punishment of Rome in her decay.

CHAPTER VII

MONASTIC WRITINGS OF THE WEST IN THE FIFTH CENTURY

Partly in discontent with the existence of ease and luxury which lay behind Salvian's fiery reproaches, partly in quest of some new thing, partly inflamed by a longing for the highest they could attain of spiritual endeavour, a multitude of men and women had by this time already withdrawn from worldly associations in that great tide of enthusiasm for the ascetic life so intimately connected with the fourth and the fifth centuries of our era. It is, of course, well known that monastic practice among Christians was developed by St. Anthony, who instituted at the beginning of the fourth century the rule of solitary living in cells amid the deserts of Egypt near Alexandria. The movement progressed with great rapidity in the East under St. Basil and St. Gregory of Nazianzus, spreading through Asia Minor and Palestine and attaining great power in Constantinople. There St. John Chrysostom, who had already won fame by the publication of the three books of his *Adversus oppugnatores Vitæ Monasticæ*, vigorously defended true monasticism against the laxity and indulgence into which many of its professed adherents had already fallen. In the West monasticism was first preached in Rome by St. Athanasius, who in 340 told many eager hearers there of the life of the monks of the Thebaid and their ascetic discipline. He had moreover brought with him thence for the better instruction of the faithful two monks, Ammonius and Isidore, who were to show by example the force of his counsels. This preaching, followed by the publication of the *Life of Saint Anthony* written by Athanasius, had an extraordinary effect on men and women, who were only too ready to yield to the charm of monastic adventure. Especially to women this new manner of devotion appealed; and we have already seen its disciples under St. Jerome leaving all, marriage, home, country, children, for the joy of renunciation.

Nor indeed was the enthusiasm with which this hope was embraced by the solitary monks of the East wanting to men of the West, though here community life proved the ideal. Under St. Jerome, Pammachius, the senator, son-in-law of Paula, on the death of his wife forsook worldly things and devoted himself and his great property to monastic aims: "In our days Rome possesses that which the world as yet has never known," writes Jerome in triumphant congratulation to this disciple of his: [1] "Once rarely were found men wise, powerful and of noble birth, who professed the Christian Faith; now many are monks who are both wise and powerful and nobly-born. And among them Pammachius, my friend, is wiser, more powerful, more nobly-born than all; great among the great, first among the foremost, an ἀρχιστρατηγὸς among monks. . . . For who would believe that the descendant of Consuls, the glory of the Furian stock, would walk forth among the purples of Senators clad in a tunic of dark and sober hue, yet would not blush to meet the eyes of his fellows nor to laugh in mockery himself at those laughing him to scorn?" Pinianus, husband of Melania the younger, founded a monastery at Thagaste, birthplace of Augustine in Africa; St. Jerome translated the famous Rule of Pachomius, the Egyptian pioneer abbot; [2] St. Augustine both lived under Religious rule himself and directed others in the same way.

Amid all those who genuinely strove to reach perfection

under this discipline it is not surprising that some were found
moved by less worthy desires. Among so many adherents
there were naturally a minority who wore the monastic habit
with conformity of outward but by no means of inward life,
as was revealed in Alexandria, in Ephesus, and in Chalcedon.[3]   There were also complaints of a different kind,
from prejudiced sources.   Jerome, writing to Paula on the
death of her daughter Blaesilla, who had herself forsaken
this present world, tells of the behaviour of the crowd at the
funeral, when Paula was carried away fainting through
grief: "When from the midst of the funeral procession they
carried you away as one dead, thus did the people whisper
one to another: 'Is not this what we said again and again?
She grieves for her daughter killed by fastings, because she
has gained no grandchildren from her child's happy marrying.   How long must we wait till this hateful race of monks
be driven from the city? till it be overwhelmed with stones?
till it be hurled into the waves of the sea?' "[4]   We may recall the remarks cast at Salvian's monk in the streets of
Carthage and the scorn of Rutilius Namatianus as he passed
the monastic settlements in the Mediterranean Sea.

In the matter of literary interest especially fruitful are
the Religious centres of Gaul, where, also in the fourth century, practice of monastic Rule was first established by
St. Martin of Tours.   His *Life,* supplemented afterward
by three *Dialogues,* was written by his disciple Sulpicius
Severus about 400 and had an immense influence in Western countries.   Postumian, represented as a friend of Sulpicius, remarks to him in the first of the *Dialogues:* "But in
truth I will tell you how far that book of yours has made
its way, that there is scarce any spot in the whole world
where the substance of so happy a history is not spread
abroad in fame.   First, your most zealous friend Paulinus

introduced it to Rome.   Then, when it was being seized upon
with emulation in all parts of the City, I saw the book-
sellers rejoicing in triumph at this most profitable article in
their stock which sold so readily and at so high a price.   It
far outstripped the course of my journeying; for, on reaching Africa, I found it being read throughout the whole of
Carthage. . . . In Alexandria almost every one knew it
better than you do yourself; it passed through Egypt, Nitria,
the Thebaid, and all the kingdoms of Memphis.   I saw some
old man reading it in the desert . . ." (par. 23).   We have
already noticed the *Chronica* of Sulpicius, composed shortly
after this date.[5]   The *Life of Saint Martin* and the *Dialogues*
are written in the same exquisitely clear and graceful Latin.

In the former we read the story now so familiar, beginning with Martin's birth in Pannonia of parents of respect-
able station though pagan creed, his endeavour to escape
from home at the early age of ten to join in church the
Catechism class, his eagerness at twelve to depart for a
hermit's life in desert solitudes.   Then we learn of his military service and record unstained in the midst of temptations that beset this calling.   The incident of the gift of
half his soldier's cloak to a beggar at Amiens, followed
by a vision in the night of the Lord wearing the severed portion, is told in the simplest words.   After receiving baptism
and leaving in consequence his military career, Martin
sought Hilary, Bishop of Poitiers, who desired to ordain
him to the sacred ministry, but he would only accept the
humble office of exorcist.   A journey ensued, fraught with
peril of robbers, back to his home country in Pannonia
for the conversion of his parents, of whom "he freed his
mother from pagan error though his father persisted in
evil."   His first formal attempt in the following of monastic
counsels was made at Milan; but soon, because of the at-

tacks of Arians, he retired to the island Gallinaria near
Alassio, where with one companion, a priest of saintly character, he lived on frugal diet of herbs.   Once indeed he suffered poisoning by unwarily eating of hellebore, but the
power of prayer saved him from death.   We next find him
settled by help of St. Hilary near Poitiers in a little place
now known as Ligugé.   "It was the first monastery in Gaul,
the pattern, probably, of many later groups of little cells, a
place which St. Patrick must have seen, the forerunner of
Bangor, Clonmacnois, Iona, Inysvitryn, and Lindisfarne." [6]
Here he developed the regular life which was subsequently
to form the foundation of the monastery of Marmoutier,
consecrated after he was obliged by the people of Tours to
become their Bishop in 371, and situate just without his
cathedral city.   It was hard for Martin the monk to take
on him the public care of Chief Pastor, especially when to
his own love of his cell was added the jealousy of his brothers in sacred office.   Only, the story goes, when on the plea
of a sick woman's need had he been enticed from his secret
retreat did the chance reading in the day's Lesson of the
words—*ut destruas inimicum et defensorem* (*Ps.* viii, 2)—
quell the strenuous opposition of his most formidable an-
tagonist, the Bishop Defensor, by the triumphant outcry
of the people, ever devoted to holy Martin, that the Lord
had openly proclaimed their will to be his own.

Yet still he held his monastic home, at Marmoutier.   And
Sulpicius thus describes the discipline practised there: "In
such wise did he, full of authority and grace, fulfil the dignity of bishop that he never forsook his purpose and godly
living as monk.   And therefore for some time he made use
of a cell adjoining unto his church; but when he could not
endure the turmoil of those who crowded thither about him,
he appointed for himself a monastery some two miles out-

side the city, a place so secret and retired that it lacked
not a hermit's solitude. For on one side it was girt around
by the sheer cliff of a high mountain, and the level space on
the other sides the river Loire had enclosed by a slight
bend; by only one and the same exceeding narrow path
could it be approached. He himself had a little cell built
of logs, and many of the brethren likewise, though a goodly
number had wrought retreats for themselves from hollowed
rock in the overhanging mountain. There dwelt some eighty
disciples who were trained after the example of their blessed
master. None possessed aught of his own, but all things
they bestowed in common. Nor was it permitted to buy or
sell anything, as is the wont among many monks, and no art
was practised there save that of scribe, to which, however,
were assigned the younger brethren; the elders gave themselves to prayer. Rarely did any one go forth without his
cell, unless at the hour of Office; all broke fast at the same
time; of wine none tasted unless compelled by infirmity.
Most were clad in camel's hair, for softer habit was deemed
there an offence. Now this is of necessity the more marvellous since many among the number were of noble birth and
had constrained themselves to this humility and patience
after usage far different; and many of these we saw as
bishops in later days. For what city or church was there
which did not desire a priest from Martin's monastery?" [7]

The narrative of the *Life* is attractive with stories which
in their simple telling remind one of the *Fioretti*. The
Bishop in his work of love heals the sick, and the possessed
of devils, even embraces the leper for his cleansing. In
the strength of unremitting prayer he brings miraculous destruction upon the work of the pagans who vehemently
oppose this casting out of superstition, raises the dead—a
thing, as his disciples joyously declare, no Egyptian hermit

ever did—and conquers Satan himself in many a solitary encounter. As Sulpicius tells the tale: "Oft-times the devil by a thousand guilty arts strove to deceive the holy man and appeared unto him in very sight under most diverse forms; now he presented the semblance of Jupiter, frequently again of Mercury, and often was he seen in the features of Venus or of Minerva. But ever without fear did Martin protect himself by the sign of the Cross and by aid of prayer. Many times were heard words of abuse in which the rabble of demons reviled him with taunting words; yet all he knew for false and vain and was not moved thereby. Some of the brethren even declared that they had heard the devil foully accusing him that he had received within his monastery certain as brethren who had lost the grace of baptism by their errors, though afterward converted, and expounding the iniquities of each among these. Then heard they Martin steadfastly withstanding the devil and saying that by the mercy of the Lord those are to be absolved of their sins who have ceased to sin. When therefore the devil opposed him, saying that guilty men have no part in forgiveness and that no clemency can be shown to those who have once fallen away from God, then Martin cried aloud in answer: 'If thou thyself, O wretched one, wouldst cease from troubling men and wouldst repent thee of thy deeds even in this time when the day of judgment is at hand, I in very truth, trusting in our Lord Jesus Christ, would promise mercy even unto thee.' " [8]

Another story is yet better known: "On a certain day after the hour of Office, the devil, encircled with ruddy glow of light the more easily to deceive, adorned in royal vesture and diadem of precious stones and gold, with shoes overlaid with gold, of tranquil countenance and merry face, that last of all things might he be thought to be the devil, stood before Martin as he was praying in his cell. And since Martin at his first appearing had been struck with dimness of sight, for long space of time both kept silence. Then first spake the devil: 'Know, O Martin,' said he, 'him whom thou beholdest! I am the Christ; I have willed in coming down to earth to reveal myself before all others to thee.' But when Martin held his peace and made no answer, the devil dared to repeat his bold profession: 'Martin, why doubtest thou to believe what thou dost see? I am the Christ.' Then he, when the Spirit gave him vision, said: 'Not clad in purple nor gleaming with diadem did Jesus our Lord declare that he would come. I will not believe that Christ has come save in that appearance and form wherein he suffered, save with the marks of the Cross.' Whereupon the apparition vanished straightway as smoke, filling the cell with foul stench, and proving thereby that this was very devil." "And that this," continues Sulpicius, "was done as I have told I learned from the lips of Martin himself, that none may hold it to be fabled tale." [9]

Full of love as was Martin to the poor and distressed, to the proud and unrepentant he appears in stern authority of his calling. Of all the bishops gathered around Maximus, the usurper-Emperor, "in Martin alone," we read, "remained the dignity of the Apostles." Never would he accept the royal bidding to banquet, declaring he might not eat with a man who had driven one emperor (Valentinian the second) from his throne, and another (Gratian) from life. Only when Maximus protested that necessity of ruling had been thrust upon him by his army, with further argument and prayer, was Martin prevailed upon to sit at the King's table. Even then he astonished the assembled courtiers by passing on the loving-cup, deferentially presented to him by Maximus that he might drink first from it, to his chaplain-

priest rather than directly back to the expectant sovereign
for his partaking. "What was a king," interprets Sulpicius,
"or a king's courtier, to drink of the cup before a priest?
But no other bishop would have done thus even in the feasts
of petty judges."

The three *Dialogues* [10] of Sulpicius have as their object
the further narrative of the marvels wrought by Martin, and
his pre-eminent glory as compared even with bishops,
monks, and solitaries of the Egyptian deserts. The framework is probably supplied by fiction. In the first of them
Sulpicius represents himself as welcoming home his friend
Postumian, who has spent many months in visiting in Egypt
the famous disciples of St. Anthony; in the company of a
third "character," of Gallic nationality, great discussion goes
on of the merits of saintliness in East and West. "What of
the lives of priests in Gaul of this day?" asks Postumian.
"No better than before," is the answer, "in their attacks
upon us" (the disciples of ascetic life). And so the visitor,
bidden to recount the wonders he has seen, launches into his
tale of hardships endured, wild beasts tamed, miracles
vouchsafed. Small indeed, he declares, are the powers of
self-discipline possessed by the faithful of Gaul in comparison with those of the dwellers in the Thebaid (a fact which
was most wisely realized by the founders of monasticism in
Gaul). Here we read that Postumian was accorded greet-
ing by an old man living alone in a hut amid the desert land
on the Cyrenean coast, who spread before him and four
companions a banquet of hospitality prodigious, of dimen-
sions the most slender. At which Sulpicius, as he relates,
turned with a quiet smile to the representative of Gaul:
" 'Tell me, Gallus,' I said, 'what think you of a breakfast
for five men on a bundle of herbs and half a loaf of bread?'
Our friend with his usual modesty blushed slightly at my

teasing words: 'Just like you, Sulpicius,' he replied, 'you never lose any chance of teasing me for my love of food. It is cruel of you to make us men of Gaul live on angels' dieting.' " [11]

All, however, was not joyous even in Egypt; for in Alexandria the traveller was dismayed by the strife occasioned by Theophilus, its bishop, through persecution of monks for their reading of Origen. Here again Sulpicius shows a calm discrimination. For of Origen he declares (in the person of "Postumian"): "I marvel that one and the same man could have been so contradictory in himself; since where he is approved, he surpasses all since the days of the Apostles, where he is rightly blamed, he falls into the most unsightly errors." [12]   And error it was, according to Sulpicius, not heresy, including Origen's teaching that the devil himself would be saved by the Passion of the Lord. It may be that Sulpicius remembered those words of Martin to the devil which we have just remarked. In any case, he decides "though doubtless obedience is due to bishops, they have no right to persecute for such cause as this so great a multitude of those confessing Christ." [13]

From Alexandria Postumian travelled to Bethlehem, and tarried a while with Jerome, "a man most learned; it was strange that he vacillated so in his judgment regarding Origen." The Gallic member of the party remembers Jerome for other cause—his bitter attack in the celebrated letter to Eustochium on the self-indulgent living of monks in Gaul, which won for the Doctor lasting unpopularity.[14] But perhaps, thinks "Gallus," he was carping at Eastern Religious rather than those of the West; for "appetite among the Greeks is gluttony, among men of Gaul it is but nature."

The narrative now turns to the life of solitaries of the

Egyptian desert, and we read of such marvels as are told
in the *Lives of the Fathers:* of the taming of wild creatures,
the lioness who ate from a hermit's hand, the wolf crouch-
ing in penitence for its secret theft of a cake of bread, the
ibex picking out for a holy man wholesome from poisonous
herbs; and of extraordinary rigour of abstinence, as of the
hermit who was said to live on six dry figs a day, and un-
derwent voluntary humiliation because he was assailed by
temptations of pride. "Alas," mourns Sulpicius, "which of
our clerics does not rejoice in the salutation of any low-born
fellow, which is not puffed out with pride at the flattering
words of one silly woman? No sooner is he ordained than
he mounts his prancing charger, builds himself a goodly
house, craves soft raiment, and accepts fine cloaks and man-
tles from the spinning-wheels of adoring maidens." [15]

Yes. Great were the hermits of Egypt, but greater holy
Martin.   Jealous indeed were his brother clerks at the
sanctity of his life, declares Postumian, and hands over his
part of the narration to the friend from Gaul.   "Gallus"
then gladdens the hearts of all the company with further
marvels of Martin's working in the second and the third
of the *Dialogues.*   So marvellous are these that repeatedly
we hear references to incredulity; subsequently the Gelasian
Decree numbered them among the *Apocrypha.*   But they
are as attractive as the stories of the *Life.*   We read of
Martin in his very Cathedral secretly stripping off his under-
tunic for a beggar's sake, and, even as his people await him
before the altar for Mass, pulling on in haste the rough
prickly garment a haughty Archdeacon has deemed sufficient for the poor man's need.   There are tales of proud
rulers subdued: of the Emperor Valentinian the first, who
scornfully refused to rise when Martin, bent on errand of
mercy, entered his presence, but leaped speedily to his feet

when fire broke out in the seat of the chair whereon he sat;
of Avitian, governor of Tours, called by an angel from his
bed to open right unwillingly the door to the man of God
in middle of the night.   There are narratives of Martin's
dealings with women.   Never one was allowed even to minister to him, save the queen of Maximus, who through her
humility and persistent prayer was once suffered to prepare
and serve with her own hands food for her husband and her
beloved Saint.   The zealous maiden, who refused in her en-
closure to receive the Bishop's blessing because she would
never be looked upon by man, called forth his praise, and
he departed from his custom in accepting from her the gift
she sent.   More ecstatic were the nuns of the convent near
Tours who rushed to gather the precious straw on which in
the church's chapter-house he had lain for sleep.

Three letters give some additional details: one to the
priest Eusebius, telling of the miraculous escape of the Saint
from a burning cell; a second to the deacon Aurelius, in
which Sulpicius pours forth his grief on receiving the news
of his patron's death, who, he says, appeared to him in a
vision at the very moment of departing; the third to his
mother-in-law, Bassula, describing the last days and death
of the Saint as the writer himself had heard the account
from eye-witnesses.   The narrative of these last scenes of
Martin's life is of special beauty in its unadorned words,
which, in distinction from the symbolic truth of much of
the miraculous story, we may readily believe to be the record
of actual fact.[16]   When the holy Bishop perceived that his
strength was waning, "gathering to him the brethren, he told
them that now his parting was at hand.   Then verily was
there mourning and grief of all and the sound of those that
smote the breast: 'Why, Father, dost thou forsake us? to
whom does thou leave us desolate?   Fierce wolves invade

thy flock. When our shepherd is smitten, who will keep
us from their jaws? Surely do we know that thou longest
for Christ, but thy rewards are safe nor will they suffer by
delay. Have pity rather on us whom thou dost leave forlorn.' Then he, moved by these tears, as ever in all his
being did he abound in compassion in the Lord, is said to
have wept, and turning to God he replied with these words
only: 'O Lord, if yet to thy people I am needful, I refuse
not toil. Thy will be done' . . . Then thus he prayed:
'Grievous indeed is the fight of fleshly warfare and sufficient unto me has been the strife; but if still in this same
labour thou biddest me stand before thy stationed army, I
hold not back nor will I plead my wearying age. With devoted service will I fulfil thy charge, beneath thy standard
as long as thou shalt command me will I fight. And though
rest is welcome to the old, yet is my spirit victor over years
and knows not how to yield to time. But if thou sparest
my age, good is thy will to me, O Lord; and these for whom
I fear, them thou thyself wilt guard."

Then comes the tradition of the last moments on earth:
"And so though now for some days he was held in the grip
of fever, yet did he not cease from the work of God. Watching by night in prayers and vigils, he compelled his tired
members to serve his spirit, lying on that well-renowned bed
of ashes and haircloth. And when his disciples besought of
him that at least he would allow common coverings to be
spread beneath him: 'It is not fitting,' he replied, 'for a
Christian to die save in ashes; if I leave other example to
you, then have I sinned.' So still with his eyes and hands
ever stretched toward heaven he relaxed not his uncon-
quered spirit from supplication. Then by the priests, who
at this time had come together to him, he was asked to
turn aside a little his body for relief. But, 'suffer me,' he

prayed, 'suffer me, brethren, to behold heaven rather than earth, that my spirit about to depart on its own journey may be directed unto the Lord.' When thus he had spoken he saw the devil stand near beside him. To whom, 'Why standest thou here, savage beast?' he said. 'Thou wilt find nothing in me, thou deadly one. The bosom of Abraham receiveth me.' With these words he yielded up his spirit, and they who were present testified to us that they beheld his face as it had been the face of an angel. . . ." [17]

The example set at Marmoutier was followed in the monastery of Lerins on the island known to Pliny as Lerina and situated in the Mediterranean near Cannes. There about the beginning of the fifth century a group of earnest men had settled in their zeal for the practice of monastic life after the Egyptian model [18] under the direction of Honoratus, whose character has been described for us in glowing words by his devoted disciple, St. Hilary, in later years destined to succeed him as Bishop of Arles. In his *Sermo de Vita Sancti Honorati* [19] we read that the future Abbot of Lerins was born of a family of noble and consular rank but pagan faith in Gaul, very probably in the neighbourhood of Arles.[20] The panegyric develops in that same strain of wholehearted love and admiration which we have seen in the writing of Sulpicius. The young Honoratus, discontented with the blandishments of the world, encounters his father's wrath in his determined desire for Christian baptism. As the father of Paulinus of Pella had shared his son's sport and games in concern for the boy's health, so the father of Honoratus threw himself into his son's diversions in a desperate attempt to ward off the conversion he feared. But in vain. With the answer *Delectat haec vita sed decipit,* Honoratus not only persevered in his chosen way, but attracted to it his elder brother Venantius, and with him so eagerly pursued ascetic discipline that his father mourned him as one dead to life. The two brothers then, in dismay at their growing reputation for holiness among their own countrymen, departed in quest of retirement in foreign lands under the guardianship of Caprasius, an old man of great piety. After his brother's death in Methone in Greece, Honoratus finally settled at Lerins under the episcopal charge of Leontius, who ordained him priest. Hilary describes the island in most unalluring terms: "uninhabited by reason of its exceeding wildness and the fear of poisonous creatures." [21] The Christians of the country hard by tried eagerly to dissuade Honoratus from embarking on so dangerous an adventure; but he would have none of their warnings, and confidently proclaiming: "Thou shalt trample under foot the lion and the dragon," he went boldly forward, "and drove away the fear of his brethren by his own confidence. The terror of the desert fled, the multitude of serpents gave place to them." [22] The pages which follow tell of his loving care as abbot of each of those who came to share his life from different parts of the world, of his sympathy with the distressed and tempted, of his kindly rebuke to the sinner, of his hospitality to strangers who visited the island, drawn by his renown, of his zealous correspondence with those who sought his direction from afar. A like faithfulness, Hilary declares, marked his government as Bishop of Arles, to which he was called in 426. For two years he ruled his people and died in 429.

Among those who lived the life of prayer and discipline at Lerins under Honoratus were others known to us for their writings. Eucherius, afterward Bishop of Lyons, lived there for a while before departing with his wife Galla to follow a like practice on the neighbouring island of Lero, named in later times Sainte-Marguerite. Of the *Letters* of the great Paulinus who had himself fled worldly things to the retirement of Nola in Campania and had there for his holy character been elected its bishop in 410, there is one, full of friendliness and good wishes, addressed to Eucherius and Galla as residents on the island.[23]   When he had thus retired, Eucherius left his two sons in the monastery for their instruction.   Of these, one, Veranus, either followed his father as Bishop of Lyons, or was called to the bishopric of Vence—we are not sure of this detail;[24] the other, Salonius, has already been described as Bishop of Geneva.

To each Eucherius addressed one of his longer works. The *Formulæ spiritalis intellegentiæ*, written for Veranus, consists of explanations in a metaphorical manner of terms used in Holy Scripture, including words treating of God, of things of the heavens and things of earth, of man, and of the Scriptural use of numbers.   To Salonius were dedicated the two books of *Instructions*, which seek to explain various problems presented by the writings of the Bible: In the Old Testament, "What is meant by the statement that God walked in Paradise?   Since God is the Author of all things, whence came evil?   Since God is omniscient, how could he be described as saying 'Adam, where art thou?'   What is meant by the finger of God by which the Tables of the Law were inscribed?   Why was honey forbidden in sacrifice?   How can God be said to repent him?   How to feel passions, such as anger or fury?"   Similar questions are propounded for the New Testament, with discussions on the meaning of words such as Alleluia, Amen, Hosanna, and others.   One of the shorter works still considered genuine (a number of those given by Migne, including ten *Homilies to Monks*, and the *Epitome of Cassian's Institutes*, are held as spurious or doubtful by Bardenhewer[25]) is a tract *In Praise of the Desert*, addressed to Hilary and containing an enthusiastic description of Lerins, far different from the mournful account of its barrenness of old. As Eucherius now beholds it, it appears "abounding in streams, green with herbs, radiant with flowers, a paradise of vision and fragrance."[26] There is one fragment of a Homily, quoted for us by Claudianus Mamertus in his well-known work *De statu Animœ*, which shows that Eucherius was a preacher of some vigour. It seeks to confront those who are sceptical of the union of the Divine and human in Christ with the common mystery of the union of body and soul, the corporeal and incorporeal, in every human being.[27]

The founder of the monastery at Lerins was succeeded by one of his monks, Maximus, who was subsequently elected to the see of Riez in Provence (in ancient days Reii). Maximus handed down his office of abbot in 433 to Faustus, destined himself as bishop of the same diocese in the latter half of the fifth century to be a leader in thought and action of the Church in Southern Gaul. He was of British birth, as we learn from a letter of Avitus, Bishop of Vienne, to Gundobad,[28] that Arian King of Burgundy who interested himself so much in questions of religion. Apollinaris Sidonius in a laudatory poem, *Carmen Euchariston ad Faustum Episcopum*,[29] speaks of visiting him and his mother at Riez, thanks him for instructing a brother at Lerins, and mentions the island as once the home, not only of Faustus, but of Honoratus, Maximus, Eucherius, and Hilary. One of the letters of Sidonius is written to the same bishop, and dated c. 477. In it he counsels intermission of correspondence for the present on account of the danger of interception of such missives by enemy invaders, but praises Faustus highly for his power as orator and writer.[30]

The life of Faustus was full of controversy, beginning even during his direction of the island monks; for we are told that about the year 455 a Council was held at Arles to decide differences of judgment between Faustus and his Bishop, Theodore of Fréjus. In 474 he appears as one of the four bishops of Gaul appointed to negotiate concerning the fate of Auvergne, the native country of Sidonius, with Euric, King of the Visigoths, a commission which, as we have seen, did not prevent the cession of the entire region into Euric's hands. In his old age he was exiled from his diocese, probably by the same ruler in his wrath at the Bishop's writings against the Arians.

Certain of the *Letters* of Faustus are of interest. Thus he writes to Græcus, a deacon entangled in Monophysite heresy,[31] that "it is vexatious to write on so obvious an error; however, the humility which has led Græcus to this enquiring of the truth is a hopeful sign. He has evidently been reading and fasting overzealously; excess of study is as bad for the spirit as excess of wine for the body. The best remedy will be submission of life and conscience to the direction of some reverend and well-esteemed Father of the Church." The counsel given to one Paulinus was not so admirable.[32] Paulinus had been thrown into great perturbation of spirit by a holy hermit Marinus, who declared to him that death-bed repentance does not avail for those who have sinned mortally against the flesh. In answer to his enquiry Faustus maintained that repentance at the last moment is indeed insufficient; good action is necessary as well as passive acceptance of forgiveness. This statement was referred by Gundobad to Avitus in the letter mentioned above. The Bishop vigorously denied such doctrine, and would not even allow it to be attributed to Faustus of Britain, but laid it to the charge of a Faustus of Africa, tainted by Manichæan heresy. There is little doubt, however, that the letter belongs to the Bishop of Riez, because he discussed in it the same doctrine of the nature of the soul which he put forward in another letter addressed to an unknown official of the Church, probably some bishop.[33] In this doctrine he maintained that only that which is not included in time and space, that is God, is without body; hence the soul of man and the invisible and heavenly substance of angels are both material. Such teaching called forth in opposition the three books of the *De statu Animæ* from Claudianus Mamertus, brother of the St. Mamertus, Archbishop of Vienne, renowned for the institution of Rogation Days.[34]

As Bishop, Sidonius tells us in the *Euchariston,* Faustus practised the same rigour of life which he had followed at Lerins, at times retreating to desert places and mountains for prayer as the disciple of Egyptian Fathers, at times returning to visit the island monastery and his brethren of former days. In active life as Chief Pastor of Riez he tended the sick and prisoners, cared for the dead, and taught from the altar steps the people who eagerly drank in his salutary exposition of the Law.[35]

But it is in connection with the famous strife of theological parties which still sprang from the following of Augustine that Faustus was best known; for he was conspicuous in the school of "Semi-Pelagians," which held its stronghold in Southern Gaul of this time—the middle party which accepted neither the full strictness of Augustinian teaching on Predestination and Grace nor the doctrine of the innate power of free will in man held by Pelagius. The fact that Faustus embraced this midway position is shown by a letter written to him as Bishop of Riez by a priest of the name of Lucidus, who was accused of harbouring extreme theories on Predestination. The Bishop's emphatic answer demanded refutation of this in detail from the enquirer; and his two

books *Concerning the Grace of God* were written to condemn this teaching on Predestination at the request of the
bishops assembled at the Council of Lyons in 474. If, however, in Gaul Faustus was eminent, at Rome his works were
held in disfavour. About 520 his treatise *De Gratia* evoked
criticism from certain Scythian monks dwelling at Constantinople; for they saw in it no insisting on prevenient
grace and suspected the writer of Pelagian error. The matter was referred by the African Bishop Possessor, at that
time in Constantinople, to the Pope Hormisdas, who rebuked his petitioners for worrying their minds with the doctrine of a book not included among those deemed appropriate
for study by the faithful. Thus checked, the monks
appealed to a number of African bishops residing in Sardinia, and especially to Fulgentius, Bishop of Ruspe in
Byzacena, exiled from Vandal Africa under the sovereignty
of the Arian King Thrasamund. To this appeal the bishops
answered in a long letter, and Fulgentius subsequently
about 523 in seven books *Against Faustus,* which are now
lost.[36]

Some six years later we find an ending of the "Pelagian
controversy" so-called, by the zeal of Cæsarius, that great
Bishop of Arles in the sixth century, and himself at one
time a dweller in Lerins. At the Second Council of Orange
in 529 the heresy of Pelagius in its whole and in its partial
form was officially quelled,[37] and the teachings of Augustine
on Grace, prevenient and habitual, without, however, the
terror of Predestination, were restated as Catholic doctrine
of the Church.

More interesting, however, than Faustus from the literary
point of view is the famous Vincent, whose name is ever connected with the monastery of Lerins. Under the description
of Peregrinus, "least of all the servants of God," he sets out

to snatch from the robber hand of time in his peaceful retreat a record of the great facts of Catholic tradition, briefly
compiled in convenient form under the title of *Commonitorium* [38] for the refreshment of his memory by constant perusal. The language is to be simple, such as ordinary folk
may understand—*facilis communisque sermo*—an aim which
is entirely realized, while at times one glides into a passage
of distinct beauty and eloquence. The author seeks to
answer the query, "What is the foundation of Catholic
Faith?" by directing search, first, to the Scriptures—*divinæ
legis auctoritas;* secondly, to the Church as interpreter of the
Scriptures—*ecclesiæ catholicæ traditio.* The content of this
is then defined as follows: "In the Catholic Church we must
make it our great care to hold that which everywhere, which
always, which by all men, has been believed; for this is truly
and properly Catholic, as the reason and meaning of the
word 'catholic' show, comprehending all things in general.
Then, and only then, will this come to pass if we follow
universality, antiquity, and general consent. Moreover, we
shall follow universality if we confess this one faith to be
true which all the Church throughout the world professes;
and antiquity, if in no manner we withdraw ourselves from
those concepts which it is clear that our holy ancestors and
fathers held fast; and general consent likewise, if we follow
closely the definitions and decisions of all, or at least almost
all, of the priests and teachers of the Church in ancient
days." [39] The third test, of "general consent," is to be obtained, if possible, from the authority of the General Councils of the Church. If this be not available, then from the
agreement of a majority of those Fathers whose fidelity to
the Faith throughout their lives has been as marked as their
power of intellect.

Only by this threefold means may heresies be detected

when they spring up as noxious weeds among the wheat; to
wit, new heresies, for, of course, tradition cannot help us
against old ones, which must—if hitherto uncondemned by
the Church—be vanquished by the truth of Holy Scripture.
Many are the evil teachings which Vincent mentions as of
late days attacking the peace of believers. Among them he
describes in detail the errors of Nestorius, Apollinaris, and
Photinus, as "furious dogs barking against the Catholic
Faith," [40] refutes the "mockery and madness" of the Mani-
chæans and Docetists, distinguishes by their several marks
of condemnation the profane Pelagius, Caelestius his "mon-
strous" follower, the sacrilegious Arius, the accursed Sabellius, and Novatian in his utter cruelty. The more gifted
the heretic, the greater his power of tempting the faithful;
hence the special danger of the brilliant genius of Origen
and Tertullian. Of a truth for this reason has God not
stayed heretics from their course of wickedness that he may
find in these trials a means of testing the faithful. Especially evil is the treacherous use of Holy Scripture. As those
who try to disguise ill-tasting medicine for children or to
hide the true nature of poisonous draughts, these false teachers try to find in the sacred books support for their evil
words. Wretched indeed is the state of those who have
fallen victims to such perils, even if they are not lost for
evermore: "For on this account without the most secure
haven of the Catholic Faith are they tossed, smitten, and
well nigh slain by divers storms of perplexities, that they
may be fain to furl the sails of their swelling minds, wrongly
filled out by the winds of strange doctrines, and bring themselves back to the most safe harbourage of their tranquil
and gracious Mother. . . ." [41]

Among such matters the attitude of Vincent toward even
Augustinian teaching has called forth energetic comment

from the seventeenth century onwards, and has made this writer of Lerins also noted in the company of the "Semi-Pelagians." Here it will be sufficient to mark the words in which Vincent has been thought to allude to the extreme followers of Augustine, though nowhere does he mention him by name, as he does mention Pelagius: "Now verily through those promises which follow have heretics been wont to deceive unguarded men in wondrous fashion. For they dare to warrant and teach that, in their own church, in the assembly of their own communion, there is some great and special and entirely individual grace of God. Wherefore without any toil, without any zeal, without any diligence, though they neither seek nor pray nor beat upon the door, yet do those, whosoever they may be who are of their own number, receive such dispensation of Divine aid that, borne by hands of angels, that is, saved by angelic guarding, they can never smite their foot against a stone, never stumble." [42]

Equal, however, in importance to the condemnation of divers errors in the *Commonitorium* is the loyal praise and acknowledgment of the Church as the guardian of the Faith once delivered to the Saints, and the clear exposition of the fundamental truths she holds as her inheritance from age to age. For Vincent was not content to condemn heresy by negative criticism, but rather made it his special work to declare in positive terms those basic articles of the Catholic creed which had in more recent times been attacked by those who saw not the Trinity in Unity nor the Unity in Trinity, nor the perfect union of God and Man in the Christ.

If, then, the doctrine of Mother Church be defined as that held *ubique, semper, et ab omnibus,* how is this compatible with that march of progress inevitable within a living Church which shall bring forth things both new and old from her

treasury? The problem was foreseen by Vincent himself:
"But perchance some one will declare: 'Shall there then be
no progress of religion in the Church of Christ?' Yea,
clearly, and most great. Who is so envious to mankind, so
hostile to God, that he would essay to prevent this? Yet
of such sort is it that it is progress of faith, not change; for
truly it pertains to progress that each thing be enlarged in
its own same self, to change that it be transferred from one
self to another. So then is it meet that understanding, that
knowledge, that wisdom grow and progress greatly in eager
advance, both of men singly and in general, of each man and
of the whole Church, through ages and centuries, but each
necessarily in its own kind, that is, in its own doctrine, with
the same concept and the same reasoning." [43]   "Growth,
therefore, of the corpus of the Church's doctrine," continues
Vincent, "is to resemble the growth of the human body, ever
one and the same, though the flower of boyhood differ far
from the maturity of age. For if the regular course of Nature be not developed by each creature according to its own
species, then deformity must ensue."

What, we may ask in this case, of statements of doctrine
explicitly put forward by the Church as matter of her Faith
in early or in later centuries following the time of the Apostles? If these declarations conform with the Vincentian
canon, it must result that they do but proclaim as binding
for the faithful those truths which have flowered in the spiritual vision of the Church from seeds implanted in the first
sowing of the Christian Faith in Christ—seeds imbedded in
Holy Scripture, to be cherished and ripened in the course of
time by increasing knowledge of Christian folk till at last
fully recognized in the general consent, belief, and practice
of the universal body of her loyal children. [44]

Of the two books which originally appeared in the *Com-*

monitorium, only one is left to us in complete form; of the second, dealing at length with the acts of the Third Œcumenical Council at Ephesus in 431, only a summary remains. As the writer states that this Council was held about three years before the composing of his work, we are enabled to date it in 434. Much discussion has centred round the similarity of its language with that of the "Athanasian" Creed, and we may indeed think it not unlikely that this Creed, so specially associated with the Church in Gaul, also found origin in the island-monastery, or was written by one who at some time dwelt therein. We cannot, however, identify the author with Vincent himself in exact detail.[45]

And now last of all, but most important and interesting for the student of monastic life in this century, we come to the great writer of the *Institutes* and *Conferences,* John Cassian, of Marseilles, where about 415 he founded two Religious houses, one for men and one for women. He was born about 360, of Scythian nationality according to Gennadius,[46] a statement which may be explained as referring to Roman Scythia (Dobrudja), near the mouth of the Danube.[47] He tells us that he was trained in Religion in the East, and resided in a monastery at Bethlehem,[48] that he travelled in Egypt and Palestine, observing the life and rule of various communities and acquiring from many solitaries in the desert lessons in spiritual discipline. It was approximately in the year 426 that, at the request of Castor, Bishop of Apta Julia in Gallia Narbonensis, Cassian proceeded to embody the learning gained by his residence in the East in the twelve books *Concerning the institutions of Cœnobitic Monks and concerning remedies for the eight principal faults.* The preface, addressed to the Bishop, tells that Castor in his desire to establish a monastery, hitherto lacking, in his diocese, has requested Cassian to describe his experience of the East in these matters, and especially the practices current among monks of Egypt. This, therefore, he will try to undertake in spite of his faulty memory of those long past years, and of the fact that others of noble life and distinguished learning, such as Basil and Jerome, have treated of such subjects. His language will be simple, he declares, a promise which he fulfilled, for his works are written in clear and easy Latin, with no pretensions to high or eloquent style. He will not tell of miracles, though he has seen them wrought under his own eyes, but will devote himself entirely to instruction. The sane and sober sense, springing from the deep knowledge of human nature and character which marks all Cassian's writings, is seen already here. He intends, as he states, to moderate such severe ordinances in the Egyptian Rule as on account of rigour of climate or difference of customs would be impracticable for monks of Gaul: "for if a measure, reasonable and duly within one's power, be maintained, there is found the same perfection of observance even in unequal capacity of attainment."

The first book deals with the habit to be worn by monks: "It will be fitting to discuss the interior character when we have arranged the exterior part. Let the monk then be ever ready, girded in his girdle as a soldier of Christ; so we read of the girdles of Elijah, of John the Baptist, of Peter and of Paul. The habit itself in general should not differ from those of other monks in colour or in appearance or, again, in marks of affected zeal for shabbiness and neglect; but should merely follow the universal standard of monastic dress, distinct from that of the world. Whatever is ex-

traordinary or practised only by individuals is not of necessity, but rather of vain-glory. Only those parts of the
Egyptian dress should be worn in Gaul which the region
and its uses permit; for instance, neither sandals nor linen
tunics nor the wearing of one tunic alone are permitted on
account of the cold weather in winter, and a tiny cowl or
goatskin garment would be more likely to evoke mockery
than edification in beholders of the West."

From exterior habit Cassian passes in the ensuing three
books to exterior practice, and tells of the Rule regarding
the canonical Hours of the Night and of the Day in Egypt.
At one time there was the greatest divergence in the practice
of the East with relation to the number of psalms proper
for the Night Office; but finally the number was fixed
throughout Egypt and the Thebaid as twelve. The origin of
this ordinance is given in one of those many stories which
season the instruction throughout the work: "When, therefore, the perfection of the glorious Church of primitive days
was still of fresh and unimpaired memory in the minds of
men and the fervent faith of the few had not yet grown
tepid as spread abroad among the multitude, the reverend
fathers took thought with watchful care for later generations
touching the manner of rule for daily use throughout the
whole body of Religious. And so they met with one accord,
that they might hand on their inheritance of piety and peace
to their descendants free from all strife and discord. . . .
And when each one for his own fervour of spirit counselled
that that number of Psalms should be determined which he
judged most easy in his own vision of faith and power, without heeding of what was possible for the general body of the
brethren, amid which of necessity there is found very great
share of weakness, in divers manners they vied with one
another in ordaining a number surpassing great. For some

thought meet fifty Psalms for each Night Office, others sixty; others again were still not content but desired to exceed this amount; and there arose among them such holy difference of contention for their sacred Rule that the hour of Vespers broke in upon their conference. Then rose up one of their number in the midst to sing Psalms unto the Lord, while the others remained seated, as is the wont yet in parts of Egypt, and all hearts were intent upon his words as he chanted eleven Psalms interspersed with prayers in even declaiming. Then, ending the twelfth Psalm with response of Alleluia, he was suddenly withdrawn from the eyes of all, and brought to conclusion both the questionings and the Office rite! Whereupon the holy Council of fathers, understanding that by an Angel's directing in ordinance of the Lord the general ruling had been given to their congregations, decreed that this number should be observed in assemblies both of Vespers and of the Night." [49]

The monks of Egypt, continues Cassian, are not in a hurry to fall on their knees for prayer after the Psalms have been sung, hoping to arrive as speedily as may be at the end of the Office, nor do they remain long in prayer prostrate on the ground. Would monks did not in Gaul, for therein they seek oftentimes relaxation of body rather than profit of spirit. The silence of these Egyptian Religious is intense. No spittings, no coughs, no sleepy noddings, groans or sighs disturb during the Office those who pray; nothing interrupts the voice of the priest except perhaps a slight sound from one whose burning spirit cannot altogether control its emotion. Brethren whose tepidity of mind causes them to shout their prayers (a rather interesting conclusion!) or who sin in any of the ways described above, are judged double offenders, by reason of their own negligent offering and their disturbing of their neighbours. Here once more Cassian's sound sense appears; for he commends the Egyptian practice of brief prayers and frequent, wherewith men may avoid those fiery darts of the evil one which beset them more especially as they pray. "It is better to sing a few verses with understanding than to gabble a whole psalm in a hurry to reach the end of the allotted number."

The Night Office is followed in Egypt by the nocturnal vigil, spent by the brethren in manual labour or in prayer in their cells; work serves as an anchor to the unstable movements of the heart and to wavering thoughts. Among the Day Hours that of Matins, according to Cassian,[50] was first instituted in his monastery in Bethlehem, in order to prevent laziness in rising, and had the happy result of completing in monastic use the Seven Canonical Hours. Sleep is permitted between the nocturnal vigil and the Office of Matins to forestall the "necessity of resuming during the day what we have taken from the night."

The counsel regarding practice of exterior things is now applied to the life in the monastery, especially as it concerns its junior members. Illustration is taken again from Egypt, with special reference to the community established by Pachomius early in the fourth century at Tabennisi in the neighbourhood of Denderah.[51] There monks remain till bowed with age, though so severe is the discipline that in Cassian's memory no one in Gallic monasteries has ever endured such for one whole year. The aspirant must lie for ten days or longer keeping watch before the entrance to show his humility and perseverance, prostrate at the feet of all the brethren passing by and purposely scorned by all. Not only must he leave all his possessions behind him, but he is not even allowed to bestow his goods upon the monastery at his entering, lest either he be puffed up with pride or, in case of rejection, demand back what he has previously given. When duly admitted he is clothed in the habit, and his own secular dress is finally given to the poor after his fitness for the life and perseverance have been tested by length of time. For a year he dwells in the Guest-House, ministering to the wants of strangers and visitors. If then he has proved faithful, he is allowed to associate with the brethren under care of a senior member of the cloister. Strict obedience is exacted. The thoughts of the novice must be discovered to his Master and reviewed for judgment; in no case may he leave his cell without permission; nor may he use, without pain of penance, the word "my" in speaking of anything he employs. Public penance is exacted for such faults as breaking a jar, stumbling in singing a psalm, delay in returning to the cell, talking with a cellmate without permission, and so on. Graver faults are punished by beating or expulsion. Well-known in this connection is the story given here by Cassian as example of monastic diligence, of the monk who was suspended from joining his brethren at the Office because he had unconsciously let fall three beans while at work in the kitchen and thus had neglected the sacred store of Community goods. Further stories are told of most literal obedience to command: of Abbot John who as a novice for a whole year faithfully fetched water twice a day from a distance of two miles for the tending of a dry and withered twig, of Abbot Patermucius who had likewise proved his submission to discipline by readiness to plunge his little son in a stream to death at his Superior's will. There is also the pleasant narrative regarding Pinufius, this time no novice, but a mitred abbot, who fled from his reverencing brethren in deadly fear of pride to a far-off community. There, unknown and scorned as an aged refugee from the satiety of this world's pleasures, he served in most menial tasks till rediscovered and brought home again by his distracted monks.[52]

The remaining eight books are devoted to consideration of the eight principal sins to which the monk is prone. First, the spirit of Gluttony. In dealing with this Cassian again shows moderation. No uniform rule, he says, can be laid down with regard to fasting; this must differ according to differences in strength and age and sex. Every one cannot fast for a week or even for three or for two days; many cannot fast till sunset without suffering. Differences, too, must be made in actual diet; for unseasoned vegetables and dry bread are not appropriate for all men. The infirmity, however, of the flesh which prevents men from austere fasting does not harm their purity of life, provided that pleasure be not their aim; even more delicate fare may be taken for the sake of health, if the conscience be sincerely obeyed. The fast may also be broken for reasons of hospitality: "Fasting, although useful and necessary, is yet an offering of free will, but the work of charity is of obligation." At the departure of the guest the monk will practise stricter abstinence in atonement. Moreover, bodily fasting by itself does not suffice, unless it be accompanied by fasting of the soul from sin. On the other hand, so hostile to the pursuit of perfection is the sin of gluttony that there is no time at which we may more keenly feel that we are in danger of being turned away from our spiritual course than when we are driven to care for the body's weakness by taking food.

Various tales follow: of old Maches who had obtained from the Lord this grace that he always fell asleep when foolish or slanderous tales were told; of the brethren who sank into slumber during spiritual exhortations but awoke straightway and pricked up their ears joyfully when an anecdote was introduced; of Abbot Theodore who was not gifted intellectually, but was led by Divine grace to the solution of a difficult problem after seven days and nights of persistent prayer.

Book VI deals with the spirit of Fornication, and Book VII with that of Covetousness. Here the temptations that beset the monk in thought are skilfully portrayed. "The food supplied in this monastery"—so Cassian pictures his meditation—"is not enough to keep a man in health. Supposing he should get ill, what would support him in this need? Sick people are horribly neglected by the Community; if he doesn't look out for himself, he will die a miserable death. Then the clothing is insufficient; no, he cannot stay in this place much longer. But he has no money for travelling. How can he get at least a tiny sum, somehow or other?" With these reflections he decides to fashion some article of his skill, sell it and provide himself with means. This sum he then tries to double and so on. The evil has set in.

In dealing with the spirit of Anger Cassian remarks that some have tried to excuse this most harmful disease of the soul by pointing to anger on the part of God against sinners. "But how," he argues, "can anger be literally predicated of God, any more than sleep or standing or sitting or drunkenness—words which are all applied to him in Holy Writ? or human form and limbs? Such terms are used symbolically and mystically; his eyes are the width of his vision, his hands his providence and care. But anger is a sin in general among men; it blinds the eyes of the heart and suffers it not to behold the sun of justice. The only objects of wholesome anger are our own selves. When then monks are tempted to long for solitude that they may flee the annoyance caused them by other men, let them remember that their highest peace and progress in good does not depend on another's will which they cannot indeed control, but is laid within their own power. Not by another's virtue shall they escape anger but by their own exercise of patience."

Especially interesting is the ninth book, on the sinful spirit of Melancholy, a vice which separates men from the contemplation of God, suffers them not to behave gently to their brethren and renders them impatient in all offices of their Religion. Sometimes this sadness comes upon them from no clearly seen cause but by subtle perturbation of the devil, so that their friends and relations, though dear to them, only provoke annoyance by their approach and words. The ground of the trouble is inward frailty; the remedy is quiet endurance, inspired by constant thought on spiritual things and hope of the promised joy to come. This will prevail against depression, whether it arise from a previous attack of anger or from some external misfortune or from some injury done or from the aforementioned *inrationabilis mentis confusio*. Closely connected with these counsels are those addressed in the following book against *Accidie* (Discontent, leading to sloth of spirit).[53] Such weariness, we are told, specially attacks solitaries dwelling in the desert, and is apt to occur about the hour of noon. Some holy men who have lived long call it that demon of noontide of which we read in the ninetieth Psalm. The section which comes next so well describes the feelings which at times beset all serious workers whether in religious or secular pursuits that it seems worth while to reproduce it in detail: "When this evil spirit has seized upon its victim, it brings forth within his mind hatred of his monastery, loathing for his cell, scorn and contempt for the brethren whether living together with him or elsewhere. How lazy and unspiritual they are! Then he becomes dull and indisposed for all manner of work which awaits him within the walls of his dormitory. His trouble allows him neither to sit quietly nor to attend to his reading. Again and again he groans that he is doing nothing by staying here so long time, thus bound down. Still he sits, empty and bereft of good to his soul in this place, a man who could even rule others and be of help to great number —yet never a single one has he been able to edify or profit by his instruction! Then he thinks enviously of monasteries far away, pictures places more advantageous for his progress and better suited for his soul's health, imagines in fancy pleasant conferences with brethren in such Houses, full of spiritual intercourse. Here, on the contrary, everything is crude and stupid. Not only is there no inspiration in the brethren who live their lives out here, but great toil is needed even to find food enough to keep one's body alive. . . . Now it is the fifth, now the sixth hour; he feels as tired and as hungry as if he had come in from a long journey or ended a most heavy piece of work, as if he had been fasting for two or three days. Presently he looks about eagerly here and there, and grumbles that none of the brethren is coming to see him; in and out of the cell he walks, and keeps on looking at the sun. Surely it is setting more slowly than ever to-day. . . . Had he not better have a good sleep if no one really is coming in?—Ah, yes! Now he remembers—he owes some calls himself (are not calls a proper act of courtesy?) —then there are those sick people, and some of them living at a distance, too—and ought he not to go more frequently to see his relatives, both men and women? What about that holy woman so devoted to God? She has no relations to help her—it would be a great act of charity to call on her quite often and see she doesn't lack any necessary thing, neglected and despised as she is. Such acts are much more the work of charity than sitting in a cell doing no good to oneself or any other." [54]

The cure is hard work. In Egypt therefore monks are obliged to work not only for their own sustenance, but for the extending of hospitality to strangers and to neighbours in want. There is a saying, Cassian remarks, among the oldest Fathers in Egypt that "a hard-working monk is beset by one devil, a lazy one is confounded by innumerable spirits." It was this conviction that drove Abbot Paul, who lived so far in the desert that he could neither help any one by the fruits of his labour nor even sell them because the cost of carriage would surpass the price of his work, to burn up every year what he had wrought by his toil that he might yet labour on to provide for his daily needs in healthful occupation of mind and body.

The work ends with the consideration of Vainglory and of Pride. Vainglory attacks both the flesh and the spirit; in fact, so many points of attack does it find in the frailty of man, seeking as point of vantage for itself both his vices and his virtues, that it has been likened to a bulbous plant from which the removal of one layer only discovers one beneath. It tempts the monk to be elated because of his victories over sin, to try to do more than his physical powers allow, to dwell on what he might have accomplished had he stayed in the world, to desire even good things, such as the ministry of priest or deacon, that he may edify others for his own praise. In this folly he is reduced at times to rehearse imaginary sermons and to conduct in his thoughts public services within the seclusion of his cell. Let him therefore flee all such thoughts; let him desire conversation neither with women, nor with bishops, who interrupt by offers of goodly cures the peace of quiet meditation, and let him lay to heart the grievous sin of preferring the glory given by the world to the glory which belongs to God.

That the *Institutes* were written not later than 426 is shown by the dedication to Bishop Castor, who died in that year. His death is mentioned in the preface to that later work of Cassian, the *Collationes*, or records of conferences held by Cassian himself and his fellow-student in the ascetic life, Germanus, with abbots governing communities of cœnobites in Egypt.[55] The two journeyed thither from the monastery at Bethlehem in which they had both been studying, and visited fifteen abbots, some of whom dwelt in the desert of Scete and some in the neighbourhood of Panephysis and of Diolcos, towns on the Nile. Twenty-four conferences are reported, collected in three sections. The first part, consisting of ten of these, interviews with abbots of the desert of Scete, is dedicated to Bishop Leontius and to Helladius, a brother; the second part, containing the account of seven interviews with abbots dwelling near Panephysis, is dedicated to "brothers Honoratus and Eucherius," which fact shows that both of these parts were published before the end of 426, as Honoratus, here called simply "brother," became Bishop of Arles in that year. The third part gives us also seven conferences, this time with abbots residing near Diolcos; it seems to have been written before Honoratus died in January, 429, as the dedication to him, now as Bishop, in the preface includes no reference to death. The date of the publication of the *Conferences* would then appear to be between 426 and 429 A.D.

Their subject matter yields a veritable mine of spiritual instruction, and strives to lift seekers after holiness to a higher stage than that of the *Institutes*. This former work, as we have seen, dealt with the exterior behaviour of monks and the mortification of vices; but the *Conferences*, as the preface tells, are to lead their readers to consider the invisible bearing of the inner man and his ascent of the heights of Prayer. The first interview reported (the method of reporting is that of discourses from the different abbots, interrupted only seldom by questions from Germanus when in perplexity or discouragement at the high ideal set before the youthful couple) was with Abbot Moses on the end and aim of monastic life. The end is Heaven, the aim is purity of heart, rooted and grounded in humility. All religious practices, fastings, watchings, meditation, monastic life, whether solitary or coenobite, are subsidiary and means to this end, the instruments of perfection, not perfection itself. Similar instruction was given by the same Abbot in the second conference, on spiritual discretion: "For Discretion is the mother, the guardian, and the ruler of all virtues." Men may even fast and watch and abound in charity, yet without the grace of discretion come to a miserable end; as did the venerable monk Heron, who after fifty years of exemplary abstinence in the desert was tempted by Satan to throw himself into a well, presuming for his safe passage on the sanctity of his past life, and died wretchedly three days after, narrowly escaping the censure of suicide. For there is no more fatal error for a monk than foolish trust in his own judgment. Then Abbot Paphnutius, who dwelt in the wilder and more remote solitude of the desert, desiring to flee the sight of men that he might attain to God, and was believed to enjoy daily conversation with angels, discoursed in Conference III on the threefold call to renunciation as exemplified in the command to Abraham: *Exi de terra tua* (worldly possessions) *et de cognatione tua* (natural conversation and evil inclinations) *et de domo patris tui* (memory of this visible world). There followed visits to Abbot Daniel, who talked on the combat between the will of the flesh and of the spirit, in the fourth conference, and to Abbot Sarapion, whose instruction, in the fifth, repeated much that had already been written on the eight principal sins. Next the two eager disciples sat at the feet of Abbot Theodore, in the sixth interview, and asked him why God allowed certain monks of holy life to be killed by robbers. "God," answered the Abbot, "has never allowed evil to befall his monks against their will." "What then does Isaiah mean when he speaks of God as creating evil?" "He means salutary affliction, hard to him who suffers it for his correction. Things may be divided into three classes: good, bad, and indifferent; the death of a good man at the hands of a robber is a thing bad for the robber but indifferent for the good man, who proceeds to his reward." "But how," asks the intelligent Germanus, "is the robber deserving of punishment, in that he has hastened the saint on his way to blessedness?" "He deserves condemnation," is the answer, "because he willed evil, though the character of his victim frustrated his will."

In Lent the pair called on Abbot Serenus to help them in their unceasing distractions of thought from holy things; and they obtained much interesting instruction (in Conference VII) on the nature of devils and their methods of attack. Devils do not know men's inner thoughts, but only conjecture from external behaviour how to tempt them. Sometimes holy men are permitted by God to encounter great trouble for their penance and cleansing. Such befell Abbot Paul, who once by accident met a woman outside his monastery, and ran back to his cell straightway in horror at the dangerous sight; for which extreme fear he was rendered absolutely helpless by seizure of paralysis and had to be tended till he died, more than three years after, by a community of holy virgins, for no male nursing could minister to his need. Yet far different now, we read, is the combat with devils from what it was in the first days of solitaries in the desert, when so vehement and persistent was the attack that the monks in turn were forced to watch and pray to guard their brethren while they slept.

Among these instructions we may recall here two of Abbot Isaac on Prayer (Conferences IX and X), in which he emphasizes the well-known lesson of "remote preparation," divides Prayer into supplication for pardon, vows of amendment, intercession and thanksgiving, and gives counsel on the Prayer of Simplicity. Others of note are that of Abbot Joseph in Conference XVI on friendship, in which he agrees with Cicero that the bond of concord can only exist between men of like purity and virtue, and that of Abbot Piamun in the eighteenth interview on the three classes of monks, Cœnobites, Anchorites, Sarabaites, "of which two are excellent, the third is lukewarm in nature and by all means to be avoided." Of interest in worldly matters is the seventeenth Conference, in which Abbot Joseph talks on the ethics of keeping or breaking promises, induced by the perplexity of Cassian and Germanus as to whether they ought forthwith to return, as they have promised, to their monastery in Bethlehem or to stay longer to derive further much needed spiritual benefit in Egypt. They are told that "if they really believe that their souls will profit more from further stay among the abbots of the desert than by returning to Bethlehem, they had better take upon themselves the guilt of one lie or one broken promise, which, after all, is only one sin committed once for all, than lose spiritual stimulus and thereby fall into permanently tepid life"; for one's word is not as important as one's spiritual progress. This strange teaching from a Master of the spiritual life Abbot Joseph then endeavours to illustrate by words culled from Holy Scripture.[56]

The plaint of Germanus is also worthy of notice in which he mourns to Abbot Nesteros in the fourteenth Conference, on spiritual learning, that his "humble knowledge of secular letters" does easily distract him in time of prayer; so that "when chanting psalms or imploring mercy for his sins the shameless memory of poetry rises before him, or pictures of warring heroes in pagan tale hover before the eyes of his mind" (c. 12). So Jerome feared in the vision on his bed of sickness; so Augustine accused himself in the *Confessions*. Yet the former defended study of Gentile learning in the letter written to the Roman orator who had been induced by Rufinus to demand why Jerome quoted from such in his work; and Augustine taught that knowledge of history and science avails in the study of Holy Writ.[57]

The charge of adhering to the views of Pelagius brought against Cassian by Prosper of Aquitaine, the indefatigable champion of Augustine's doctrine as expressed in the *De Prædestinatione Sanctorum* and the *De dono Perseverantiæ,* written to combat "Semi-Pelagianism" in Gaul in 428-429, just about the date of publication of the *Conferences,* was based on the celebrated thirteenth Conference, that held by Abbot Chæremon.   In his account of this Cassian clearly shows his sympathy with this teaching by his insistence on the real power of man's innate capacity for good bestowed on him at his creation.   His attitude may be briefly illustrated by two passages from this section, both quoted afterwards by Prosper in his book *Contra Collatorem,* aimed at Cassian, though it does not mention him by name.   The first comes from the twelfth chapter of Cassian's work, paragraph 5: "Wherefore we must beware lest we in such wise refer all the merits of the Saints to the Lord that we ascribe to human nature nothing save what is evil and perverse"; and the second from the same chapter, paragraph 7: "Therefore it cannot be doubted that there are indeed in every soul by reason of its nature the seeds of virtues implanted by the gracious act of the Creator; but unless these by the favour of God have been stirred to vigour they will not be able to attain to the increase of perfection."

Both in his own and in later ages Cassian exercised much influence in matters of ecclesiastical and religious concern. The leading part he played in affairs of his day is shown in two ways: first, by his journey with his friend Germanus to Rome in 405 as ambassador for the clergy of Constantinople and their exiled Archbishop John, and by his pleading with Innocent I against the deeds of Theophilus; and secondly, and more clearly, in the request made to him by the Roman Archdeacon Leo, afterwards the Pope Leo of the "Tome" so fiercely debated at Chalcedon, that he defend the Church against the heresy of Nestorius. This request bore fruit about 430 in the seven books of his treatise *Against the Nestorians concerning the Incarnation of the Lord.* His importance in later time appears in the wide use made of his writings. A short Epitome of the *Institutes* is extant under the name of Bishop Eucherius; [58] St. Benedict prescribed the *Collationes* as proper reading for his brethren, and recommended in the ending chapter of his *Rule* the *Conferences of the Fathers* and the *Institutes* as "instruments of virtues for loyal and obedient monks." And indeed the influence of Cassian on the Benedictine Rule is a matter familiar.[59] In the same sixth century Cassiodorus Senator in his *De institutione Divinarum Litterarum,* drawn up for the instruction in sacred literature of his monks at Viviers in Calabria, also bade that they "read diligently and gladly hear the *Institutes* of the Priest Cassian"; although he warned them against Cassian's words concerning free will (in the thirteenth Conference) as rightly censured by blessed Prosper, and mentioned an expurgated edition prepared by Victor, Bishop of Martyrites in Africa.[60] Another expurgated edition was published in the fifteenth century by Denys the Carthusian (van Leeuwen), the "Ecstatic Doctor," with the purpose, as he tells in his preface, of rendering Cassian's difficulty of interpretation and style easier for the simple reader.[61] The ill-fated matter of the thirteenth Conference is here replaced by other doctrine through the zeal of Denys.[62] The work of Cassian, or some part of it, was also translated into Greek.[63]

As may be readily understood through his Pelagian tendency, Cassian has never received canonization in the Western Church, though he is usually alluded to informally as *beatus*.[64] In the East he has received higher honour, and is included among the Saints of the Church's kalendar. It is interesting also to note that his name was found among the "faults and follies" of the second of the draft kalendars of Cranmer, prepared as studies for the Prayer Book of 1549.[65]

CHAPTER VIII

SECULAR PROSE: MARTIANUS CAPELLA

We have travelled far since we left our pagan writers. But if after this long course of study of sacred things in works of Christian poets and teachers and saints, if after these many pages given to matters theological and spiritual alike, we turn back for a moment to secular literature, we find its record in prose as well as in the verse of Claudian and Namatianus, though unmarked by their spirit of devotion to Rome. For evidence points to the earlier part of the fifth century [1] as the time when that old gentleman with hoary head, Martianus Minneius Felix Capella, to give him his name complete, was delighting his soul in the province of Africa with composition of a medley "Satire" full of heathen learning, and shot through with courtly romance after the model of the *Cupid and Psyche* of his own fellow country-man, Lucius Apuleius. Here again the hero is a god. The lady, however, is no untutored girl, but a learned maid, the most accomplished that may be found. The *Nuptials of Mercury and Philology* was, possibly, the work of a Car-thaginian man-of-law, composed in his hours of leisure from the "strife of forensic rabble" which, he complains, dulled his vision of better things.[2] Its matter is cast in the form of a *Satura Menippea*, in which prose is mingled with verse in no fewer than fifteen different metres, and dialogue finds place side by side with narrative. Its crude and rough style drew from Scaliger the description of "barbarus scrip-tor" for its author.[3] Capella tells us himself that this is an old man's tale. And it resembles indeed an unfiltered stream poured out in careless haste with blending of solid learning and rustic fancy till it fills nine volumes with its copious flow. As no one save determined students of Latin is likely to read it in the original and there is no English translation, it may be worth while to give in some detail the chief features of its strange content.

The first "scene" shows us Martianus Capella senior engaged in meditation, which he suddenly interrupts with a jovial song carolled forth in honour of the God of Marriage, to the astonishment of his son, who cannot think such levity becoming in one of Capella's reverend appearance and years. The father explains that he is recalling to mind a "fabella," which Satura [4] devised for his instruction in the winter evenings, and proceeds to tell the tale straightway, after this manner. Once on a time Mercury would get him a wife, stimulated thereto by the loves of his fellow-Gods and by his mother who deemed him full ready for the wedding day. Then followed long pondering as to who the maid should be; for Sophia would not wed, because she was dear to Pallas, and Mantice loved Apollo, and Psyche was vowed to Cupid. At length by counsel of Virtue the would-be bridegroom set out in her company to consult his brother Apollo. Through shrines and caves they sought him, in Helicon and in Delos, till Fame turned their steps to Parnassus, where they met the array of Fortunes of cities and kings and all peoples, encompassed by seven rivers on which the Fortunes are buffeted and tossed. Across the seven rivers they saw Apollo seated on a height with four urns about him—the *Vertex Mulciferi*, the fiery urn wrought of iron, the *Saturni Exitium*, the urn of cold and frost, the *Risus Jovis*, the silver urn, full of sweetness, and the *Junonis Ubera*, of the colour of the sea and filled with all the elements of air. From the two former Apollo brought forth affliction, and from the latter, joy for mortal men. Here, then, the needed counsel was given; for Apollo burst out into hexameter verse for the praise of the maiden Philology.[5]

Whereupon Virtue, overcome with joy, unbent from her usual severe demeanour, declaring that this maid was indeed the patron of the belauded Mantice, that she had bestowed much endowment upon Sophia and had trained Psyche in her crudeness. Mercury declared his willingness, and Virtue bade both brothers seek consent of Jupiter. As they journeyed, the heavens smiled on Apollo and the earth was bright with flowers at the coming of Mercury, the god of Spring, while the Muses made harmony in the spheres of the Planets. On Apollo's pleading Jupiter enquired the will of Juno; and since Phœbus had always a soothing way with him and she had a soft heart for lovers and liked Mercury to boot, she counselled that the marriage take place forthwith to keep him from mischief's lure. Yet Jupiter feared lest he be rendered slothful by the loving care of a wife and, steeped in nuptial joys, might refuse to obey commands; but Juno waxed eloquent on the sleepless vigilance of Philology, warranted to spur on her spouse.

Just now Pallas appeared on the scene, and Jupiter laid his hesitation before her. But Pallas as a true spinster was wrathful in outraged modesty at such an appeal. She had no love for marriages, and Mercury would no doubt be spoiled. Surely Jupiter could ask the married gods and the older matrons of Olympus to discuss so delicate a matter in Council? So Jupiter's secretary was bidden convoke an assembly, especially of Gods of Senatorial rank—the *Dei Consentes*. Many others also came of varying dignity, even such lesser powers as Health and Strength and the Fruits of Spring. From all the Sixteen Divisions of Heaven they flocked to this attractive debate. Janus was the door-keeper, and Fama announced the arrivals by name, while the three Fates took notes of the proceedings. When all in full array according to their differing glory were assembled, Jupiter delivered his desire in dactylic tetrameters catalectic; and all the Council voted that it should be as he willed. Juno then bade all foregather at dawn on the following day for the nuptial banquet, and the meeting was dismissed.

In the watches of the night Philology pondered anxiously on her coming marriage; for she feared lest her mortal limbs might not be able to endure the fiery sphere of Heaven, till her mother, Phronesis, brought her raiment wrought for protection against this peril. And now the dawn broke, and maidens and Muses each in varying metre chanted songs at the doors of Philology's home. Four sober matrons, Prudence, Justice, Temperance, and Courage, came to seek the bride, and the three Graces bestowed gifts upon her brow and lips and breast. Then appeared a royal chair in which the maid should travel to Heaven in charge of the reverend Lady Athanasia. No mortal might travel therein, not even Philology herself till she had disgorged the burden of learning she carried within her. And therefore a marvel; for from her mouth there flowed forth matter which was speedily converted into books of all kinds and appearances. At length she was exhausted by the effort of giving out, and received gladly a sweet draught from the Lady Apotheosis, who stood near to consecrate the stream of books. This draught bestowed the gift of immortality, and for it Philology offered thanksgiving.

Now she entered the chair, but the ascent was so difficult that she sought help of her dear fosterchild Labour, who travelled with her to Heaven. On her way she met Juno, who explained to her the office of those who dwell betwixt Heaven and Earth: the Guardian Angels, the Heroes, and the Manes. Through the Planets they journeyed on, till they reached the palace of Jupiter in the Milky Way, and found the Gods assembled there. Mercury came forward to greet his bride, attended not only by fellow-deities and the sons of Jupiter, but by the souls of great men of olden days, Linus and Homer and the Mantuan bard, Orpheus and Aristoxenus making melody, Plato and Archimedes rolling golden spheres, burning Heraclitus, Thales steeped in water and Democritus girt about by atoms. Philosophers, too, were there: Aristotle seeking Entelechy through the heights of heaven, Epicurus bearing roses and violets and all enticements of pleasure, Zeno escorting a lady of discretion. When all were seated, the mother of the bride asked that the Lex Poppæa be now read and that the gifts of bridegroom to bride be offered, a service performed by Phœbus, who presented seven fair slaves from Mercury's home. These were seven of the nine Liberal Arts, and each in order now described the principles of her skill.

The Art of Grammar spoke first. She was indeed of great age, but most attractive grace, and bore in her arms medicines whereby faults of speech might be remedied. Her flood of exposition was at length interrupted by Minerva *propter superi senatus Iovisque fastidium;* and Dialectic took her place, a figure somewhat paler in complexion, with keen and flashing eyes and curling hair around her head. A serpent was coiled in one hand, and in the other lay waxen tablets furnished with a hook to draw men toward the serpent's bite. Whereat Bromius attempted a joke, but was sternly suppressed by Pallas, who said the lady was no subject for mirth. A nod from the impatient Mercury brought her long periods to an end, and with a parting shot at Bromius, which cast awe on many of the Gods, she made way for Rhetoric, a tall and distinguished woman, girt with helmet and glittering weapons. The crash of her arms in conflict was like thunder-bolts of Jupiter. This speaker made a deep impression on the Congress by her familiarity with Pallas and Mercury. On her retiring she saluted the head of Philology with a resounding embrace; for she could do nothing quietly, even had she wished. Geometry, who next appeared, had the good sense to bring her lecture to an end herself by snatching his works from Euclid, who was present, and offering them to the audience if they would know further of her art; whereupon she was judged most skilled and well-pleasing in charm. By this time Pleasure was growing anxious and whispered, in hexameters, to Mercury her wonder that he could put off nuptial joys so long. Venus also tried to persuade him with her eyes, till checked by a grim look from Juno.

The next discourse, given by Arithmetic, was followed by so much admiration that Phœbus forbore to introduce the sixth maiden, and there was reverential silence for a space, broken suddenly by a loud snore from Silenus, who had fallen asleep through weariness or premature festivity. At this the Assembly shook with laughter, and Cupid woke him up with a slap of the hand. Satura vigorously disapproved of this merriment in one of those short dialogues with Capella which break the tale now and again; but Astronomy now arrived in a ball of light and held forth till Venus once more protested at the delay. Mars uttered long yawns, and Luna declared she could only spare time for one more speaker, as much of her course was yet to run. No time, then, remained for Medicine and Architecture; besides, they were busily engaged among men on earth. Jupiter decided that Harmony should bring the learned proceedings to an end; she was skilled to soothe cares and delighted all with her song ere she passed to expound the matter of her art.

When she had ended, Jupiter arose and the whole company went with joy unto the marriage feast.

Such is the story of the work that was to reign supreme as a manual of instruction during the Middle Ages. Its only interest to us lies in the extraordinary influence it exercised on future programmes of learning; for it was largely through its currency that the famous Seven Liberal Arts of the *trivium* and *quadrivium* were so firmly defined and established in the pedagogy of later days. It was not in itself pioneer in describing these Arts, for it drew upon the work to which that fame belongs, Varro's *Disciplinarum Libri Novem* and in which Varro had described the Medicine and Architecture for which Capella found no space. St. Augustine followed Varro in writing of the Arts. He tells at the end of his life [6] that he once began to write *Disciplinarum Libri* when he was awaiting his baptism in Milan; that he only finished the work on Grammar, and, after his baptism and return to Africa, six books on Music; [7] that he had, however, begun treatises on Dialect, Rhetoric, Geometry, Arithmetic, and Philosophy. It has not been difficult to understand why Augustine in his horror of theurgy and magic should prefer Philosophy, sister of Theology, to Astronomy, whose presence might lead to acquaintance with Astrology, her less worthy relative.

Yet it was to neither of these manuals that Gregory of Tours already in the sixth century referred as the standard of pedagogical training in his time. In the ending of his *History of the Franks* he begs any priest who has been instructed in the Seven Arts by Martianus, that is, who has received a proper education, not to delete any of his words even should they be deemed lacking in grace. [8] It was very probably the influence of Cassiodorus in the similar work, *De Artibus ac Disciplinis Liberalium Litterarum*, written in the same century for the instruction of his monks at Squillace, which stimulated among Christian men study of the manual by the pagan Capella.[9] The sixth century saw also the editing of Capella's work by Securus Memor Felix, a Christian rhetorician of Rome; and in the ninth century we find Irish scholarship busy with its pages. Especially was it indebted for commentary to John the Scot, that lover of Capella who arrived at the court of Charles the Bald about 845 and brought the wrath of Prudentius of Troyes upon his head for his poisonous teachings on Predestination, for which Prudentius declared his study of Capella was to blame.[10] Another commentary was written in the ninth century by Remigius of Auxerre, famous as teacher at Rheims and at Paris, where he instructed Odo of Cluni in *Capella on the Seven Arts*.[11] Later on, John of Salisbury knew well his work.[12] In the *Anticlaudianus* of Alain de Lille the carriage of Wisdom is fashioned by the work of these same seven handmaidens. And indeed in this twelfth and the following century so great was the reputation of the *farrago libelli* of Capella that his bridesmaids supplanted colder conceptions of the Arts.[13] Not only did their doctrines fill the lecture rooms of universities where men studied the Three and the Four Branches of civilized learning, but in pictured representation alike of book, of glass, and of stone, they left their evident trace.[14] At Chartres, home of John of Salisbury, of Bernard and Theodoric his brother, the Liberal Arts of Capella found long and illustrious life. In the sculptured or pictured representations of cathedrals their figures are still to be seen, at Chartres and at Laon, at Sens and Auxerre, at Clermont and at Rouen. For in the Middle Ages the "Arts" were of greater interest to scholars than the classic poets and writers of prose from whom were drawn the precepts of which they told; so the *Hortus Deliciarum,* that picture-book made by the Abbess Herrad of Landsberg in the twelfth century for the edification of her convent, shows them to us as they sit in majesty with the emblems of their profession, while down below into the ears of poets evil spirits are whispering their pernicious words.[15] Martianus Capella had drawn his work from Latin writers, from Cicero and Vergil, from Varro and Pliny, and others of lesser note, from Solinus and Aquila Romanus and Aristides Quintilianus. The Middle Ages drew at third hand from the dry and dreary compilation he sought to vivify with his romantic frame. As Orosius provided a convenient refuge for those who cared not to probe into original records,[16] so Capella afforded a general education for students who cared not to learn from those who originally had created the details of his work.

Ex libris magistrorum. The Middle Ages preferred it thus. From this fifth century they garnered much harvest for the mind—their knowledge of universal history from Orosius, followed in future days by a line extending from Gregory of Tours to Otto von Freising,[17] their academic instruction from Capella, their concept of the meaning of history from Augustine's *City of God.* Not only in matters of Church and State, but also of education and intellectual training, this last age of the Western Empire, for the better or for the worse, was of deep and enduring import in the seeds it sowed during its days. For the worse. For it carried secretly the conception of far-reaching political power within spiritual domain, of spiritual dominion which should not only hold sway among the things of God, but should rigidly control the things of man, levying fear and torment in time to come. It taught men to receive rather than to create, to obey convenient dictates of authority in the realm of spirit and of mind, rather than freely and frankly to reason out the truths that await their disclosing to those who have patience and leisure to seek. The practical bent of Latin thought could not forget its present necessity in the lengthy theorizings of the East; nor indeed had its immediate sorrows allowed it to forget. And the very existence in itself of God, the Source and Lord of all, keeping within his will and knowledge the names of those who should be saved, was held sufficient motive for inspiration of man in his helplessness. To the few was it left to probe with reverent curiosity into God's dealings with the world, into the mysterious and hidden ways in which he might make usage of all created life as worker together with himself. But again, for the better. For by the very strife and disasters of its troubled course it brought light to the darkness of distant lands, uniting peoples in one common fellowship of the Church Catholic rather than of an Empire's secular bond. It nurtured and protected the growing Church by its ancient tradition and power. It held before mortal men the noble image of their integral part in that infinite progress of creation, which leads from God before the birth of history to God when time and its recording shall be over and gone. If the East of this century knew the throes of nascent belief, the West in problems of daily order and practice aided Christian men to live—by conflict with enemies that subjugated the physical dominion of Rome but were themselves conquered by her spiritual power, by rooting out of weeds of heresies that threatened to stay free growth and progress in grace, by transplanting from the East to a new soil those counsels of holy living which should bear so great abundance of fruit in future years. It left to the world, through Martin and through Monnica, some clearer understanding of the strange and quickening force of prayer in those to whom it is given to travail for men; it left, through Augustine, some further revelation of the witness declared by Paul and John, of a life that loses not its fellows as it struggles on and ever to lose itself in longing for that Wisdom which sitteth by the throne of God.

ABBREVIATIONS

P. L.   = Migne: *Patrologia Latina.*
C. S. E. L.   = *Corpus Scriptorum Ecclesiasticorum Latinorum* (Vienna).
M. G. H.   = *Monumenta Germaniæ Historica, Auctores Antiquissimi,*
                 (Berlin).
P. L. M.   = *Poetoe Latini Minores.*
P. W. R. E. = Pauly-Wissowa : *Real-Encyclopädie.*
C. R.   = *Classical Review* (London).
H. S. C. P.   = *Harvard Studies in Classical Philology.*
T. A. P. A.   = *Transactions of the American Philological Association*
                 (Boston).
C. J.   = *Classical Journal* (Chicago).
C. I. L.   = *Corpus Inscriptionum Latinarum.*

NOTES

CHAPTER I

[1] Mackail, pp. 266 ff.; Philip S. Allen, *The Romanesque Lyric*, 1928, p. 98.

CHAPTER II

[1] See Bibliography for Claudian and list of works of general reference.
[2] The dates assigned are: *De cons. Stil.*, written 400 (Vollmer), published Feb. 400? (Birt); *De bello Goth.*, 402; *De VI cons. Hon.*, 404; *Ep. ad Serenam* (*Car. Min.* 31), after Jan. 404 (V.), 400 or 401 (B.); *Laus Serenæ* (*Car. Min.* 30), after 398 (V.), 404 (B.); *De sene Ver.* (*Car. Min.* 20), before autumn 401 (V.), before 401 (B.); *In Iacobum* (*Car. Min.* 50) 401.
[3] *Life and Letters of the Fourth Century*, p. 217. The cause of his disappearance from the literary world is not known. One suggestion views him as living after 404 in retirement in Northern Africa on the estate of that wife whom Serena had aided him to win; Vollmer thinks he may have died on his way home from a honeymoon celebrated in Africa in 404 (*P. W. R. E.*, col. 2655).
[4] Suidas, *s. v.* Κλαυδιανός; Apoll. Sid., *Carm.*, IX, 274.
[5] Birt, ed., pp. 417 ff.; Koch, ed., pp. 311 ff.; *Ep. ad Probinum* (*Car. Min.* 41), 13 f.
[6] *De cons. Stil.*, I, 328 f.; II, 296 f. See Birt, ed., p. x.
[7] See on this power over two tongues Boissier, *Fin du Paganisme*, II, p. 238.
[8] *C. I. L.*, VI, 1710.
[9] Birt, præf. ed., p. xliv.
[10] *De cons. Stil.*, præf. III, 21 ff.; on the comparison with Ennius, see Birt, p. xix.
[11] *De cons. Stil.*, I, 30 ff.
[12] *Ibid.*, I, 291 ff.
[13] Zosimus (V, 11) is our only authority for this tale; see Bury, *Later Roman Empire*, I, p. 122.
[14] Bury, p. 120. For this second intrusion Stilicho was condemned at Constantinople as a public enemy: Zosimus, V, 11.
[15] III, 133 ff.
[16] Crees, *Claudian as an Historical Authority*, ch. VII.
[17] Glover, p. 220.
[18] *De bell. Goth.*, 213 ff.
[19] *Car.*, XXVI, 29 ff.
[20] Lines 708 ff. For these references see Birt, præf. ed., pp. xlix f.
[21] The place has been disputed: see Crees, p. 163 note; Birt, p. li.
[22] *De bell. Goth.*, 267 ff.
[23] *Ibid.*, 453 ff.
[24] Cf. Prudentius, *Contra Symm.*, II, 714 ff.
[25] *De VI cons. Hon.*, 127 ff.

[26] *Ibid.,* 300 ff.

[27] *De bello Goth.,* 95 ff.

[28] On the side favourable to Stilicho see Vogt, pp. 40 ff.; Hodgkin I, ii [2], p. 724; Crees, p. 175; against him Bury, *L. R. E.,* I, p. 163, and *Invasion of Europe by the Barbarians,* 1928, pp. 87 f. Among ancient historians see Zosimus, V, 29; Orosius, VII, 37.

[29] Boissier, II, pp. 246 f.

[30] Vogt, pp. 18 ff.

[31] Hodgkin, I, ii[2], p. 725, remarks this.

[32] Lines 135 ff.

[33] Mackail, *Lat. Lit.,* pp. 267 ff.; Glover, ch. X.

[34] *De Civ. Dei,* V, 26.

[35] *Hist. adv. paganos,* VII, 35.

[36] *Fin du Pag.,* II, pp. 242 ff.

[37] *De III cons. Hon.,* 163 ff.; *In Ruf.,* I, 334 ff.; *De VI cons. Hon.,* 185 f. See for these and other details noted here Arens, pp. 1-22.

[38] *De VI cons. Hon.,* 597 ff.; the other passage occurs in *De cons. Stil.,* III, 202 f.

[39] Birt, p. lxiv, note 5.

[40] Arens, p. 17; Glover, p. 240.

[41] *In Eutrop.,* II, præf., 39 f.

[42] *Ibid.,* I, 312 f.

[43] There is a spirited translation of this poem by Glover, p. 241.

[44] *Car. Min.,* XXXII.

[45] Birt, præf. ed., pp. lxiii ff.; also *De fide Christiana quantum Stilichonis ætate in aula imperatoria occidentali valuerit,* Marburg, 1885, p. x; Vollmer, *P. W., s. v. Claudianus,* col. 2656; Bardenhewer, IV, pp. 124 f.; Rolfe, *Claudian,* pp. 140 f.; Schanz, p. 32; Platnauer, I, p. xix. Two other Christian poems, Nos. XX (*Laus Christi*) and XXI (*Miracula Christi*) of the Appendix to the *Carmina Minora* in Birt's edition were assigned to Claudian by Camers in his edition of 1510, but are not of his work. The *Laus Christi,* under the title of *De Christo,* has been assigned to Merobaudes (see my page 45). Two little poems of Christian character are included among the *Carmina Græca*—Nos. VI and VII, both entitled Εἰς τὸν σωτῆρα; but Birt doubts (præf. ed., p. lxxiv) whether they are by the Claudian with whom we are concerned.

[46] To which Arens retorts by quoting Augustine: *Enchiridion On Faith, Hope, and Charity,* c. 4: "He who opposes these is either a total stranger to the name of Christ or a heretic."

[47] Yet we may remember Symmachus and Rutilius, among others.

[48] Duchesne, III, p. 6.

[49] We may here recall the fact that the official Roman "panegyric," as Boissier has traced it in its development from Cicero, Pliny, and Fronto, remained persistently pagan in character; it would be natural for Claudian to follow the tradition in his official capacity (*Fin du Pag.,* II, p. 220).

[50] I, 19 ff.

[51] I, 47 ff.

[52] I, 131 ff.

[53] For detailed argument on this evidence see Keene's edition, pp. 7 ff. The modern names of places visited by Rutilius are also taken from this work.

[54] I, 383 ff.

[55] I, 439 ff.
[56] I, 515 ff.
[57] Keene, ed., p. 231.
[58] *Miscellaneous Works,* vol. 5, 1814, pp. 435 ff.
[59] See pages 26 f.
[60] See Keene, ed., pp. 37 ff.
[61] Beugnot, vol. II, ch. XII, pp. 182 ff.; cf. J. S. Reid, *Encycl. Brit.,*[13] p. 942.
[62] See on this attitude to monasticism my page 184.
[63] *Les derniers écrivains profanes,* 1906, p. 251.
[64] Procopius, *De bello Vandalico,* I, 4.
[65] *Excusatorium ad Felicem,* 297 ff.
[66] Sirmond, ed. Apoll. Sidonius, 1652, *ad loc.;* Niebuhr, ed.[2] Merobaudes, 1824, p. vii.
[67] *C. I. L.,* VI, 1724.
[68] See my note 45.
[69] Niebuhr, ed. of 1824, pp. viii f.
[70] The following interpretations are given in his edition, pp. 3 ff.
[71] Cf. the equally laudatory description of Aetius quoted by Gregory of Tours from the History of Renatus Profuturus Frigeridus, a writer of the fifth century: *History of the Franks,* trans. O. M. Dalton, 1927, II, pp. 48 f.
[72] The career and writings of Sidonius have been fully and excellently described in various works mentioned in the bibliography.
[73] See Dalton, I, p. xxxiv.
[74] The Frankish nationality is inferred from the letter: Dalton, *ibid.,* p. xciii.
[75] Epp., I, 2; IV, 20; I, 5; III, 3; VIII, 3.
[76] *Ibid.,* II, 2; II, 9; V, 19 and *passim.*
[77] *Ibid.,* IV, 3; cf. V, 2; IV, 18; IV, 25; V, 17.
[78] In a letter (VII, 1) written to Mamertus in 474.
[79] See Dalton, *List of Correspondents,* I, pp. clx ff.

CHAPTER III

[1] The *Latin Heptateuch,* p. lv.
[2] For accounts of Sulpicius Severus see Glover, *Life and Letters in the Fourth Century,* ch. XII, and André Lavertujon, *La Chronique de Sulpice Sévère,* I and II, 1896-1899.
[3] Epp. 1, 5, 11, 17, 22-24, 27-32, ed. de Hartel, *C. S. E. L.,* XXIX, 1894; Gennadius, c. 19.
[4] This incident is of doubtful standing: see Glover, p. 301.
[5] He tells us himself (II, 9) that he continued his chronology till the time of Stilicho's consulship, *i.e.,* till 400 A.D.; and it has been observed (see Bernays, p. 3, note 4) that the story of *Chronica,* c. 33, agrees in substance with a letter written to Severus by Paulinus of Nola in 403.
[6] Cf. *Exod.,* XX, 8 (Old Version): "Memento diem Sabbatorum sanctificare eum" with *Chronica,* I, 17, 7: "Sabbato nullum opus facies"; and *Exod.,* XXI, 12 f. with *Chron.,* I, 18, 2; and Bernays, pp. 31 ff.
[7] Bernays, *ibid.*
[8] These are noted in the translation by Dr. Roberts. Lavertujon thinks that Sulpicius did not use the *Vetus Itala* of the Codex Lugdunensis, I, pp. 149 ff.

9 Ep. XXXI, 4 f.
10 Glover, pp. 291 ff.
11 Cazenove, in *Dict. Christ. Biog., s. v.* Martin, p. 845.
12 See Dr. Scott Holmes (*Christian Church in Gaul*, "The Tragedy of Priscillian," chs. VIII and IX), who defends Priscillian (as also Babut, *Priscillien et le Priscillianisme*, 1909, p. 120) ; Dr. Kidd (*History*, II, ch. XI), who sums up: "no heresy, perhaps, but a system which the Church's tradition could not assimilate" (p. 309) ; Dr. Burn (*Church Quarterly Review*, April, 1912, pp. 142 ff.), who pronounces him "a good man led astray into very serious heresies" (p. 144) ; and works cited by these authorities. The writings of Priscillian are to be found in the edition of Schepss, who discovered them, *C. S. E. L.*, XVIII, 1889. St. Martin was forced afterward (Sulpicii *Dial.*, III, 11 ff.), when in peril to his own life, to obtain respite for Priscillianists in Spain by joining in sacramental fellowship with Ithacius and his party; we read that he never attended a Synod thereafter.
13 Schenkl, ed., pp. 346 f. ; Bardenhewer, IV, p. 637. Another reading gives *tres libros.*
14 103 ff.
15 119 ff.
16 I, 98 ff.
17 I, 211 f.
18 I, 325 ff.
19 I, 245 ff.
20 I, 390 ff.
21 I, 409 ff. Cf. St. Ambrose (whose *Hexameron* was used as source by Victor: Schanz, p. 364), *De Paradiso*, 13, 61: "in quo licet advertere idolatriæ auctorem esse serpentem."
22 I, 453 f. Cf. St. Augustine, *Conf.*, IV, 9: "No man loses Thee, save he who refuses Thee: and he who refuses Thee, whither does he go, or whither does he flee, save from Thee in gentleness to Thee in wrath?"
23 II, 231 ff.
24 69 ff. This "inexactitude" is the only point in which the Abbé Gambier finds just cause of reproach in Victor's theology (*Le livre de la Genèse*, p. 58).
25 90 ff. (addressed to Christ as Redeemer). Cf. (with Gambier, p. 57) the Church's cry: *O certe necessarium Adami peccatum, quod Christi morte deletum est! O felix culpa* . . . (from the *Blessing of the Paschal Candle*).
26 It was doubtless for his free treatment of the Biblical narrative that Victor met with disapproval from Gennadius: Labriolle, p. 626.
27 *Par. Lost*, 10, 1078 ff. For comparisons, including some given here, of the work of these writers with that of Milton, see G. Sigerson, *Easter Song of Sedulius*, Dublin, 1922; and P. Parizel, *Saint Avite*, Louvain, 1859.
28 II, 54 ff.
29 II, 106 ff.
30 III, 225 ff.
31 Migne, *P. L.*, vol. L, coll. 1287 ff.
32 Mayor, p. xliii; Peiper, ed., pp. xxvi f.
33 Peiper, pp. xxv f. Mayor assigns him to the sixth century.
34 Mayor, p. xli; Labriolle, pp. 422 ff.

[35] See the Bollandist Life, Acta SS., 5 Feb., I, 667 ff., Antwerp, 1658; and Ado of Vienne, *Chron. ætatis sextæ*, Migne, *P. L.*, CXXIII, 105.

[36] Ep. LI (45), p. 79, ed. Peiper.

[37] *Lit. d. Mittelalters*, p. 398.

[38] II, 1 ff. Cf. *Par. Lost*, IV, 319 ff.

[39] II, 89 ff. Cf. the soliloquy of Satan as described by St. Ambrose, *De Paradiso*, 12, 54.

[40] II, 145 ff.

[41] II, 185 ff. Cf. *Par. Lost*, IX, 684 ff., 735 ff.

[42] II, 217 ff.

[43] II, 240 ff.

[44] *Par. Lost*, IX, 984 ff.

[45] II, 275 f.

[46] III, 358 ff.

[47] VI, 165 ff.

[48] III, 362 ff.

[49] VI, 190 ff.

[50] III, 103 ff.

[51] *Par. Lost*, 10, 888 ff. Cf. St. Augustine, *De Genesi contra Manichæos*, II, ch. XVII; *De Genesi ad Litteram*, XI, ch. XXXV.

[52] V, 156 ff.

[53] V, 696 ff. Cf. Rand, p. 204 f.

[54] In 1499; Schanz, p. 373.

[55] The name Cælius has been attributed to him on doubtful authority.

[56] *Cod. Vindob.* (85).

[57] Huemer, *Commentatio*, p. 17.

[58] I, 122 ff.

[59] I, 273 ff.

[60] I, 322 ff.

[61] II, 28 ff.

[62] V, 188 ff.

[63] IV, 251 ff.

[64] Ebert, I, p. 363.

[65] For other translations see Julian, *Dictionary of Hymnology*,[2] 1907, pp. 4 f.

[66] See Bury, I, pp. 244 ff.; Ludwig Schmidt, *Gesch. der Wandalen*, 1901, p. 35; and in the *Cambridge Med. Hist.*, I, 1911, ch. XI, p. 305.

[67] Leclercq, p. 207.

[68] Vollmer, ed., 1905 (*Mon. Germ. Hist.*), p. vi (with note); ed., 1914, p. viii and p. 237.

[69] Lines 11 ff. Cf. on this St. Th. Aquin. on *Romans*, ch. IX, and St. Aug., *De Grat. et Lib. Arb.*, XXI, 43, and see for these citations the note in Arevalo's ed. of Dracontius (*P. L.*, LX, col. 904).

[70] Lines 53 ff.

[71] 287 ff.

[72] 311 ff.

[73] I, 180 ff. Cf. *Par. Lost*, IV, 214; 246 ff.

[74] I, 245.

[75] I, 348 ff.

[76] I, 437 ff. Rand, p. 202, notes "It is strange that Dracontius, so far as I know, is the only poet of the story of creation who has described the feelings of our first parents when the blackness of the first night came on."

[77] *Par. Lost,* IV, 703 ff.; *De Laud. Dei,* I, 454 ff.

[78] I, 465 ff.

[79] II, 621 ff.

[80] II, 273 ff.

[81] Avitus, II, 176, 196, 214 (pomum letale), 241, 261; III, 101, 115; Victor, I, 417; Cyprian, *Genesis* 78.

[82] Lines 4 f. Although Fortunatus may very possibly have had "apple" in mind, the word "pomum" does not justify that translation here with certainty.

[83] *Par. Reg.,* II, 349; cf. *Par. Lost,* IX, 585, X, 487. Avitus himself may not have advanced as far as the definite restriction to "apple"; for when the devil first comes upon the pair, "carpebant iuvenes viridi de palmite mala," where "palmes" may mean "branch," not of a vine, but of any tree, and "mala" may mean any "fleshy" fruit.

[84] II, 210 f.

[85] Cyprian, 66 ff., 77 f. Cf. Du Cange, *s. v. pomum.*

[86] II, 208 ff.

[87] For enthusiastic comment on his work see Boissier, *L'Afrique Romaine,* 1895, pp. 261 ff.

[88] See Mark Pattison, *Milton,* 1900, p. 118; S. H. Gurteen, *The Epic of the Fall of Man,* 1896, pp. 128 ff.; M. Woodhull, *The Epic of Paradise Lost,* 1907, ch. V.

[89] Pattison, *op. cit.,* p. 99.

CHAPTER IV

[1] P. Pithœus, in his *Vett. aliquot Galliæ theologorum scripta,* 1586.

[2] Teuffel, III, p. 391.

[3] Two outbreaks of plague are mentioned as occurring about this time: (1) by St. Ambrose, *Comm. in Luc.,* X, on c. XXI, 9, dated variously between 387 and 389; (2) by Rufinus, *Hist. eccles. præfat.,* in which he speaks of a cattle-plague which coincided with Alaric's invasion of Italy; Piper, pp. 89 f.

[4] 105 ff.

[5] Fabricius, in his edition, col. 349; cf. Migne, *P. L.,* LXI, coll. 969 f.

[6] Wernsdorf, in his edition, p. 103.

[7] So concludes Schenkl in his (the latest) edition on the evidence of a statement made by the chronicler Hydatius that Paulinus, Bishop of Biterræ (Béziers) wrote in a letter of many dread deeds done in his region. But, as Schenkl himself admits, the suggestion is weak enough. The text owes a deep debt to this scholar, who restored it from the bad state in which it remained since the editing of Gagny. Migne assigns it to Cl. Marius Victor; the title in the *Codex Parisinus—S. Paulini Epigramma*—has caused also a suggestion of Saint Paulinus of Nola. The interpretation given here is that of Schenkl, ed., pp. 500 f.

[8] So at least Schenkl suggests from the words "care pater" in line 103.

[9] 15 ff.

[10] 30 ff.

[11] Dill, p. 316. Doubtless, as he remarks, "there may be a good deal of exaggeration in these descriptions, and a good deal of sacred rhetoric with a religious purpose."

[12] 11 ff.

[13] 27 ff.

[14] 554 ff.

[15] 820 ff.

[16] *Gesch. d. christlich-lat. Poesie,* p. 212.

[17] There is no authority for the name, which, however, was applied to the work by Sigebert de Gembloux (1030-1112 A.D.) in his work *De vir. ill. sive scriptoribus eccles.,* c. 34, as one well suited to the content; see Bardenhewer, IV, p. 641.

[18] Acta SS. Maii I, 1680, I, 69 ff.

[19] II, 181 ff.; see F. R. M. Hitchcock, *Class. Review,* XXVIII, 1914, pp. 41 f. The lines refer, it seems, to the invasion of barbarians in 406.

[20] Bellanger, p. 74.

[21] I quote from Haverfield, *Class. Review,* XIX, 1905, p. 127.

[22] *The Commonitorium of Orientius,* Oxford, 1903, p. 17.

[23] I, 51 f., 170, 197 f., 257 ff., II, 313 ff., 325 ff., 85 ff., I, 405 f., 387 f., II, 43 f., I, 585 ff. There are also five short poems of uncertain authorship connected with the name of Orientius, and two *Orationes* in iambic trimeter, surviving out of a total of twenty-four. The literary merit of these poems is insignificant.

[24] *La Fin du Paganisme,* II, p. 404.

[25] See Brandes, *Prolegomena* to his edition, pp. 266 ff., where he vigorously opposes the theory of Seeck, proposed in his edition of Symmachus, pp. lxxvii ff., that Paulinus was the son of Ausonius' daughter.

[26] 159 ff.

[27] 205 ff. Bury (*L. R. E.,* I, p. 199) justly quotes lines 296 ff. as illustrating Paulinus' "doggerel."

[28] Paulinus had indeed been appointed "keeper of the privy purse" by Attalus, the puppet king set up in Gaul as Emperor by Alaric and, later by Athaulf; but, as Paulinus complained, Attalus was helpless and forced to rely on the Goths for aid. See Bury, pp. 180, 198 f.

[29] 580 f.

[30] See his edition, pp. 315 f.

[31] An excellent description and criticism of Paulinus and his work found in Dill, 178 f.; 346 ff.

CHAPTER V

[1] Prosper of Aquitaine in his *Chronicle* places his death in 420. Cavlera (II, p. 63) favours the date 419 on the ground that no works ca from his pen after that year, which is however explained by inabi through illness. Grützmacher remarks that Augustine knew nothing Jerome's death when he wrote to Optatus of Mileve in 420: *Hieronyr* I, p. 97; III, p. 279.

[2] CVII, I.

[3] E. G. Sihler, *From Augustus to Augustine,* 1923, pp. 306 ff.

[4] CVII, 2.

[5] CXIV, I.

[6] CXXII, 4.

[7] CXXIII, 17.

[8] CXXXVII, 12.

[9] CXXXVIII, 4.

[10] XCIX.

[11] CVIII, 6.

[12] CXXVII.

[13] *Ibid.*, 5. Cf. LXV, 1: and Preface to the Comm. on Zephaniah.

[14] CVII.

[15] CXXVIII.

[16] CXXV.

[17] CXXX. This is the Demetrias also mentioned in connection with Augustine, on page 138.

[18] CXVIII.

[19] CXX.

[20] CXXI.

[21] CVI.

[22] CXVII.

[23] CXXIV.

[24] CIX.

[25] 406 A.D.

[26] The father of Vigilantius was an innkeeper; and Jerome repeatedly in coarse fashion charges the son with dissipated living; in the first paragraph of this work he calls him "iste caupo Calagurritanus."

[27] LXXXIII.

[28] *Contra Rufinum*, I, 3, 6.

[29] LXXIII, 6.

[30] *sc.* Theophilus and Anastasius.

[31] *Contra Ruf.*, III, 9.

[32] For references see Fremantle in *Dict. Christ. Biog., s. v. Hieronymus*, p. 43.

[33] *Contra Pelagianos*, III, 6.

[34] CXXXVIII, 1.

[35] CXXXIX, 1.

[36] CII and CV.

[37] XXII, 30; see A. S. Pease, *T. A. P. A.*, L (1919), pp. 150 ff.

[38] LXXI.

[39] CXV, 1.

[40] CXXXIV.

[41] CXLI.

[42] See (*Hieronymi LI*) the letter in which Epiphanius excuses to John, Bishop of Jerusalem, the enforced ordination of Jerome's brother, Paulinian, to serve as priest the monastery of Jerome in Bethlehem; and Fremantle, *Dict. Christ. Biog.*, p. 32. Sulpicius Severus indeed remarks (*Dial.*, I, 8, in Postumian's narrative of his visit to Bethlehem): "ecclesiam loci illius Hieronymus presbyter regit: nam paroechia est episcopi, qui Hierosolymam tenet"; but this does not necessarily mean that Jerome administered the sacraments as priest.

[43] Cf. Fremantle, p. 50.

[44] Cavallera, p. 338: "il est de ceux à qui leurs œuvres suffisent."

[45] *Dial.*, I, 8 f.

[46] The story appears at length in the Life *Plerosque nimirum:* Migne, *Patrol.*, XXII, coll. 210 ff. See Cavallera, II, p. 141.

[47] See Migne, *P. L.*, XLVI.

[48] LIV. This letter contains (8) the famous statement on the "observance through all the world" of Fasting Communion.

[49] XCII.

[50] CXXX.

[51] XCV.

[52] CLXXXVIII.

[53] CCVIII.

[54] CCLXIII. Cf. Tillemont, XIII, p. 222, who notes that Augustine had already expressed clearly his wish regarding gifts in a Sermon (356, coll. 1579 f.). He asked his people that no offerings of cloak or linen tunic and so on be made except for the common use of the Clergy House; a gift of a costly cloak, for instance, might be fitting indeed for a Bishop, but not for "Augustine, a poor man, born of poor parents."

[55] CCLXII.

[56] CXXXVI.

[57] CXXXII, CXXXVII.

[58] CLVIII f.

[59] CXL.

[60] CX, 6.

[61] CII, 38.

[62] CXVIII, 1.

[63] *Vita*, c. 8.

[64] LXI, 1.

[65] LXXXVII, 3.

[66] The Rogatists were a sect of Donatists, professing less extreme views.

[67] XCIII, 48.

[68] *Ibid.* Cf. similar teaching in Augustine's *De Baptismo*, dated c. 400, attacking the Donatist appeal to St. Cyprian, and *Contra litteras Petiliani*, dated 400-402; at the same time he declares firmly that deliberate choice of Baptism "per aliquam mentis perversitatem" at the hands of one separated from the Catholic Church forfeits for the baptized, not indeed the validity, but the benefit of the Sacrament (*De Bap.*, 3).

[69] LXXXVII, 7. *Contra litt. Pet.*, III, c. 49.

[70] LXXXIX, 3.

[71] LXXXVIII, 8.

[72] *Vita*, c. 12.

[73] CV, 4.

[74] *Vita*, c. 13.

[75] CXXVIII; cf. *Retract*, II, c. 39. The minutes of the Conference are given in Mansi IV, 7 ff., and, as summarized by Augustine, in Migne, *P. L.*, XLIII, 613 ff.

[76] *Codex Theodosianus*, XVI, V, 52, 54, 55.

[77] *Vita*, c. 14.

[78] CXXXIII, 2. Cf. CXXXIV, CXXXIX.

[79] XCIII, 4.

[80] *Ibid.*, 17, 18.

[81] The technical discussion of this struggle belongs to theologians, and may be sought in their works; for a few of these see lists of books at end.

[82] CXLV, 8.

[83] *De peccatorum meritis*, III, 1.

[84] *De gestis Pelagii*, c. 46.

[85] I, 11; cf. *De Civ. Dei*, XIII, c. 14.

[86] I, 15.

[87] I, 24 f.

[88] I, 21. Martyrdom for the sake of Christ avails for the as yet unbaptized in the same manner as Baptism (*De Civ. Dei*, XIII, 7).

[89] Cf. *Sermon* 174, sect. 9.

[90] I, 68; II, 48. Augustine teaches in the *City of God* (XIII, 23) that man was not given absolute immortality in Paradise, but gained perpetual freedom from death by partaking of the Tree of Life.

[91] These same refutations of Pelagian doctrine were given from time to time in simple language to the people in the Sermons; cf. here *Sermons* 154 ff.

[92] *De dono Perseverantiæ*, c. 53.

[93] Letter of Pelagius, in *P. L.*, XXXIII, coll. 1099 ff., of Jerome, CXXX; of Augustine, CLXXXVIII.

[94] Sect. 21.

[95] Cf. *Sermon* 156.

[96] It has, of course, repeatedly been pointed out that the Bishops would be inclined *à priori* to be favourable to Pelagius in that the Eastern Church was especially zealous in maintaining the doctrine of freedom of will.

[97] *Sermon* 131, end. For the documents sent by Councils and Bishops to Innocent see *Epp.* CLXXV ff., for his answers *Epp.* CLXXXI ff.

[98] *Retract.*, II, 67.

[99] See *Sermon* 26, wherein the Bishop declares that his own human heart is not unmoved by the thought of those who perish unbaptized (*Sect.* 15). We may compare the troubled perplexity regarding the suffering of little children, which he shows in his letter to Jerome on the origin of souls (CLXVI). The teaching here developed had already found expression in 397, in the work *On divers questions addressed to Simplicianus;* Batiffol, p. 353.

[100] *Contra Julianum Pelagianum*, 422 A.D.; *Contra secundam Juliani responsionem imperfectum opus*, 429-430 A.D. For study of these matters before, during, and after the time of Augustine, see Dr. N. P. Williams, *The Ideas of the Fall and of Original Sin*, 1927, with bibliography given in his preface and notes, and *The Doctrine of Grace*, 1930.

[101] CCXI. From this letter sprang the Rule of Augustinian Religious orders.

[102] These "acts" are included by Migne among the Letters as No. CCXIII.

[103] See pages 6 and 81.

[104] CLXXXIX. Augustine also wrote him in 417 a long letter on the Donatist Controversy (CLXXXV).

[105] CCXX.

[106] CCXXVIII; reproduced by Possidius, *Vita*, c. 30.

[107] CCXXIX ff.

[108] CCXXIX, *sect.* 2.

[109] I have been constantly indebted in this section to the excellent commentary by Heinrich Scholz; also to the works of Troeltsch, Mausbach, Seidel, Figgis, and others, mentioned in the bibliography for Saint Augustine. Augustine himself described shortly his *City of God* in the *Retractationes*, ii, 43, 1 f.

[110] The feeling of Augustine toward Rome has been a disputed point; various views of modern writers are given shortly in *The Sources of the First Ten Books of Augustine's De Civitate Dei*, by S. Angus, Princeton, 1906. With the indifference expressed above (*Quantum enim pertinet ad hanc vitam mortalium, quæ paucis diebus ducitur et finitur, quid interest sub cuius imperio vivat homo moriturus, si illi qui imperant ad impia et iniqua non cogant?* Civ. Dei, V, 17), and the re-

peated warning that Rome will pass away with the rest of the world in God's good time (as in *Sermones,* 81 and 105), we may compare Augustine's praises of the natural virtues of the ancient Romans expressed in *Civ. Dei,* V, cc. 12, 17, and 18; for which, as Augustine declares, they have received their temporal and passing reward in this world. The truth seems to be that he cared so passionately for the City of God that he could bear without undue perturbation the news of the fall of the Roman city on earth, especially in its state of present wickedness and devotion to worship of demons (*Civ. Dei,* II, 19; XVIII, 41). Angus contrasts the human cry of anguish wrung from Jerome (*Ep.* 127, quoted by me on page 111) with Augustine's calmer words in his sermon *De urbis excidio* (Migne, *P. L.,* XL, coll. 715 ff.).

111 Augustine writes with sadness of Plotinus and his followers that they see veiled in shadow and from a far distance the Fatherland which is their goal, but perceive not the Way by which they must travel: *O si cognovisses Dei gratiam per Iesum Christum Dominum nostrum ipsamque eius incarnationem, qua hominis animam corpusque suscepit, summum esse exemplum gratiæ videre potuisses* (*Civ. Dei,* X, 29). See on his debt to Plotinus and his contempt for the "magic" practices of later Neoplatonism, Dean Inge, *Christian Mysticism,* 1921, pp. 128 ff. Harnack has an interesting note (*Die Mission und Ausbreitung des Christentums,* Eng. trans.², vol. I, 1908, page 505) on the difference between Augustine and Jerome in their treatment of Porphyry; Augustine describes him as *"philosophus nobilis, magnus gentilium philosophus, doctissimus philosophorum, quamvis Christianorum acerrimus inimicus,"* Jerome as *"stultus, impius, blasphemus, vesanus, impudens, sycophantes, calumniator ecclesiæ, rabidus adversus Christum canis."*

112 *De Civ. Dei,* XIV, 3; cf. XIX, 13.
113 XIV, 11.
114 *Ibid.*
115 XXI, 25.
116 XII, 7; cf. XI, 22.
117 XIV, 13.
118 XIV, 11.
119 XIII, 23.
120 XV, 4 f.
121 XV, 7.
122 XV, 1.
123 XIX, 15. See A. J. Carlyle, *History of Mediæval Political Theory in the West,* I, pp. 126 f.
124 II, 19.
125 XVIII, 2.
126 XIX, 16.
127 IV, 3.
128 *Rep.,* 433, A, E.
129 II, 21.
130 XIX, 21.
131 IV, 4: *Remota itaque iustitia quid sunt regna nisi magna latrocinia?* This famous sentence, as is well known, evoked the theory that Augustine condemned the State *per se.* Scholz (pp. 102 ff.) deems it "wie er dasteht, ein reguläres Todesurteil über den Staat" in its pagan form, because of the lack of Divine justice. He thinks, however, that the text may be corrupt, and admits that Augustine, in practical as dis-

248 NOTES

tinct from theoretical conclusion, did admit merit to the State and a measure of *iustitia civilis.*

132 Ep. 138, 18. Cf. Mausbach, p. 340.
133 XIX, 24. Cf. II, 21, where Augustine calls his own definition "more practicable" (*probabilior*).
134 The distinction of Faith and Unbelief as the basic difference between the members of the two Cities is emphasized in the Commentary of Scholz.
135 I, 35. Cf. XVIII, 47.
136 XIX, 17.
137 See his work, pp. 21 ff.
138 Scholz remarks (p. 108) on the chapters from *De Civ. Dei,* IV, 15; V, 19; IV, 3: "Das ganze Programm des mittelalterlichen Priesterstaates ist in diesen Deduktionen enthalten oder kann wenigstens aus ihnen herausgelesen werden."
139 See A. J. Carlyle, *Hist. Med. Pol. Theory,* I, pp. 150 ff., p. 169, on the influence of St. Augustine on St. Gregory the Great's teaching regarding the absolute God-given authority of rulers, influence drawn from *De Civ. Dei,* V, 19 and 21.
140 XX, 9; XVI, 2.
141 See Mausbach, pp. 344 ff; Seidel, pp. 45 ff.
142 Troeltsch, pp. 77 ff.
143 XIX, 19. Of this passage Dom Cuthbert Butler (*Western Mysticism,*2 p. 297) remarks that it "set the standard in the West" for the mixed life, contemplative and active.
144 XIX, 27 f.
145 He was probably influenced in his conception of the Two Cities and in his apocalyptic teaching by Ticonius, a Donatist of his own country of Africa, who lived toward the end of the fourth century. Ticonius wrote a Commentary on the Apocalypse, now lost, though part of its content may be found in the *Tyconius-Studien* of Hahn (see Scholz, pp. 78 ff.). Augustine dealt at some length in his *De doctrina Christiana,* III, 30 ff., with another work of Ticonius, the *Book of Rules* (for which see F. C. Burkitt, vol. III, i, *Texts and Studies,* Cambridge, 1894). On Ticonius (Tyconius) see also Paul Monceaux, *Hist. litt. de l'Afrique chrét.,* V, pp. 209-219.
146 Augustine was originally an adherent of early Chiliasm (*De Civ. Dei,* XX, 7); but, as he tells us, revolted from the carnal conception held of the reign of the faithful with Christ after their resurrection, and declared that the era of this present world was indeed the reign of a thousand years of the saints with Christ. Harnack remarks with emphasis (*Hist. of Dogma,* Eng. trans., V, 1902, pp. 152 f.) that this placing of the millennial kingdom here on earth by Augustine carries with it the theory that the Church has supreme authority over secular power; though, as he observes: "Augustine neither followed out nor clearly perceived the hierarchical tendency of his position." Harnack also notes the same preparation for spiritual dominion in Augustine's interpretation of the Bishops of the Church as the judges of the Apocalyptic vision.

CHAPTER VI

1 See, for the details of this section, J. B. Bury, *Ancient Greek Historians,* 1909; Moriz Ritter, *Die christlich mittelalterliche Geschicht-*

schreibung, Hist. Zeitschrift, CVII, 1911, pp. 237 ff.; Heinrich Scholz, *Glaube und Unglaube in der Weltgeschichte,* 1911, pp. 137 ff.; H. N. Figgis, *The Political Aspects of S. Augustine's 'City of God,'* 1921, ch. II; J. T. Shotwell, *An Introduction to the History of History,* 1923, pp. 322 ff., and *s. v. History* in the *Encycl. Brit.;* W. M. T. Gamble, *Orosius,* in *Church Historians,* ed. Peter Guilday, 1926, pp. 30 ff.

[2] Bury, *A. G. H.,* pp. 162 ff.
[3] *Histories,* III, 1. Cf. XXXIX, 19.
[4] *Ibid.,* I, 4; Bury, *A. G. H.,* pp. 200 f.
[5] *A. G. H.,* pp. 203 ff.
[6] R. D. Hicks, *Stoic and Epicurean,* 1910, p. 345. See the work of Scholz, pp. 137 ff., for this and the following remarks.
[7] *De Civ. Dei,* XXII, 2.
[8] *Op. cit.,* p. 45.
[9] Ritter, p. 262.
[10] *s. v. History* in the *Encycl. Brit.,* 1926, p. 529.
[11] Gennadius, c. 40 (39), thus describes him. His birth has been connected with Tarragon in Spain and with Braga in Portugal, where he seems to have carried on his ministry; Schanz, p. 485; Gamble, p. 34.
[12] Ep. CLXVI, 2.
[13] *Hist.,* III, 20, 5 f. In 414, after his arrival in Africa, Orosius addressed to Augustine a *Consultatio sive Commonitorium de errore Priscillianistarum et Origenistarum* (Migne, *P. L.,* XXXI, coll. 1211-1216); at the beginning he remarks: "I have been sent to you by God. . . . I do not know why I have come—without desire on my part, without compulsion, without mÿ consent I set out from my own country, driven by some secret constraint. . . ."
[14] The *Liber apologeticus de arbitrii libertate* is printed in the *Corpus script. eccles. lat.,* vol. V, rec. C. Zangemeister, pp. 601 ff., and in the *Patrologia* of Migne, vol. XXXI, coll. 1174 ff.
[15] *Prol.,* 11; *Hist.,* VII, 43, 19.
[16] *Prol.,* 9, 10.
[17] *Hist.,* I, 17, 3.
[18] II, 3, 6-8. Orosius' chronology, borrowed from St. Jerome, is marked by a beautiful symmetry; 64 years, he declares, intervened between the beginning of the rule of Ninus and the restoring of Babylon by Semiramis, 64 years between the first year of Proca's rule and the founding of the city of Rome by Romulus. About 1164 years intervened between the founding of Babylon and its capture by the Medes, and 1164 years between the founding of Rome and its invasion by Alaric: *Hist.,* II, 2 f.
[19] II, 19.
[20] IV, 12, 8.
[21] IV, 17, 5 ff.
[22] V, 1, 12.
[23] Cf. Dill, p. 314.
[24] V, 2, 5 f. Augustine had even written (*De Civ. Dei,* XIX, 17) of the "terror of the great number" of Christians to their adversaries; the evidence for this is to be found in Harnack's *Die Mission und Ausbreitung des Christentums,*[2] 1906 (Eng. trans.[2] by Dr. Moffatt, 1908), Book IV, cited by Dr. Welldon in his note on the passage.
[25] *The Letters and Sermons of Leo the Great;* Migne, *P. L.,* LIV, Ep. 52.

[26] Gore, *Roman Catholic Claims*,[11] 1920, pp. 106 ff. On Leo the Great and the See of Rome, cf. Edward Denny's *Papalism*, 1912, pp. 98 ff.
[27] VI, I, 24.
[28] *Cod. Theod.*, XVI, 10.
[29] VII, 36 ff.
[30] VII, 38 f.
[31] VII, 37, 9.
[32] VII, 40, 2.
[33] VII, 43, 4 ff.
[34] Gamble, p. 53.
[35] VII, 41, 8 f.
[36] It was known in later days under the title *Ormesta*, the origin of which is not clear. Possibly it was derived from *Or(osii) M(undi) Hist(oria)* or from *Orosii de miseria mundi*. See *s. v. Orosius* in *Encycl. Brit.* (drawing from the work of Mörner).
[37] Hodgkin, I, 2, p. 919.
[38] *De Gub. Dei*, VII, 40.
[39] VII, 39.
[40] Pauly in his edition brackets the word (Treveros) on which this tradition is based: *De Gub. Dei*, VI, 72.
[41] Ep. I, 5.
[42] *Vita Hon.*, 4, 19; Migne, *P. L., L.*, col. 1260.
[43] *Eucherii Lugdunensis Instructionum Lib.*, I, *præf. ad Salonium.*
[44] III, 44.
[45] IV, 30.
[46] V, 17 ff. It must be remembered here, in the midst of Salvian's sympathetic dwelling on the misery of the poorest and most lowly class, that the lot of the provincial officials, the *curiales*, was almost as bad, as may be seen from the twelfth book of the Codex of Theodosius. They were obliged to make good from their own private purses any deficiencies in the land taxes of their districts, and were subject to all kinds of grievous restrictions and penalties through their calling, from which they constantly sought escape by actual flight or by adopting some other career: see Dill, pp. 245 ff.; 320 f.
[47] V, 22.
[48] V, 44.
[49] VI, 40.
[50] VII, 6.
[51] *Italy and her Invaders*, I, 2, p. 923; Salvian, *De Gub. Dei.*, IV, 74.
[52] VII, 12.
[53] VII, 24.
[54] VII, 44.
[55] VII, 63 f.
[56] VIII, 21 f.
[57] *E.g.* see Dill, pp. 321 ff.

CHAPTER VII

[1] Ep. LXVI, coll. 641 ff. M.
[2] The translation is dated 404; see Migne, *P.L.*, XXIII, coll. 62 ff.
[3] Bury, *L. R. E.*, I, p. 387; where references to the Theodosian Code and to Mansi may be found.

4 Ep. XXXIX, Migne, XXII, col. 472.
5 Pages 51 ff.
6 Holmes, ch. VII, p. 195.
7 *Vita*, 10.
8 *Ibid*, 22.
9 *Ibid*, 24.
10 In certain MSS. the division is made into three dialogues; in others the first dialogue is divided into two parts.
11 *Dial.*, 1, 4.
12 *Ibid.*, 6 f.
13 c. 7.
14 Ep. XXII; 384 A.D.
15 c. 21.
16 Holmes, ch. VII, p. 208; Labriolle, pp. 512 ff. (Eng. trans., pp. 383 ff.), discusses the merits of the Life of Martin as "history." The Saint is delightfully described by Professor Rand.
17 The work of Sulpicius Severus on St. Martin was used freely as source by Paulinus of Périgueux in five books of his *Life of St. Martin,* written in hexameter verse about 470 A.D. at the request of Perpetuus, Bishop of Tours. A sixth book was added by him on later miracles of Martin, based on an account sent him by the Bishop. This version is vastly inferior to the prose of Sulpicius; it has been edited in the *Vienna Corpus,* XVI, 1888, by Petschenig. Other narratives are those (1) of Venantius Fortunatus, friend of St. Radegunde and author of the *Pange lingua* and the *Vexilla Regis,* who wrote in the sixth century four books of verse on the Saint, also based on the tradition of Sulpicius (ed. Friedrich Leo, *Mon. Ger. Hist.,* IV, 1881, pp. 293 ff.), and (2) of Saint Gregory of Tours (538-594 A.D.), written in four books of prose and telling of miraculous doings wrought by the intercession of Martin after his death (ed. Bruno Krusch, *Script. Rerum Merovingicarum,* I, 2, 1885, pp. 584 ff., and also H. L. Bordier, for the *Société de l'Histoire de France,* II, 1860, with translation into French).
18 As Dom Cuthbert Butler explains, *Historia Lausiaca of Palladius, Texts and Studies,* VI, 1, Cambridge, 1898, pp. 246 f.
19 Migne, *P. L.,* L, coll. 1249 ff. This is, of course, the Saint Hilary famous for maintaining the right of the Bishops of Gaul against the See of Rome under Leo I.
20 Hilary states to his own flock at Arles: "Hinc iam vobis Honoratum vestrum Christus reducit": *Sermo,* III, 15.
21 *Sermo,* III, 15.
22 *Sermo, ibid.*
23 Epp. Paulini, LI, 2.
24 Holmes, p. 286.
25 IV, pp. 563, 569.
26 c. 42.
27 *De statu An.,* II, 9.
28 Ed. Peiper, 29 f.
29 Carmen XVI, ed. Lütjohann, pp. 239 ff.
30 Ep. IX, 3, trans. Dalton, vol. II, pp. 179 ff.
31 Gennadius (*de vir. ill.,* c. 86) says "Nestorian," but, as Tillemont observes (XVI, p. 412), he seems to be in error. The letter is No. VII in the edition of Engelbrecht, *C. S. E. L.,* XXI, 1891 (pp. 206 f.).

[32] Letter V, ed. Engelbrecht.

[33] Engelbrecht, pp. xix, xxiii f. The letter is No. III in his edition, pp. 168 ff.

[34] For this work see *C. S. E. L.*, XI, 1885, also edited by Engelbrecht; the letter, No. III, of Faustus which called it forth is printed as a preface.

[35] Lines 105 ff.

[36] The correspondence is given among the writings of Fulgentius by Migne, *P. L.*, LXV, coll. 442 ff.

[37] "Pelagianism is a Phenix or at least a *revenant* as long as humanism lives": Fr. D. in *Laudate*, Dec., 1925, p. 241.

[38] The full title is *Commonitorium pro catholicæ fidei antiquitate et universitate adversus profanas omnium hæreticorum novitates.* (The word *Commonitorium* occurs repeatedly in the text, though the MS. title gives *Tractatus.*)

[39] c. II.

[40] c. XIII.

[41] c. XX.

[42] c. XXVI. Vincent has also been suggested as probable author of the Sixteen "Objections" to the Augustinian teachings which. Prosper of Aquitaine answered in turn in his *Responsiones ad capitula objectionum Vincentianarum*, Migne, *P. L.*, LI, coll. 177 ff. See on Vincent and Augustine, Kidd, III, p. 155.

[43] c. XXIII.

[44] See for the relation of the Vincentian Canon, on the one hand, to the statements put forward in defence of Christian truth by the General Councils of the undivided Church, and, on the other, to the doctrinal developments of later centuries, Bishop Gore, *The Holy Spirit and the Church*, 1924, chs. VI-VIII, and, for the latter relations, Edward Denny, *Papalism*, p. 593; for the application of this Canon to the doctrine of the Fall, Dr. N. P. Williams, *The Ideas of the Fall*, pp. 184 ff. (interpreted *"semper* quidem ab aliquibus, iam pridem vero *ubique et ab omnibus"*; cf. the Abbot of Nashdom, *Laudate*, Dec., 1927, p. 234). See also W. L. Knox, *The Catholic Movement in the Church of England*, 1923, chs. II-V, and *Essays Catholic and Critical*, 1926, pp. 107 ff., and cf. Karl Adam, *The Spirit of Catholicism*, trans. 1930, pp. 133 ff.

[45] Scholarship has suggested as author of this Creed not only Vincent, but also Honoratus, Hilary, and Cæsarius of Arles.

[46] c. LXII.

[47] See Bardenhewer, IV, p. 558; Gibson, *Prolegomena*, p. 183; Duchesne, vol. III (French edition), p. 272, note 2.

[48] *Instit., præf.*, 4; III, 4; IV, 31.

[49] *Ibid.*, II, 5, 3 ff.

[50] Dom Alard Gazet (Commentary on Cassian, Migne, *P. L.*, XLIX, col. 126) identifies this Office with Prime of later date; Procter and Frere, *New History of the Book of Common Prayer*, third impression (issue of 1925), do not connect the two.

[51] There is no evidence that Cassian knew of the life in Community of the Pachomian monks by his own witnessing of this; the Egyptian monachism which he saw in practice was of the Antonian or "Solitary" type: Dom Cuthbert Butler, *Historia Lausiaca of Palladius*, p. 236, p. 241.

[52] This story is told in English verse in *Legenda Monastica*,[4] London, 1905, pp. 35 ff.

[53] On accidie see Bishop Francis Paget, *The Spirit of Discipline*,[7] London, 1918, introductory essay and ch. I.

[54] *Instit.*, X, 2.

[55] If the teaching here given by Cassian does not reproduce the *verba ipsissima* of the Egyptian Abbots it represents the views held by them: Dom Cuthbert Butler, *Camb. Med. Hist.*, vol. I, 1911, ch. XVIII, *Monasticism*, p. 525; and *Historia Lausiaca*, I, pp. 203 ff. For the teaching of the Egyptian monks see the *Historia Monachorum in Ægypto* (Latin version, attributed to Rufinus of Aquileia, Migne, *P. L.*, XXI, 1849, coll. 389 ff., translated, with Introduction, by W. K. Lowther Clarke, in *Translations of Christian Literature*, Series I, London, 1918); the *Vitæ Patrum*, Migne, *P. L.*, LXXIII, LXXIV, 1849-1850 (Latin versions, reprinted from Rosweyd); the *Historia Lausiaca* cited above, written in 419-420 A.D. by Palladius (at one time Bishop of Helenopolis in Bithynia and later, of Aspona), as a description of lives of monks he had known, dedicated to a certain Lausus, whence its title; and, among modern authorities, Canon Hannay, *The Origin and Spirit of Christian Monasticism*, London, 1903, and *The Wisdom of the Desert*, London, 1904; H. B. Workman, *The Evolution of the Monastic Ideal*, London, 1913.

[56] c. VIII. For scathing condemnation of Abbot Joseph's decision see Kenneth E. Kirk, *Conscience and Its Problems*, London, 1927, pp. 184 ff.

[57] Jerome, Ep. LXX; c. 397 A.D. See also, for Augustine, *De doct. Christ.*, II, cc. 16, 25 ff.; and, for these references, the long and learned discussion in the note of Dom Alard Gazet on Cassian's passage (Migne, *P. L.*, XLIX, coll. 975 ff.) regarding the utility of secular studies for monks; and Comparetti, *Vergil in the Middle Ages* (trans. Benecke), London, 1895, pp. 82 f.

[58] Migne, *P. L.*, vol. L, coll. 867-894. Gennadius (c. 64) mentions an epitome of certain of Cassian's works by Eucherius, but see my page 197.

[59] See *The Rule of St. Benedict* with Commentary by Dom Paul Delatte, trans. by Dom Justin McCann, London, 1921, c. 42, c. 73, and p. xi: "The Rule is reminiscent continually of the Institutes and the Conferences of Cassian."

[60] *De instit. div. Litt.*, c. 29, Migne, *P. L.*, LXX, col. 1144.

[61] This is included in the great Carthusian edition of Denys published at Tournai, vol. XXVIII, 1904.

[62] *Ibid.*, p. 297, note.

[63] See Migne, *P. L.*, XLIX, col. 480, note of Dom Alard Gazet.

[64] His festival was instituted at Marseilles for the date of July 23.

[65] Procter and Frere, p. 336.

CHAPTER VIII

[1] So *e.g.* Sandys (*History of Scholarship*, I,[3] p. 241), Schanz, Rand. Evidence has been gathered for the dating as follows: (1) From his work, IX, 999, line 10, Dick, there seems reason to believe that he pleaded in the court of the pro-consul (though the line is corrupt): this theory, if correct, points to a date before the taking of Carthage by Gaiseric in 439, as pro-consuls were not found there after that time; (2) the words (VI, 637) *ipsa caput gentium Roma armis, viris sacrisque, quamdiu*

viguit, cæliferis laudibus conferenda seem to point to a time after the taking of Rome by Alaric in 410; (3) the words (VI, 669) *Carthago inclita pridem armis, nunc felicitate reverenda* to a time before the Vandal descent on Africa in 429. Dick in his edition of 1925 (præf., p. xxv, note 1) dates the work of Capella before 330, understanding *quamdiu viguit = omni tempore;* H. Parker likewise (*English Historical Review,* July, 1890, pp. 445 f.), on the ground that Capella wrote (VI, 657), Byzantium instead of Constantinopolis.

² VI, 577: Satura remarks to Capella: *ex illo, quo desudatio curaque districtior tibi forensis rabulationis partibus illigata aciem industriæ melioris obtudit.* But as Parker observes (p. 443) listening to disputes in the market-place does not make one a lawyer. The word *Cart(h)agin(i)ensis* is given, with Capella's full name, in the subscription at the end of Book IX.

³ G. W. Robinson, *H. S. C. P.,* XXIX, 1918, p. 160.

⁴ From this rôle of Satura in the story it has also been known by the title of *Satyricon.*

⁵ Φίλειν-λόγον: Hermes, according to Plotinus, being the λόγος. See H. O. Taylor, *The Classical Heritage of the Middle Ages,*³ 1925, p. 49, note 2.

⁶ *Retract.,* I, 6.

⁷ The six books on Music are extant: Migne, *P. L.,* XXXII, coll. 1082 ff.

⁸ *Hist. Franc.,* X, 31.

⁹ Sandys, *Hist. Class. Schol.,* I,³ p. 267. Cassiodorus does not mention Capella's treatise.

¹⁰ Migne, *P. L.,* CXV, col. 1294; *Nam ille tuus Capella, exceptis aliis, vel maxime te in hunc labyrinthum induxisse creditur, cuius meditationi magis quam veritati evangelicæ animum appulisti;* see A. B. Mullinger, *Schools of Charles the Great,* 1877, pp. 175 f. On the commentary of John the Scot, edited by M. Hauréau, see for up-to-date information the note (*Founders of the M. A.,* p. 336, 4) by Professor Rand, our authority on this mediæval scholar; also Manitius, *Gesch. d. lat. Lit. des Mittelalters,* I, 1911, pp. 335 f. For the commentary on Capella attributed in the British Museum MS. to Dunchad, an Irish Bishop of the ninth century, see Manitius, *ibid.,* pp. 525 f., and M. Esposito, *Zeitschrift für Celt. Phil.,* 1909, pp. 499 ff.; 1913, pp. 158 ff.

¹¹ Manitius, pp. 505 f., pp. 513 f.

¹² Migne, *P. L.,* CXCIX, col. 969.

¹³ Sandys, I,³ pp. 243, 553; for the description in Alain de Lille see his text edited by T. Wright, *Anglo-Saxon Satirical Poets,* London, 1872, 2, vii, pp. 304 ff.; also in Migne, *P. L.,* CCX, coll. 505 ff.

¹⁴ See Emile Mâle, *Religious Art in France in the 13th Century,*³ trans. D. Nussey, London, 1913, pp. 77-90.

¹⁵ Sandys, I,³ pp. 618 ff.; and reproduction on p. 559.

¹⁶ Ritter, *op. cit.,* p. 262.

¹⁷ His *"Two Cities: A Chronicle of Universal History to the Year 1146 A.D."* has lately been translated by Dr. C. C. Mierow, Columbia University Press, 1928.

SELECT BIBLIOGRAPHY

CHAPTER II

CLAUDIAN.

Jeep, Ludwig, *Claudii Claudiani Carmina*, ed., vols. I and II, Leipzig, 1876-1879.

Birt, Theodor, *Claudii Claudiani Carmina*, ed., *M. G. H.*, X, Berlin, 1892.

Koch, Julius, *Claudii Claudiani Carmina*, ed., Leipzig, 1893.

Platnauer, Maurice, *Claudian*, with English translation (Loeb Library), London and New York, 1922.

Vogt, Ed., *De Cl. Claudiani carminum quæ Stiliconem prædicant fide historica*, Bonn, 1863.

Hodgkin, Thomas, *Claudian: the last of the Roman poets* (Two Lectures), London, 1875.

Arens, Ed., *Claudian: Christ oder Heide? Hist. Jahrbuch im Auftrage der Görres-Gesellschaft*, XVII Bd., Munich, 1896, pp. 1-22.

Crees, J. H. E., *Claudian as an Historical Authority*, Cambridge, 1908.

Mackail, J. W., *Latin Literature*, London, 1895.

Moore, Clifford H., *Rome's heroic past in the Poems of Claudian, C. J.*, VI, Chicago, 1910, pp. 108 ff.

Rolfe, John C., *Claudian, T. A. P. A.*, vol. L, 1919, pp. 135 ff.

Vollmer, Friedrich, *P. W. R. E.*, *s. v. Claudianus*.

RUTILIUS NAMATIANUS.

Werndorf-Lemaire, *P. L. M.*, vol. 4, Paris, 1825: ed. with notes and excursus.

Itasius Lemniacus (von Reumont, A.), *Des Claudius Rutilius Namatianus Heimkehr*, ed. with translation into German verse and notes, Berlin, 1872.

Collection des auteurs latins, avec la traduction en français, publiée sons la direction de M. Nisard, *Rutilius*, Paris, 1884.

Vessereau, J., *Cl. Rutilius Namatianus*, ed. with translation into French prose and a detailed study of the author and his work, Paris, 1904.

255

RUTILIUS NAMATIANUS (Cont.).

Keene, Charles H., *Rutilius Claudius Namatianus De Reditu Suo*, Libri Duo, ed. with introduction and notes, and with translation into English verse by George F. Savage-Armstrong, London, 1907.

Heidrich, Georg, *Claudius Rutilius Namatianus*, ed. with introduction and critical notes, Vienna, 1912.

Zumpt, A. W., *Observationes in Rutilii Claudii Namatiani Carmen de reditu suo*, Berlin, 1836.

Rasi, Pietro, *In Claudii Rutilii Namatiani de reditu suo libros adnotationes metricæ, Riv. di Fil. e d'Istr. class.*, 1897, pp. 169 ff.

Schissel-Fleschenberg, Othmar, *Claudius Rutilius Namatianus gegen Stilicho, Janus* 2, Vienna, 1920 (rhetorical, grammatical, historical analysis of II, 31-60).

Beugnot, A., *Histoire de la destruction du paganisme en occident*, II, Paris, 1835, ch. xii.

Reid, J. S., *Rutilius Claudius Namatianus, Encyc. Brit., s. v.*

MEROBAUDES.

Niebuhr, B. G., *Fl. Merobaudis Carminum Panegyricique Reliquiæ*, Bonn, 1824.

Bekker, I., *Merobaudes et Corippus, Corp. Script. Hist. Byz.*, Bonn, 1836.

Migne, P. L., vol. LXI, *Carmen de Christo*, coll. 971 f.

Vollmer, Fr., *Fl. Merobaudis Reliquiæ, M. G. H.*, XIV, Berlin, 1905.

SIDONIUS APOLLINARIS.

Sirmond, Jac., S. J., *C. Sol. Apollin. Sidonii Opera*, ed. with notes, Paris, 1652.

Migne, P. L., LVIII, coll. 435 ff.

Baret, Eugène, *Œuvres de Sidoine Apollinaire*, ed. with introduction and notes, Paris, 1878.

Lütjohann, C., *C. Sollii Apollinaris Sidonii Epistulæ et Carmina*, rec. et emendavit, M. G. H., VIII, Berlin, 1887.

Mohr, Paulus, *C. Sollius Apollinaris Sidonius*, recensuit, Leipzig (Teubner), 1895.

Dalton, O. M., *The Letters of Sidonius*, translated with introduction and notes, vols. I and II, Oxford, 1915.

Chaix, L. A., *Saint Sidoine Apollinaire et son siècle*, vols. I and II, Clermont-Ferrand, 1866.

Bigg, Charles, *Wayside Sketches in Ecclesiastical History*, London, 1906, pp. 57 ff.

CHAPTER III

SULPICIUS SEVERUS: *Chronica.*
Migne, *P. L.,* XX, coll. 95 ff.
Halm, C., *Sulpicii Severi libri qui supersunt,* ed. *C. S. E. L.,* vol. I, 1866.
Bernays, J., *Ueber die Chronik des Sulpicius Severus,* Berlin, 1861.
Roberts, A., *Sulpicius Severus,* Works, translated with introduction, *Select Library of Nicene and Post-Nicene Fathers,* Series 2, vol. XI, New York, 1894.
(See also Chapter 3, note 2.)

CLAUDIUS MARIUS VICTOR.
Schenkl, C., *Claudii Marii Victoris, Oratoris Massiliensis, Alethia,* ed. *C. S. E. L.,* XVI, 1888, pp. 335 ff.
(This is the best edition. Migne (*P. L.,* LXI, coll. 937 ff.) followed the first edition by Gagny, published from the Codex Lugdunensis at Lyons in 1536, full of interpolations by its editor.)

HILARY, AND CYPRIAN OF GAUL.
Migne, *P. L.,* vol. L, coll. 1287 ff. (Hilary).
Peiper, R., *Cypriani Galli poetæ Heptateuchos: accedunt. . . .
Hilarii quæ feruntur in Genesin, etc.,* C. S. E. L., XXIII, 1891.
Mayor, J. E. B., *The Latin Heptateuch,* London, 1889.
Bardenhewer, O., *Gesch. d. Altkirchlichen Literatur,* III, Freiburg, 1912, pp. 432 f. (on Cyprian of Gaul).

ALCIMUS AVITUS.
Migne, *P. L.,* LIX, coll. 323 ff.
Peiper, R., *Alcimi Ecdicii Aviti opera quæ supersunt, M. G. H.,* VI, 2, Berlin, 1883.
Parizel, P., *Saint Avite, évêque de Vienne, sa vie et ses écrits,* Louvain, 1859.

SEDULIUS.
Migne, *P. L.,* XIX, coll. 433 ff. (ed. Arevalo, 1794).
Huemer, J., *Sedulii opera omnia, C. S. E. L.,* vol. X, 1885.
Huemer, J., *De Sedulii poetæ vita et scriptis commentatio,* Vienna, 1878.
Leimbach, K. L., *Ueber den christlichen Dichter Cœlius Sedulius und dessen Carmen Paschale,* Goslar, 1879.

SEDULIUS (Cont.).

Sigerson, G., *The Easter Song* . . . by Sedulius, the first Scholar-Saint of Erinn, Dublin, 1922 (Confuses Sedulius on the testimony of Trithemius, *script. eccl.* 142, with the Sedulius Scottus of the 9th century, on whom see Schanz, p. 369, and Huemer, *Commentatio*, p. 12). In Appendix I there are translations from Sedulius, Claudius Marius Victor and Avitus.

DRACONTIUS.

Migne, *P. L.*, LX, coll. 679 ff.
Vollmer, F., *Blossii Æmilii Dracontii Carmina*, ed., *M. G. H.*, XIV, Berlin, 1905; also in *P. L. M.*, vol. V, 1914.
Vollmer, F., *P. W. R. E.*, *s.v.* Dracontius.
Boissier, Gaston, *L'Afrique Romaine*, Paris, 1895; and *Roman Africa*, authorized English version of this book, by Arabella Ward, New York, 1899.
Leclercq, H. (Dom), *L'Afrique chrétienne*, vol. II, Paris, 1904.

GENERAL REFERENCE.

Gambier, Stanislaus, *Le livre de la Genèse dans la poësie latine au Ve siècle*, Paris, 1899.
Taylor, Henry Osborn, *The Classical Heritage of the Middle Ages*, New York, 1925.
Williams, N. P., *The Ideas of the Fall and of Original Sin* (Bampton Lectures for 1924), London, 1927.

CHAPTER IV

ENDELECHIUS.

Piper, F., *Severi Sancti Endelechii Carmen Bucolicum de mortibus boum*, ed. with translation into German and notes, Göttingen, 1835.
Buecheler, F. and Riese, A., ed. in *Anthologia Latina*, 1, 2, No. 893, Leipzig, 1906.

S. PAULINI EPIGRAMMA.

Wernsdorf, J. C., *P. L. M.*, vol. 3, Altenburgi, 1782, pp. 103 ff. (also rec. Lemaire, N. E., vol. 2, Paris, 1824, pp. 161 ff.).
Migne, *P. L.*, LXI, coll. 969 ff.
Fabricius, G., *Poetarum veterum eccles. opera chris.*, Basle, 1562, coll. 349 ff.
Schenkl, C., *S. Paulini Epigramma*, *C. S. E. L.*, XVI, I, 1888, pp. 499 ff.

CARMEN DE PROVIDENTIA.
Migne, *P. L.*, LI, coll. 615 ff.

POEMA CONJUGIS AD UXOREM.
Migne, *P. L.*, LI, coll. 611 ff.
Hartel, G. de, *C. S. E. L.*, XXX, Appendix, pp. 344 ff. (added
   to his edition of the Carmina S. Paulini Nolani after the
   example of Rosweyd).

ORIENTIUS.
Migne, *P. L.*, LXI, coll. 977 ff.
Ellis, Robinson, ed. *C. S. E. L.*, XVI, I, 1888, pp. 191 ff.
Bellanger, L., *Le Poème d'Orientius*, edited with introduction,
   Paris, 1903.
Ellis, Robinson, *The Commonitorium of Orientius*, a Lecture
   Oxford, 1903.
Haverfield, F., *Recent Literature on Orientius*, *C. R.*, XIX,
   1905, pp. 126 ff.
Hitchcock, F. R. M., *Notes on the Commonitorium of Orien-
   tius*, *C. R.*, XXVIII, 1914, pp. 41 ff.

PAULINUS OF PELLA.
Brandes, G., *Paulini Pellœi Eucharisticos*, ed. *C. S. E. L.*, XVI,
   I, 1888, pp. 263 ff.

GENERAL REFERENCE.
Clément, Félix, *Carmina e poetis Christianis excerpta ad usum
   scholarum edidit* (with notes in French), Paris, 1854.
Poizat, Alfred, *Les poètes chrétiens; scènes de la vie litteraires
   du Ive au Viie siècle*, Paris, 1902.
Kuhnmuench, Otto, S. J., *Early Christian Latin Poets from
   the Fourth to the Sixth Century*, Chicago, 1929.

CHAPTER V

ST. JEROME.
Vallarsi, D., ed. in 11 volumes, 1766-1771.
Migne, *P. L.*, vols. XXII-XXX (reproduces the edition of Val-
   larsi and gives the *Vita* by him).
Hilberg, I., *Sancti Eusebii Hieronymi Epistulæ*, Partes I-III,
   C. S. E. L., LIV, 1910-1918.
Fremantle, W. H., translated, *Principal Works of St. Jerome,
   Select Library of Nicene and Post-Nicene Fathers*, Series
   2, vol. VI, New York, 1893.

St. Jerome (Cont.).

Thierry, Amédée, *Saint Jérôme: la Société chrétienne en Occident*, Paris, 1875.

Fremantle, W. H., *Dictionary of Christian Biography, s.v. Hieronymus*, vol. III, 1882.

Grützmacher, Georg, *Hieronymus*, vols. i-iii, Leipzig and Berlin, 1901-1908.

Cavallera, Ferdinand, *Saint Jérôme, Sa vie et son œuvre*, Première Partie, tomes I and II, *Spicilegium sacrum Lovaniense*, Louvain, 1922.

St. Augustine.

Migne, *P. L.*, XXXII-XLVII.

Goldbacher, A., *S. Aureli Augustini Hipp. Episc. Epistulæ*, rec. *C. S. E. L.*, vol. XXXIV, Pars I, Epp. I-XXX, 1895; Pars 2, Epp. XXXI-CXXIII, 1898; Pars 3, vol. XLIV, Epp. CXXIV-CLXXXIVa, 1904; Pars 4, vol. LVII, Epp. CLXXXV-CCLXX, 1911.

Hoffman, E., *S. Aurelii Augustini De Civitate Dei Libri XXII*, rec. *C. S. E. L.*, XXXX, Pars I, Libri I-XIII, 1899; Pars 2, Libri XIV-XXII, 1900.

Welldon, J. E. C., *S. Aurelii Augustini De Civitate Dei, Libri XXII*, edited with introduction and appendices, vols. I and II, London, 1924.

Dombart, B., *S. Aurelii Augustini Ep. De Civitate Dei, Libri XXII*, vol. I, Lib. I-XIII, rec. A. Kalb, Leipzig, 1928.

Cunningham, J. G., *Letters of Saint Augustine*, translation, vols. I and II, Edinburgh, 1872-1875.

Holmes, Peter, and Wallis, R. E., *The Anti-Pelagian Works of Saint Augustine*, translated, vols. I-III, Edinburgh, 1872-1876.

Dods, Marcus, *The City of God*, translated, vols. I and II, Edinburgh, 1871, published also later in the *Select Library of Nicene and Post-Nicene Fathers*, Series 1, vol. II, New York, 1887.

Mozley, J. B., *Treatise on the Augustinian Doctrine of Predestination*, 1878.

Bright, William, *Select Anti-Pelagian Treatises of St. Augustine and the Acts of the Second Council of Orange*, with introduction, Oxford, 1880.

Cunningham, W., *S. Austin and His Place in the History of Christian Thought* (Hulsean Lectures for 1885), London, 1886.

Robertson, A., *Regnum Dei* (Bampton Lectures for 1901), London, 1901.

McCabe, Joseph, *Saint Augustine and His Age*, London, 1902.

Mausbach, Joseph, *Die Ethik des heiligen Augustinus*, Freiburg, 1909.

Seidel, Bruno, *Die Lehre vom Staat beim heiligen Augustinus*, Breslau, 1909 (in Sdralek, *Kirchen geschichliche Abhandlungen* IX, 1, 1909).

Simpson, W. J. Sparrow, *St. Augustine and African Church Divisions*, London, 1910.

Scholz, Heinrich, *Glaube und Unglaube in der Weltgeschichte*, Leipzig, 1911.

Humphrey, E. F., *Politics and Religion in the Days of Augustine*, New York, 1912.

Troeltsch, Ernst, *Augustin, die christliche Antike und das Mittelalter*, Berlin, 1915.

Lacey, T. A., *Nature, Miracle, and Sin: a Study of St. Augustine's Conception of the Natural Order:* the Pringle Stuart Lectures for 1914, London, 1916.

Weiskotten, H. T., *Sancti Augustini Vita scripta a Possidio Episcopo*, edited with introduction, notes, and English version, Princeton, 1919.

Batiffol, Pierre, *Le Catholicisme de Saint Augustin*, vols. 1 and 2, Paris, 1920.

Figgis, John Neville, *On the Political Aspects of St. Augustine's "City of God,"* London, 1921.

Sihler, E. G., *From Augustus to Augustine*, Cambridge, 1923.

Jauncey, Ernest, *The Doctrine of Grace*, London, 1925: ch. 5: The Pelagian Controversy.

Butler, Dom Cuthbert, *Western Mysticism: The Teaching of SS. Augustine, Gregory, and Bernard on Contemplation and the Contemplative Life*, London, 1927.

Gilson, Étienne, *Introduction à l'Étude de Saint Augustin*, Paris, 1929.

Williams, N. P., *The Doctrine of Grace*, London, 1930.

A Monument to Saint Augustine: Essays on some aspects of his thought, written in commemoration of his 15th centenary, London, 1930.

CHAPTER VI

Migne, *P. L.*, XXXI, coll. 663 ff. (Orosius); LIII, coll. 10 ff. (Salvian).

St. Augustine (Cont.)

Zangemeister, C., *Pauli Orosii Historiarum adversus Paganos Libri VII*, rec. *C. S. E. L.*, V, 1882.

Pauly, F., *Salviani Presbyteri Massiliensis opera omnia*, rec. *C. S. E. L.*, VIII, 1883.

Halm, C., *Salviani libri*, rec. *M. G. H.*, I, Berlin, 1877.

Gamble, W. M. T., *Orosius*, in *Church Historians*, ed. P. Guilday, New York, 1926, pp. 30 ff.

CHAPTER VII

Sulpicius Severus.

Migne, *P. L.*, XX, coll. 159 ff.

Halm, C., *Sulpicii Severi libri qui supersunt*, *C. S. E. L.*, vol. I, 1866.

Sulpicius Severus, Works, translated A. Roberts; *Vincent of Lérins, Commonitory*, translated C. A. Heurtley; *John Cassian, Works*, translated E. C. S. Gibson, with introduction in each case, *Select Library of Nicene and Post-Nicene Fathers*, Series 2, vol. XI, New York, 1894.

Rand, E. K., *St. Martin of Tours, Bulletin of the John Rylands Library*, January, 1927.

Watt, Mary C., Sulpicius Severus, *Vita S. Martini*, trans. from the French of Paul Monceaux, with an introduction by him, London, 1928.

Eucherius.

Migne, *P. L.*, vol. L, coll. 701 ff.

Wotke, C., *Sancti Eucherii Lugdunensis Opera*, *C. S. E. L.*, XXXI, Pars I, 1894.

Hilary of Arles.

Migne, *P. L.*, vol. L, coll. 1249 ff.

Faustus.

Migne, *P. L.*, LVIII, coll. 783 ff.

Engelbrecht, A., *Fausti Reiensis Opera*, *C. S. E. L.*, XXI, 1891.

S. Paulinus of Nola.

Migne, *P. L.*, LXI, coll. 15 ff.

de Hartel, G., *Sancti Pontii Meropii Paulini Nolani Epistulæ*, *C. S. E. L.*, XXIX, 1894.

Vincent of Lerins.

Migne, *P. L.*, L. coll. 637 ff.

Jülicher, D. A., *Vincenz von Lerinum, Commonitorium*, ed., Leipzig, 1895.

Rauschen, G., *Florilegium Patristicum*, V, Bonn, 1906.
Moxon, R. S., *The Commonitorium of Vincentius of Lérins*, edited, *Cambridge Patristic Texts*, 1915.
Bindley, T. H., *The Commonitory of St. Vincent of Lérins*, translated, *Early Church Classics*, London, 1914.
See also under *Sulpicius Severus* (in Ch. VII).

CASSIAN.
Migne, *P. L.*, XLIX-L (with the full commentary by Dom Alard Gazet, Douai, 1616, Paris, 1682).
Petschenig, M., *Johannis Cassiani Conlationes* XXIV, *C. S. E. L.*, XIII, Pars 2, 1886; *De Institutis Cœnobiorum et de Octo Principalium Vitiorum Remediis, Libri XII*, and *De Incarnatione Domini contra Nestorium, Libri VII, C. S. E. L.*, XVII, Pars I, 1888.
Lilley, A. L., *Prayer in Christian Theology*, London, 1925: Ch. III.
Trevelyan, W. B., *A Master of the Desert*, London, 1927.
See also under *Sulpicius Severus*.

GENERAL REFERENCE.
Alliez, L., *Histoire du monastère de Lérins*, Paris, 1862.
The Count de Montalembert, *The Monks of the West*, English edition, with introduction by Cardinal Gasquet, vol. I, London, 1896.
Cooper-Marsdin, A. C., *The School of Lérins*, Rochester, 1905.
Holmes, T. S., *The Origin and Development of the Christian Church in Gaul During the First Six Centuries of the Christian Era* (Birkbeck Lectures for 1907 and 1908), London, 1911.
Cooper-Marsdin, A. C., *The History of the Island of the Lérins*, Cambridge, 1913.
Butler, Cuthbert (Dom), *Benedictine Monachism*, London, 1924, ch. 2.
Armytage, Duncan, *Christianity in the Roman World*, London, 1927, ch. IX.
(See also Notes *passim*.)

CHAPTER VIII

Kopp, U. F., *Martianus Capella*, ed., Frankfurt, 1836.
Eyssenhardt, F., *Martianus Capella*, ed., Leipzig, 1866.
Dick, A., *Martianus Capella*, ed., Teub., Leipzig, 1925.
Monceaux, Paul, *Les Africains (les Païens)*, Paris, 1894, pp. 445 ff.
Manitius, M., *Geschichte der lat. Lit. des Mittelalters*, I, 1911.

GENERAL BIBLIOGRAPHY

Tillemont, Lenain de (Louis Sébastien), *Mémoires pour servir a l'histoire ecclésiastique des six premiers siècles,* vols. X, XII-XVI, Paris, 1705-1712.

Fauriel, C. C., *Histoire de la Gaule méridionale sous la domination des conquérants Germains,* vol. I, Paris, 1836.

Guizot, F. P. G., *Histoire de la civilisation en France depuis la chute de l'empire romain,* vol. I, Paris, 1853.

Histoire litéraire de la France, par les Religieux Bénédictins de la Congrégation de S. Maur, Tomes I-III, Paris, 1865-1866.

Ozanam, A. F., *History of Civilization in the Fifth Century,* translated into English by A. C. Glyn, vols. I and II, London, 1868.

Simcox, G. A., *A History of Latin Literature from Ennius to Boethius,* vol. II, London, 1883.

Ebert, A., *Allgemeine Geschichte der Literatur des Mittelalters im Abendlande,* Bd. I: *Gesch. der christlich-lateinischen Literatur,* Leipzig, 1889.

Farrar, F. W., *Lives of the Fathers,* vol. II, Edinburgh, 1889.

Manitius, M., *Geschichte der christlich-lateinischen Poesie,* Stuttgart, 1891.

Hodgkin, Thomas, *Italy and her Invaders,* vols. I and II, Oxford, 1892.

Boissier, Gaston, *La Fin du Paganisme,* vols. I and II, Paris, 1894.

Dill, Samuel, *Roman Society in the last century of the Western Empire,* London, 1899.

Gregorovius, Ferdinand, *History of the City of Rome in the Middle Ages,* trans. Hamilton, vol. I, London, 1900.

Glover, T. R., *Life and Letters in the Fourth Century,* Cambridge, 1901.

Bright, William, *The Age of the Fathers, being chapters in the history of the Church during the Fourth and Fifth Centuries,* vol. II, London, 1903.

Sandys, J. E., *History of Classical Scholarship,* vols. I-III, Cambridge, 1903-1908 (vol. I, 3rd ed., 1921).

Freeman, E. A., *Western Europe in the Fifth Century*, London, 1904.

Mommsen, T. and Meyer, E., *Codex Theodosianus*, ed., vols. I and II, Berlin, 1905.

Gibbon, Edward, *Decline and Fall of the Roman Empire*, ed. J. B. Bury, vols. III and IV, London, 1909.

Duchesne, L., *Histoire ancienne de l'Église*, vol. III, Paris, 1910; English translation by Claude Jenkins, London, 1924.

The Cambridge Medieval History, vol. I, The Christian Empire, Cambridge, 1911.

Monceaux, Paul, *Histoire littéraire de l'Afrique chrétienne*, Tomes 4-6 (on the Donatists), 1912-1922.

Teuffel, W. S., *Geschichte der römischen Literatur* (neu bearbeitet von W. Kroll und F. Skutsch), Bd. III, Berlin, 1913.

Bardenhewer, O., *Geschichte der altkirchlichen Literatur*, Bd. IV, Freiburg, 1924.

Haarhoff, Theodore, *Schools of Gaul: a study of Pagan and Christian Education in the last century of the Western Empire*, Oxford, 1920.

Schanz, M., *Geschichte der romischen Litteratur*, IV, 2 (Schanz-Hosius-Krüger), Munich, 1920.

Kidd, Benjamin J., *A History of the Church to A.D. 461*, vols. II and III, Oxford, 1922.

Bury, J. B., *History of the Later Roman Empire* (A.D. 395-A.D. 565), vols. I and II, London, 1923.

Labriolle, Pierre de, *Histoire de la littérature latine chrétienne*, Paris, 1924; English translation by H. Wilson, London, 1924.

Monceaux, Paul, *Histoire de la littérature latine chrétienne*, Paris, 1924.

Weyman, Karl, *Beiträge zur Geschichte der christlich-lateinischen Poesie*, Munich, 1926.

Raby, F. J. E., *A History of Christian-Latin Poetry*, Oxford, 1927, especially pp. 75-85; 95-110.

Rand, E. K., *Founders of the Middle Ages*, Harvard University Press, 1928.

INDEX

Accidie, 214 ff.
Adrumetum, in Tunis, 141 f.
Aetius, minister of Galla Placidia, 8, 44 ff., 81
Alain de Lille, 231
Alaric, the Visigoth, 4, 7, 19 ff., 31, 37, 111, 113, 125, 166, 170 f.
Aldhelm, 77, 90
Algasia, correspondent of St. Jerome, 114
Ambrose, Saint, 56, 126, 170
Anastasius I, Pope, 117
Anastasius, correspondent of St. Augustine, 135
Anthemius, Emperor of the West, 9 f., 11, 47, 49, 82
Anthony, Saint, 112, 182, 190
Apollinaris Sidonius, 8 ff., 12 f., 27, 34, 44, 46 ff., 53, 105, 178, 181, 198 ff.
Apronius, correspondent of St. Jerome, 120
Apuleius, 224
Arcadius, Emperor of the East, 3, 5, 18, 21, 169
Arians, 55, 66, 79, 88, 146, 186, 199
Arles, 4; Council of, 133, 199
Arts, Seven Liberal, 13, 228 ff.
Aterbius, 116
"Athanasian" Creed, 206
Athanasius, Saint, 114, 182 f.
Athaulf, the Visigoth, 4, 7, 40, 171 f.
Attila, the Hun, 8, 44, 173
Augustine, Saint, 6, 10, 15, 31, 34, 67, 98, 105, 118 f., 122 ff., 183, 204, 221, 230, 234
his philosophy of history, 158 ff.
City of God, 10, 110, 125 f., 147 ff., 158, 163, 232
Confessions, 125
Indiculus, 126
Letters, 126 ff.
Retractationes, 126, 140
Treatises written against the Pelagians, 136 ff.

Ausonius, 14, 34, 43, 103, 107, 181
Avitus, Emperor of the West, 8 f., 47, 82
Avitus, Alcimus Ecdicius, 11, 13, 51, 53, 65 ff., 85, 88, 90 ff., 198 f.
Avitus, correspondent of St. Jerome, 115

Bardenhewer, 34, 58, 77, 197
Barth, 51
Basilius, Bishop of Aix, 49
Bede, the Venerable, 90, 101
Benedict, Saint, 222
Bernays, 52
Bethlehem, 10, 108, 114 f., 117 f., 120 f., 123 f., 191, 206
Birt, 34
Blaesilla, daughter of Paula, 184
Boissier, 31, 103
Boniface, Count, 6, 44, 81, 145 ff.
Bordeaux, 103, 105 f.; Synod of, 56
Brandes, 107
Browne, Sir Thomas, 54
Bury, J. B., 159

Cæcilian, Bishop of Carthage, 131
Cædmon, 90 f.
Caelestius, friend of Pelagius, 119, 136, 140, 203
Cæsar, 172
Cæsarius, Bishop of Arles, 201
Capraria, island of, 40, 170
Carmen *Ad Uxorem*, 96 f., 101, 103
Carmen *De Providentia Divina*, 96 ff.
Cassian, 10, 15, 143, 206 ff.
Institutes, 206 ff.
Conferences, 217 ff.
Cassiodorus, Senator, 222 f., 230 f.
Castor, Bishop of Apta Julia, 206 f., 217
Chalcedon, Council of, 3, 222
Cicero, *Hortensius*, 125; *De Republica*, 152

267

"Circumcellions," 133
Claudian, 5, 7, 14 f., 17 ff., 41, 43
  De Bello Gothico, 17, 22 ff.
  De Consulatu Stilichonis, 17, 19 ff.
  De Salvatore, 33 ff.
  De Sene Veronensi, 29 f.
  Epistula ad Serenam, 17, 30
  In Jacobum, 32 f., 34
  Laus Serenæ, 17, 30
  Panegyricus de Sexto Consulatu Honorii, 17, 25 ff., 32
Claudianus Mamertus, 34, 49, 198, 200
Claudius Marius, *see* Victor
Commodian, 83
Constantius III, Emperor of the West, 6
Cyprian of Gaul, 51, 64 f., 88; *Heptateuch*, 65

Damasus, Pope, 34, 56
Darius, legate of Galla Placidia, 146 f.
Decretum Gelasianum, 77, 192
Demetrias, 114, 127, 138
Denys, the Carthusian, 223
Deogratias, correspondent of St. Augustine, 129
Dill, Sir Samuel, 97
Dioscorus, correspondent of St. Augustine, 129
Diospolis (Lydda), 59, 120, 139
Donatists, 130 ff., 155
Donatus, 131
Dracontius, 12, 34, 46, 67, 82 ff.

Ebert, 67, 98
Ecdicia, correspondent of St. Augustine, 127 f.
Eluso (Elsonne), 52
Emeritus of Cæsarea, Donatist, 132, 134
Endelechius, Severus Sanctus, 5, 93 ff.
Ennius, 19
Ephesus, Council of, 3, 193, 206
Epigramma S. Paulini, 7, 95, 102 f.
Epiphanius, Bishop of Salamis in Cyprus, 112, 116
Epistula Tractoria, 141
Erasmus, *Life of Jerome*, 124 f.
Eucherius, Bishop of Lyons, 173 f., 196 ff., 222

Eucherius, son of Stilicho, 170
Eudocia, daughter of Valentinian III, 46, 81 f.
Eudoxia, wife of Arcadius, 18
Eudoxia, wife of Valentinian III, 46, 82
Eugenius, Bishop of Toledo, editor of Dracontius, 90
Eugenius, claimant of the Western throne, 32
Eulogius, Bishop of Cæsarea, 139
Eunapius, 28
Euric, the Visigoth, 9 f., 48 ff., 199
Eusebius, *Chronicles* of, 53
Eustochium, daughter of Paula, 108, 111, 113, 123, 191
Eutropius, minister of Arcadius, 18, 32
Eutychian heresy, 66
Evodius, Bishop of Uzala, 128
Eyssenbergk, 77

Fall of Adam and Eve, 61, 68, 73 f., 87, 100
Faustus, Bishop of Riez, 49, 198 ff.
Felicia, correspondent of St. Augustine, 127
Felix of Aptunga, 131, 133
Figgis, H. N., 161
Flavian, Bishop of Constantinople, 3
Fretela, correspondent of St. Jerome, 114
Fulgentius, Bishop of Ruspe, 201

Gagny, ed. Claudius Marius Victor, 95
Gainas, general of Arcadius, 18
Gaiseric, the Vandal, 6 ff., 9, 12, 44, 46, 81 f., 146 f., 178
Galla Placidia, 4, 6, 8, 44 f., 81, 146, 165, 171
Gaudentius, son of Aetius, 46
Gaudentius, correspondent of St. Jerome, 114
Gennadius, 51 f., 58, 77
Germanus, 217 f., 222
Gibbon, Edward, 42 f.
Gildo, the Moor, 18, 20, 170
Glover, T. R., 17, 30
Glycerius, Emperor of the West, 11
Gorgona, island of, 40 f.
Græcus, Bishop of Marseilles, 48 f.

Gratian, Emperor of Rome, 56, 189
Gregory of Tours, 230, 232
Guizot, on Avitus, 91
Gundobad, King of Burgundy, 66 f., 198
Gunthamund, King of the Vandals, 82 f., 85

Hedibia, correspondent of St. Jerome, 114
Helena, Saint, 54
Hilary, Bishop of Arles, 11, 174, 195 f., 197
Hilary, Bishop of Poitiers, 185 f.
Hippo Regius, 6, 122, 126, 130 f., 136, 142 ff., 146, 162
Honoratus of Lerins, 11, 174, 195 f., 217
Honoratus, Bishop of Thiava, 146
Honoratus, correspondent of St. Augustine, 128
Honorius, Emperor of the West, 3 ff., 18, 23 ff., 27 f., 31, 33, 36, 44, 106, 133, 155, 166, 169 f.
Hormisdas, Pope, 201
Huneric, son of Gaiseric, 46, 81 f.

Idacius, Bishop of Merida, 56
Innocent I, Pope, 139 f.
Isidore of Seville, 77, 90
Ithacius, Bishop of Ossonoba, 56 f.

Januarius of Casæ Nigræ, Donatist, 133
Januarius, correspondent of St. Augustine, 127
Jerome, Saint, 5, 10, 15, 53, 78, 108 ff., 162, 183 f., 191, 221
  Apology against Rufinus, 117 f.
  Commentaries on the Prophets, 121 f.
  Dialogue against the Pelagians, 119 f., 135
  Letters, 109 ff.
  Vulgate, 65, 109, 122
Jerusalem, Synod of, 139, 163
John, Bishop of Jerusalem, 116, 139, 163
John Chrysostom, Saint, 3, 182, 222
John of Salisbury, 231
John the Scot, 231
John, Thebaid monk, 32
John, usurper of throne of the West, 6, 8, 44, 46

Julian, Bishop of Eclanum, 141, 143
Julian, correspondent of St. Jerome, 114
Juliana, correspondent of St. Augustine, 127
Julius Nepos, Emperor of the West, 10 f., 48

Lachanius, 35, 41
Læta, daughter-in-law of Paula, 113 ff.
Leo the Great, Pope, 8, 168, 222
Leo I, Emperor of the East, 9, 47, 82
Leontius, Bishop of Arles, 49
Lerins, Monastery of, 174, 195 ff.
Liguge, 186
Litorius, 7, 173
Livy, 167, 172
Lucidus, priest, 200 f.
Lupus, Bishop of Troyes, 49

Majorian, Emperor of the West, 9, 47, 82
Majorinus, Donatist, 131
Mamertus of Vienne, 49
Marcella, friend of St. Jerome, 108, 112 f.
Marcellinus, tribune, 128, 133 ff., 137, 147
Marmoutier, 186 f.
Martianus Capella, 13 f., 82, 224 ff.
Martin, Saint, of Tours, 11, 15, 49, 51 ff., 184 ff., 234
Mascezel, 20, 170
Maximus, Abbot of Lerins, 198
Maximus, Emperor of Rome, 56 f., 189 f., 193
Merobaudes, 8, 13, 34, 45 f.
Milan, Court at, 23 f.
Mileve, 59, 140, 145
Milton: *Paradise Lost,* 61, 70, 72, 75, 86, 90 ff.; *Paradise Regained,* 91
Monnica, Saint, 125, 234
Mystical Interpretation, 76, 80

Nestorius, 3, 222
New Rome (Constantinople), 3
Niebuhr, 45

Odovacar, the Scirian, 11 f.
Old Latin version of Scripture, 65

Olybrius, Emperor of the West, 11, 46
Olympiodorus, 28
Orange, Second Council of, 201
Orientius, 5; *Commonitorium,* 97 f., 102 f.
Origen, 110, 115 ff., 163, 191, 203
De Principiis, 116 ff.
Hexapla, 109
Original Sin, 68, 73 f., 136 ff.
Orosius, 6, 15, 28, 31, 34, 139, 158 ff., 181, 232
Histories, 163 ff.
Liber apologeticus, 163
Otto von Freising, 232

Pachomius, Abbot, 183, 210
Pammachius, son-in-law of Paula, 108, 183
Paula, friend of St. Jerome, 108 f., 111 ff., 183 f.
Paula, her granddaughter, 113 f.
Paulinus, Bishop of Béziers, 95
Paulinus of Nola, 23, 51, 54, 93, 127, 197
Paulinus of Pella, 13, 103 ff., 195
Paulinus of Périgueux, 11
Paulinus, deacon, 136
Pelagians, 52, 119 f., 123, 131, 135 ff., 163
Pelagius, 59, 119 ff., 136, 138 f., 140, 163, 203 f.
Petronius Maximus, Emperor of the West, 8, 81 f.
Placidia, daughter of Valentinian III and Eudoxia, 46
Plato, *Republic,* 152
Plotinus, 156
Pollentia, battle of, 22 ff.
Polybius, 158 f.
Pompeius Trogus, 158 ff.
Possidius, 126, 130, 133 f.
Postumian, 53, 124, 184, 190 ff.
Predestination, 141 ff., 161, 200 f.
Priscillian, 55 ff., 163
Prosper of Aquitaine, 97 f., 101, 221
Prudentius, 14, 23, 31

Radagaisus, the Ostrogoth, 4, 7, 24, 27, 170
Ravenna, 4, 6, 12, 45 f.
Remigius, Bishop of Reims, 49
Ricimer, 9, 11, 47, 49, 66

Ruffina, daughter of Paula, 111 f.
Rufinus of Aquileia, 116 ff., 123
Rufinus, Prefect of Constantinople, 18 f., 21, 41
Rutilius Namatianus, 5, 14 f., 28, 35 ff., 93, 170, 184

Salmasian Codex, 82
Salvian, 7, 15, 102, 173 ff., 184
Ad Ecclesiam, 174
On the Government of God, 173 ff.
Letters, 173 f.
Satan, 61 f., 69 ff., 74, 87 f., 90 f., 188 f.
Satura Menippea, 224
Sedulius, 12, 15, 34, 77 ff., 91
Semi-Pelagians, 98, 143, 200 f., 204, 221
Septuagint, 53, 122
Sigismund, King of Burgundy, 66
Sixtus, later Pope Sixtus III, 141
Stilicho, 7, 17 ff., 41 f., 44, 111, 170
Sulpicius Severus, 11, 51, 124, 184, 186, 188 ff.
Chronica, 51 ff., 185
Dialogues, 53 f., 184 f., 190 ff.
Life of St. Martin, 184 ff.
Symmachus, 23, 181

Taylor, Henry Osborn, 91
Thagaste, 125 f., 183
Theodoret of Cyrus, 168 f.
Theodoric, the Ostrogoth, 12
Theodoric I, the Visigoth, 7, 102
Theodoric II, 8 f., 47 f.
Theodorus, correspondent of St. Augustine, 132
Theodosian Code, 181
Theodosius, the Great, 3, 5, 7, 19, 30 ff., 93, 155, 169
Theophilus, Bishop of Alexandria, 110 f., 191, 222
Thrasamund, King of the Vandals, 82 f.
Toulouse, 7, 35, 40, 42, 52, 114, 173
Toxotius, son of Paula, 111 f.
Tree of knowledge of good and evil, 87 f.
Troeltsch, 154 f.

Valentine, Abbot, 141 f.
Valentinian I, Emperor of Rome,

192; Valentinian II, 189; Valentinian III, 6 f., 44, 46, 77, 81

Valerius, Bishop of Hippo, 126, 130 f.

Venantius Fortunatus, 88, 90

Vergil, 43, 80, 94, 107, 232
Æneid, 70, 103

Victor, Claudius Marius, 12, 51, 57 ff., 65, 67, 88, 95

Victory, goddess of, 31 f.

Vigilantius, priest, 115 f.

Vincent of Lerins, 11, 201 ff.

Vincentius of Cartennæ, Rogatist, 132, 134

Volusianus, 128, 147

Wallia, King of the Visigoths, 165, 172

Zeno, Emperor of the East, 11, 82 f.

Zosimus, Pope, 141

Zosimus, historian, 28